Sport, Leisure and Tourism
Information Sources

Sport, Leisure and Tourism Information Sources

A guide for researchers

Edited by Martin Scarrott

OXFORD AUCKLAND BOSTON JOHANNESBURG MELBOURNE NEW DELHI

026.79

Butterworth-Heinemann
Linacre House, Jordan Hill, Oxford OX2 8DP
225 Wildwood Avenue, Woburn, MA 01801-2041
A division of Reed Educational and Professional Publishing Ltd

ℛ A member of the Reed Elsevier plc group

First published 1999

British Library Cataloguing in Publication Data
Sport, leisure and tourism information sources: a guide for
    researchers
    1. Sports and tourist trade – Information resources
    2. Leisure – information resources
    I. Scarrott, Martin
    026.7'9

ISBN 0 7506 3864 8

£33 ·94

Composition by Scribe Design, Gillingham, Kent
Printed and bound in Great Britain by Biddles Ltd, Guildford

FOR EVERY VOLUME THAT WE PUBLISH, BUTTERWORTH-HEINEMANN
WILL PAY FOR BTCV TO PLANT AND CARE FOR A TREE.

Contents

Acknowledgements   vii

Introduction   ix

List of contributors   xiii

1   An excursion in sport, leisure and tourism research: the changing
    face of research in sport, leisure and tourism   1
    Bob Lentell

2   An introduction to the Internet as an information source for
    sport, leisure and tourism research   27
    Martin Scarrott

3   Using libraries for sport, leisure and tourism research   51
    Karen King and Martin Scarrott

4   Journals as sources of information in sport, leisure and tourism   76
    David Airey, Geoff Cole and Ruth Mitchell

5   A guide to using bibliographies, abstracts and indexes   119
    Denise Harrison

6   Finding out about statistics and market research   138
    Sarah Ward and Wendy Luker

7   Finding and using official European Union information
    sources on sport, leisure and tourism   157
    Bob Burns

8   Sport, leisure and tourism organizations   197
    C. Michael Hall

Contents

9 Finding out about sport, leisure and tourism on video   232
      Lesley Gunter

Appendix: A selection of books on sport, leisure and tourism   253

Glossary of terms   257

Index   261

Acknowledgements

Inevitably a large number of people have been involved in the compilation of this book and there are a number of people I would like to thank. First, I would like to thank all of the contributors for their hard work in producing their chapters. Secondly, I would like to thank all those people who have offered me advice and have read various drafts of various chapters. They include: Ruth Mitchell, Ben Wynne, Crispin Partridge, Bob Lentell and Michael Hitchcock. All of their advice was gratefully received. Finally, I would like to thank Kathryn Grant, Diane Scarlett and their colleagues at Butterworth-Heinemann.

Introduction

This book aims to describe the methods and principles by which information to support research in sport, leisure and tourism can be traced. It sets out to enthuse readers to use the information sources and tools which it introduces, and to make active use of libraries and information services during the research process. It should give readers a general understanding of some of the main information search tools which are available. Hence the book is essentially a guide to information sources and tools, it is not a directory. It does not pretend to offer a list of all of the possible information sources within the fields of sport, leisure and tourism, which are vast interdisciplinary fields of study. This book is a starting point in the search for information which offers advice and indicates some of the main sources which are available.

Perhaps you are preparing an important piece of work, such as a dissertation or thesis, for an undergraduate or postgraduate university degree. Perhaps you work in the sport, leisure and tourism industries and you need to assess the market for a particular product or service, or to investigate sources of funding for a particular project. Libraries and the information services and sources they provide can help you to find the answers to all sorts of problems like these, and this book will help guide you in the right direction.

In Chapter 1 we set the scene by taking a look at the process of research as it relates to sport, leisure and tourism. This chapter defines the concept of research and the difference between primary and secondary research, and goes on to consider why it is important to this field of study and to the industry. Whatever kind of research is being undertaken, information of some kind or another will be needed and very often this will be drawn from literature which has been published and research that has already been undertaken.

Chapter 2 introduces the Internet and focuses on information sources available free of charge on the World Wide Web. The Web can be a useful source of information but many people find that it is difficult to track down what they need. This chapter offers a basic introduction to the use of search engines, the tools used to find information on the World Wide Web. It also has an indicative list of some of the more useful sources which are available for researchers. More and more information is becoming available on the Web and it is referred to in all of the subsequent chapters of this book.

Having established that the Web is an important information tool, Chapter 3 reminds us that libraries are also a vital resource for researchers and that they often exploit the Web to make information available. They also often provide their users with access to fee-based information services on the Web and to services delivered through other electronic media and printed information sources. This chapter outlines the process of literature searching and also gives a brief account of how to record references to material which is found during that process.

In Chapter 4 we take a look at journals as sources of information for research. There are a large number of journal titles available in the fields of sport, leisure and tourism and many more titles which belong to disciplines such as economics or anthropology which from time to time will contain relevant material. This chapter explains the importance of the different kinds of journals and offers a general guide to the titles which are available in the subject areas covered by this book. It also offers a guide to the way in which articles from journals can be cited (referred to) in your own research.

Whilst journals are important sources of information and conveyors of knowledge many new researchers find it difficult to keep up to date with what is being published in them. Library catalogues do not generally contain details of articles published in journals and whilst browsing through individual volumes of journals can sometimes be rewarding it is not a very efficient or effective way to discover what is available on a particular topic. Chapter 5 provides a solution to this problem; it will guide you through the use of abstracts, indexes and bibliographies. It offers general advice on how to use these important search tools and it provides a descriptive list of the main titles available in sport, leisure and tourism. It also includes some titles from other disciplines which will be useful to researchers in these subject areas.

Statistics are another area in which it can often be difficult to track down exactly what is needed. All governments produce statistics in relation to sport, leisure and tourism, as do a large number of other organizations. There are also commercial organizations which carry out research into the markets for particular products or services, such as holidays for senior citizens or sports shoes. Perhaps you need to find out how many people participate in a particular sport or the number of inbound tourists to a particular country. Chapter 6 will explain how to go about finding statistics on a particular topic and it will also introduce market research information. Market research is conducted to inform marketing decisions. It can also be a useful and important source of information whether you are a student researching a particular market for some coursework or an investor thinking about entering a particular market.

The European Union's (EU) policies affect the lives of millions of people across Europe and, consequently, it produces vast amounts of information. It operates a highly developed and decentralized system of information dissemination and provision. Perhaps you need to assess EU policy in relation to tourism or find the full details of a particular directive that affects your area of work. Tracing EU policy on a particular issue, or a particular EU regulation, can seem daunting to someone with little or no experience of how official EU information is arranged. Chapter 7 offers advice on how to find official EU information including a comprehensive list of EU information providers and further sources of help. It also gives an indication of the areas of sport, leisure and tourism in which the EU publishes material.

The EU is an example of an intergovernmental organization, but there are many other intergovernmental organizations and, indeed, many other kinds of organizations such as commercial companies and national governments. Chapter 8 offers an introduction to organizations and outlines how and why they can be an important source of information for researchers in sport, leisure and tourism. It describes some directories which can be used to locate particular organizations and there is an indicative list of organizations in this field.

Having considered information which is provided by means of both printed paper and electronic delivery we turn our attention finally to information available on video. It can be extremely difficult to trace video material on a particular subject and once a particular title has been identified there can be further problems obtaining it. This chapter describes some of the main tools which can be used to identify video material by subject and also gives a list of some of the companies that produce videos in sport, leisure and tourism. It also offers some general advice about copyright.

Martin Scarrott

Contributors

David Airey began his academic career as a lecturer in tourism and economics in 1975. From 1985 to 1993 he worked for the UK Ministry of Education with particular responsibility for tourism. Subsequently, following two years as adviser on tourism management and manpower for the European Commission Phare programme based in Poland, he returned to the UK and to an academic career. Initially he joined Nottingham Trent University and in 1997 he rejoined the University of Surrey as Professor of Tourism Management in the School of Management Studies for the Service Sector.

Bob Burns has been the European Documentation Centre and Law Librarian at Queen Mary and Westfield College (University of London) since 1991. He has a first degree in international history and a postgraduate qualification in library and information studies.

Geoff Cole is the subject librarian for tourism and hospitality management, and for a number of other subjects, at Oxford Brookes University. He is a chartered librarian, with a first degree in French and German. With colleagues from Bournemouth University and the University of Surrey, he produces Articles in Hospitality and Tourism, a database and current awareness service giving details of English language articles published in hospitality and tourism journals. In 1995 he was involved in a British Government-funded project (Know How Fund for Eastern Europe) supporting tourism management education in Bulgaria, giving advice on library facilities there.

Lesley Gunter is Senior Sport and Leisure Librarian with Sheffield Libraries and Information Services. She has been developing the Sports Library for the past nine years and is also the Marketing and Development Manager for the Music and Video Library. She is the Chair of the Sport and Recreation Information Group (SPRIG), a non-profit organization which seeks to co-ordinate and disseminate information resources in sport and recreation for the benefit of both researchers and those who work in the library and information profession.

C. Michael Hall is based at the Centre for Tourism, University of Otago, Dunedin, New Zealand. He was previously Professor of Tourism and Services Management at Victoria University of Wellington. His most recent works are *Tourism: People, Pleasure and Places*, *Tourism Planning* and *Tourism in the Pacific Rim*, all three published by Addison Wesley Longman, and *Connecting People with Places: Values, Principles and Practice of Heritage Management* (with Simon McArthur) and *Rural Tourism* (with Richard Butler and John Jenkins) published by John Wiley and Sons.

Denise Harrison is Head of Lending Services at the University of Sheffield, Main Library. She is also Faculty Librarian for Education and Leisure Management. Her main commitment to the field of leisure, sport and tourism research is her work on Sport and Leisure Research on Disc, a new database, listing research carried out at postgraduate level at fifteen UK universities. A new edition of the database will be produced annually and new contributors are welcomed. Denise has a BA Honours Degree in German, a Diploma in Education, an MA in Librarianship and is an Associate of the Library Association.

Karen King graduated from Leeds Metropolitan University with a first-class Honours Degree in Information and Library Studies. She is now the Information and Technology Officer with Humberts Leisure, one of the UK's leading leisure surveying practices, and is currently working towards her Chartership with the Library Association.

Bob Lentell is Senior Lecturer in Leisure Management at the University of North London. His research interests include sport and recreation services management and public policy in leisure and tourism. He has held several previous posts during eleven years' professional experience in the leisure industry, including Deputy Director of the Action Sport Programme at the English Sports Council.

Wendy Luker is an Information Adviser at Sheffield Hallam University, where she works in the team supporting, amongst other subject areas, leisure, tourism management and sport.

Ruth Mitchell is an Assistant Librarian at the University of Surrey where her duties include being the Academic Liaison Librarian for the School of Management Studies for the Service Sector. She is a chartered librarian, with a first degree in geography. With colleagues from Bournemouth University and Oxford Brookes University, she produces Articles in Hospitality and Tourism, a database and current awareness service giving details of English language articles published in hospitality and tourism journals. In 1995 she was involved in a British Government-funded project (Know How Fund for Eastern Europe) supporting tourism management education in Bulgaria, giving advice on library facilities there.

Martin Scarrott has been the Subject Librarian for Leisure, Tourism and Hospitality Management at the University of North London since 1991. He is also Publicity Officer for the Sport and Recreation Information Group (SPRIG) and information provider for Travel and Tourism to the Web resource discovery project, Bized. He has a postgraduate qualification in library and information studies and is a chartered librarian.

Sarah Ward is an Information Specialist at Sheffield Hallam University where she is responsible for a range of subjects including leisure and tourism management and sport. In 1991–92 she was seconded to UMIST to work on a British Library funded research project on the growth of electronic information sources in academic libraries; the findings were published as a British Library (BL) research report.

1

An excursion in sport, leisure and tourism research: the changing face of research in sport, leisure and tourism

Bob Lentell

Introduction

This chapter is intended to give the reader a sense of the scale, scope and place of leisure and tourism research. Moreover, it is intended to introduce the reader to some issues that face researchers, whether they are engaged full time upon large-scale research projects, or are involved in research as part of their professional activities or studies. This should help the reader by giving a research framework to his or her exploration of information sources in leisure and tourism.

What the chapter does not do is provide an outline of research methodologies appropriate to leisure and tourism. The issues involved, both philosophical and practical, are too complex to be dealt with in a relatively short piece. Fortunately, other authors have written upon the subject and details of their work may be found among the Further reading section at the end of this chapter.

Modern times: the 'research society'

In all developed countries research is a major feature of society. Much of it is conducted in a highly organized and collective manner with universities, commercial organizations and government departments or public bodies commissioning or undertaking research activities. What is not often fully appreciated is how recent is this institutionalization of research. The growth of the natural sciences in the Enlightenment of the seventeenth and eighteenth centuries was essentially an individual, small-scale enterprise, accompanied by the formation of societies to support research and its dissemination. However, the strong links between religion and the universities meant that it was not until the nineteenth century that scientific research achieved a prominent place in Higher Education; the universities' research role only fully flowered in the twentieth century (Bernal, 1965: 505). The research and development laboratory, now a central component of any manufacturing enterprise, was originated as late as 1876 by the inventor Thomas Edison (Josephson, 1961). An indication of the change which occurred in the nineteenth century is towards the midpoint of that century when researchers felt the need to distinguish their rigorous investigations from speculation, increasingly using the word 'scientist' in place of 'natural (or social) philosopher' (see, for example, Roberts, 1993: 703).

Of course not all research is institutionalized. Much of it is still undertaken on a much smaller scale, by students or by professionals in pursuance of a project or by individuals following a personal interest.

None of this is to say that there is anything very new in the act of research itself. On the contrary, some ancient civilizations undertook sophisticated research projects. For example, many such civilizations constructed impressive astronomical observatories and knew how to use their research to construct calendars and to calculate eclipses.

What is new to modern times is the intimate connection between research activity, production and the way we live our lives. Industrial capitalism led to a premium being placed upon technological advancement, and this itself has led to continuous research activity developing at the heart of production processes. The great significance of this growth in scientific research was apparent to those who theorized about how industrial societies were different from their predecessors. If we look, for example, to some of the founders of sociological thought, such as Durkheim, Marx and Weber, we find that they attached great significance to the growth of scientific research. It was becoming clear to them that this growth was related to many other changes, which one can summarize as being of both a social and mental character.

First there is clearly a connection between scientific research and technological development; the latter leads to social changes that occur as a result of the new industries, products and ways of living which it enables. As long as there is no prospect of an end to research there is no prospect of an end to the process of social change. Second, and perhaps less obviously, these changes have impacted upon the mind-sets of people. In previous societies, people had tended to look to the past as a guide for what to do in the present. It was the accumulated wisdom of the past, as represented by tradition, scripture or the pronouncements of elders which provided guidance. But the Enlightenment period introduced the notion of 'progress' and industrial capitalism put that notion into practice. The future will not resemble the past which can therefore no longer provide the framework for behaviour. One response to this has been to look to science itself, particularly to the social sciences, for clues about how to guide individual or social action. Another has been for people to look to the 'rational' procedures of the institutions of modernity, government agencies, professional bodies, work organizations and so on, as a way of providing them with a code by which at least a part of their lives can be lived.

However, the application of science has not led to the stable condition of universal betterment hoped for by many proponents of the Enlightenment. Previous societies had to face the uncertainties of nature, such as famine, disease and pestilence. They also encountered the uncertainties of arbitrary government and war. Modern societies have largely controlled natural dangers, but success in overcoming politically or socially generated uncertainty and risk is much harder to establish. In fact, we live in an era of new risks and dangers of our own making. The conditions of modern times are ones of rapid change, uncertainty and, even, unpredictability. On every front – environmental, industrial, technological, military, commercial, social and cultural – the situation is one of accelerating flux and shift. This is particularly true of leisure and tourism which are greatly influenced by fashion, new technologies and global media. Giddens (1990: 36–45) has pointed out that it is through analysing their changing circumstances that individuals, organizations and governments attempt to respond to these changes and to elaborate strategies to survive and succeed. Thus the response to turbulent modern conditions is to let reflection upon them be the guide to action, that is, of reflexivity. We can better understand the place of research if we consider the ways in which reflexivity operates.

First let us consider individuals acting for themselves. Writers such as Lasch (1980, 1985) have commented upon how the self has become a 'project' for people living in the contemporary era. We are no longer content to leave ourselves unconsidered and unaltered. The self – physical, mental, spiritual – is analysed and subjected to improvement activity. This is of interest to scholars of leisure and tourism because much of this activity takes place through leisure and tourism experiences. For example, exercise regimes are undertaken to 'sculpt' the body to the desired shape, the mind is expanded through 'cultural tourism' or adult education, or the spirit is healed through rest at a resort or through any one of a myriad of personal growth therapies. The language of more formal research is sometimes used in this context, people speaking of, for instance, 'researching' their holiday destination or family history. It is also the case that many formal pieces of research work are undertaken for purely personal interest, because the subject matter happens to have engaged the individual.

Next, let us consider the professional working in a leisure or tourism organization. It is no longer the case that any occupation can remain essentially unchanged during a lifetime career. The rapidity of change means that professionals are continually having to learn from experience, undertake in-service training or even change professions altogether. The 'rational' codes of professionals may have served well enough in past eras, but today they are insufficient. Schön (1991) writes of the need to develop 'reflective practitioners'. He suggests that whilst more traditional technical rationality (applying rules or thinking procedures to existing knowledge) is appropriate for problem-solving, it is not very successful in identifying and framing new problems thrown up by new circumstances. This implies that professionals need the ability to think beyond the boundaries of their current knowledge, and he calls this 'reflection-in-action'. Many issues arise from this concept, but if professionals are to be able to analyse their environment, both within their own employing organization and more widely, it is clear that they need to understand research. This not only means being aware of research undertaken in their own field, but also to undertake their own research projects or to commission others to undertake them.

Profile of a reflective practitioner

Maureen Taylor is Managing Director of Taylor Made Solutions, a management consultancy specializing in the development and marketing of projects in the fields of leisure, tourism and urban regeneration. Her past career includes a Master's Degree in Planning Studies from the London School of Economics, lecturing in Higher Education, and eleven years' working in the community arts and leisure sectors, including four years as Director of Leisure Services and Tourism for an Inner London local authority. She says:

> As a leisure and tourism professional I had little time available for reading academic journals, although as a former academic, I was certainly aware of their existence. I read, however, on a regular basis, the practice-related journals such as Leisure Management and Leisure Week, the trade-based Travel GBI and professional Tourism Society Journal, as well as the Local Government Chronicle and Municipal Journal. Articles there which influenced my practice were mostly on specific topics for which I was responsible, library service reviews and urban tourism strategies, for example. As a practitioner, therefore, it was not 'pure' research that interested and influenced me but rather applied research, in the areas in which my professional judgement was being sought and my actions required.
>
> As a Director of Leisure Services and Tourism I commissioned this type of research. For example, shortly after I took up that post I was alerted to a project in progress to convert one of the municipal swimming pools into a leisure centre. A component of the scheme was the provision of additional features through the use of private sector finance which would be repaid over a period by the local authority on the basis of the increased income from centre users that would be generated. The prospect was the achievement of something which could not be afforded using a conventional funding arrangement.
>
> I rapidly assessed this part of the project as financially unsound, but as one of the leading local politicians was committed to it, and I was a new Director, I recommended that external consultants should examine the viability of the proposed scheme. The research would need to begin almost at once, taking three weeks straddling the Christmas/New Year break. I invited three firms of consultants to tender for the work, all three did so and I selected one. Their report confirmed that the deal was non-viable and as a result this part of the project was cancelled. This probably saved the local authority £250,000 a year, and prevented a public relations disaster. It could not have been achieved in my view without the research support.
>
> Leisure and tourism professionals find that they need to employ a variety of research methods. Sometimes I simply asked colleagues to review the literature that related to a particular project or topic. I was frequently involved in reviews of our service and organizational restructuring, and

tapping into the experience of colleagues about those issues was important, for example by circulating a questionnaire which could provide the basis for more detailed discussions. I also ran a lot of what could be classified as focus groups of key stakeholders, since much of our problem-solving and policy development was carried out with other agencies. When our parks and grounds maintenance people developed some specialist computer software, we wondered if other local authorities might find it useful too; we did a telephone survey of parks and grounds managers which led to sales of the software to several other authorities.

Now, as a consultant, I have to use a wide range of research methods, or manage other researchers to do them. I have carried out consultancy for corporations such as British Telecom, professional bodies like the British Medical Association and public sector bodies such as local authorities. Every consultancy project is different and the research method is tied to the needs of the client.

(*Source:* Personal interview with Maureen Taylor)

Now we shall turn to organizations involved in providing leisure and tourism services. How can they survive and succeed in their especially fast-moving circumstances? How can they keep pace with changes in customer tastes and preferences, market conditions and government regulations? How can they learn from successes and failures, both their own and those of other service organizations? It might seem sensible to turn to management studies or organizational theory for clues about how organizations can do this. In fact, these disciplines have a strong heritage from the first half of the twentieth century in which the relationship between the organization and its environment was all but ignored (Morgan, 1986: 72). More recently the questions of how organizations can explore their environment as it changes and adapt themselves in response to it have moved to be a central concern. Senge (1990; Senge et al., 1994) has written of the need for work organizations to become 'learning organizations', adapting to their changing conditions. The leisure and tourism industries have a great need for research which produces intelligence about their changing environments, and which suggests possible adaptations to them. They are substantial consumers of information produced by government departments, national tourism organizations, universities and commercial consultancies. Many of them frequently research their own customers or market.

We next consider government, both local and national. The involvement of governments in leisure and tourism research is complex because they have a multiplicity of roles within the sector (see, for example, Hall, 1994; Henry,

1993). One role is directly to deliver some services, for example art galleries, museums, parks, heritage sites and public sector leisure centres. They are also directly involved in providing some key aspects of the tourist system, such as airports. Another role is regulation: encouraging leisure forms thought to be socially or economically desirable and discouraging those thought of as harmful. Additionally, leisure and tourism are very significant in the economy of many countries, for example in the UK accounting for some £125 billion, or roughly 27 per cent of gross domestic product (GDP), and usually have a major impact upon trade balances and currency management. Many localities or regions wish to stimulate leisure and tourism investment so as to promote economic development or urban regeneration. Thus government, as part of its macroeconomic management, also has a need to know how these industries are functioning. It is not surprising therefore that government departments, public sector agencies and local government are all active in researching leisure and tourism, sometimes conducting their own research, but often 'buying in' researchers under contract.

Last, we consider the role of supranational or international organizations in leisure and tourism research. In this category we include bodies which are very different in constitution and powers. The supranational bodies of the European Union are essentially governmental in character, functioning in a framework of European Law. Other international agencies, such as the World Tourism Organization, are the result of governments agreeing to work together. Yet other international bodies, such as the international sports federations, or the World Travel and Tourism Council, are voluntary associations which bring together various national organizations, or businesses.

Each international organization has its own agenda, and the degree to which they commission or undertake research varies according to these objectives and the resources available to them, some being important sponsors of research. Generally, tourism research receives a higher profile from international bodies than does leisure research. Clearly international tourism involves issues of international travel and co-operation which render it a particularly suitable topic for research by international agencies. Moreover, the significance of tourism in economic development means that it has sometimes been researched, perhaps as part of wider studies, by agencies which primarily have an economic remit (such as the World Bank, or the Directorates of the European Commission responsible for rural development or regional policy). Often the research sponsored has a strongly practical or applied character, aimed at assisting policy development, for example through the creation of tourism master plans.

The above provides a clue about why so much research is conducted in the economic and social sciences. When people write about what is special in the modern era, they usually mention the role of technology and the associated research and development in the natural sciences. Yet in many ways it is the social sciences which characterize modern times (Giddens, 1990: 40–5). Without their investigation and representation of the social world, it would not be possible to conceptualize, interact with and develop the complex networks upon which our system of production is based.

Leisure and tourism research is mostly based in the social sciences and provides an excellent illustration of this point. Take, for example, the concept of tourism multipliers. This idea aims to specify the knock-on effect upon a host economy of spending by incoming tourists. It derives from research in the interwar years which attempted to model the effect of exports on the economy (see, for example, Archer, 1991). Other researchers have applied the concept to tourism in order to gain an understanding of its economic effects. Governments have taken up the idea as a way of justifying the promotion of tourism development, and it is now an integral part of the policy formation process. Of course, to calculate multipliers and to check the actual economy against the predicted one, continual research into the tourism economy is required. For example, most states compile extensive statistics, such as those on the number of tourist arrivals and on spending by tourists.

This brief section has attempted to show that research is very far from being an esoteric activity conducted by white-coated people in ivory towers. On the contrary, it is a vital part of the reflexivity processes which form part of everyday life in the modern era. In some ways, we can consider ourselves as living in a 'research society' in which the natural and social environments are continually investigated and analysed with the results being returned to society as a possible basis for action. Leisure and tourism research is a vibrant part of these processes.

Knowledge and information

The purpose of reflexivity, and of the research which is part of it, is the generation of knowledge; that is, knowledge in the form of an elaboration of the concepts that enable us to better understand what is being researched (*wissenschaft*), or 'know-how', in the sense that Edison understood it, of applied knowledge which enables us to do something new.

Information, on the other hand, is the raw material for knowledge. By itself, information has little utility. When it is brought into a relationship with other pieces of information, perhaps to demonstrate a correlation between two variables, or when it is incorporated into 'know-how', it becomes powerful.

It is often remarked that the modern age is one of an abundance, indeed an over-abundance, of information. Castels (1989), for example, writes about our 'informational society'. The advent of the broadcast media, and now computer-based communications, has enabled much wider and more rapid dissemination of information; information generated in any global location can now be instantly accessed anywhere in the world. This in turn is altering the economics of information production, encouraging the provision of more information sources. Thus the problems for researchers in leisure and tourism studies have transformed in recent years. Much more information is available to them, providing that they know how to navigate their path through the sources and to access relevant information when they find it. Hence the need for a book such as this.

However, budding researchers should keep in mind that although information is abundant, knowledge and know-how are not (Storper, 1997). Information included in research reports should always be related to the aim of the research. Moreover, information usually needs to be processed in some way to render it meaningful to the subject of enquiry.

The case study of the research on the UK National Lottery (see below) illustrates some of these points. It did not merely assemble dispersed research upon lotteries, but also processed it through developing a classification scheme and through expert commentary. Thus, this research used previous studies to produce new knowledge and new information sources.

What is research?

Having discussed the place of research in today's societies, and having reflected upon the difference between information and knowledge, it is important to consider more closely what research is. *The Oxford Modern English Dictionary*'s definition of research is as follows: '... the systematic investigation into and study of materials, sources etc., to establish facts and to reach conclusions; an endeavour to discover new or collate old facts by the scientific study of a subject or by a course of critical investigation (Oxford University Press, 1992).

Three elements are significant. First, research involves 'finding things out' by identifying aspects of the natural or social world. Such research may generate information either of a quantitative or qualitative kind. However, to create knowledge from information there needs to be some link between the different things which have been found out. Often this link is an explanatory one, that is, a link which provides an apprehension of cause and effect. Thus 'explanation' is the second aspect of research. The third aspect is understanding. Explanation itself can be the source of a deeper appreciation of the relationship between the elements studied, and of how they relate to other bodies of knowledge, that is, of understanding or *verstehen* (Giddens, 1976: 52).

It might be argued that other enquiries apart from scientific research, would be covered by the preceding paragraph, for example detective work. To clarify a demarcation of scientific research we should add two further points. First, research should take account of the scientific principles and methods appropriate to the research object and objective. Second, the results of the research should be communicated to the outside world, which in practice usually means one of a myriad of scientific or professional communities. Communication of the research, perhaps through journal papers, conference presentations, reports or practitioner seminars is a highly important component because it affords an opportunity for critique and evaluation; it also permits others to consider the research when planning their own investigations.

Research may involve the discovery of new facts, but it need not necessarily do so. Some of the most valuable research relies not on new factual evidence, but upon devising new ways of 'seeing' what is already known (e.g. Jarvie and Maguire, 1995; MacCannell, 1989; Urry, 1990). The critique of existing concepts and models and the elaboration of new ones is a key part of major research, particularly that undertaken by academics (e.g. Hargreaves, 1994; Wilson, 1993).

More about research

Natural and social sciences

Making a distinction here between the natural and social sciences may be helpful to the reader. In the former, the intention is usually to be able to make statements about how the object of study behaves under certain circumstances. If other researchers choose to replicate these conditions, then the object should behave in the same way. Experiments are a means of establishing cause and effect by keeping most variables constant while adjusting the particular variables under study. There are many occasions when experiments in the strict meaning of the word cannot be done, for example in astronomy and palaeontology. In these circumstances natural sciences must make a systematic use of observation.

The situation of researchers in the social sciences is different. Replication of circumstances is usually impossible. Although experiments can be performed in certain cases, there is always the concern that in the 'real world', factors other than those tested will come into play, effectively making the experiment irrelevant. And in many circumstances experiments are not possible at all. Thus the social sciences must rely more completely upon counting and measurement (enumeration and mensuration), and upon observation, than is usual in the natural sciences. However, because the object of study in the social sciences is human beings and their actions, the researcher can choose to *interact* with the researched (for example by asking questions) to find out about their circumstances and motivations. But this highlights a key issue for the social science researcher, which does not arise in the natural sciences: human beings can be aware of the research and the researcher and can adjust their behaviour in the light of it.

Of course, researchers, whether in the natural or social sciences, are human beings too. This means that they are influenced by social factors. A host of cultural, linguistic, societal and familial factors influence what people research, how they choose to investigate and the terms in which they conceptualize their research (Foucault, 1970; Kuhn, 1962). In this sense there can be no truly 'objective' and 'unbiased' research because social factors will always influence how we think about society and the natural world. What researchers can do, however, is to be aware, at least to some degree, of their own philosophical, political or cultural predispositions, and to acknowledge them.

Primary and secondary research

Researchers often speak of 'primary' and 'secondary' research. Primary research involves the researcher directly studying the object under investigation, and generating his or her own data on it. Secondary research involves using data collected by others. For example, a researcher interested in the extent of participation in a particular sport could conduct a survey; alternatively, use could be made of surveys conducted by others, for example in the UK material might be obtained from the General Household Survey (GHS) conducted as part of the Census. Whether primary research is necessary depends very much upon the objective of the research as compared with that which generated the secondary source. Returning to the example, if we wished to find out how many hours per week were spent playing the sport by those who took part in it, then the GHS would be of little help because it asks about who takes part, rather than about the duration of participation.

It is not at all necessary for a research project to find out new things, explain them and generate understanding. In fact it is much more usual to concentrate upon one or other of these elements. Veal (1992) refers to three types of research: descriptive, explanatory and evaluative. Descriptive research identifies or maps phenomena. Explanatory research concentrates upon discovering causal relationships. Evaluative research is explicitly a part of intervention in the natural or social world, since it seeks to throw light upon the strengths and weaknesses of policies, strategies and programmes.

An example of primary research: London's Royal Parks

This research project was undertaken by the Centre for Leisure and Tourism Studies (CELTS) at the University of North London, UK, for London's Royal Parks Agency between 1993 and 1996.

The research had its origins in the decision of the Government to create a separate body to manage the nine Royal Parks in London. The new 'government-at-arms-length' agency, the Royal Parks Agency, came into being in 1993, aware that it would be important for them to be able to demonstrate the results they were achieving with the public money they received. Thus the primary aim of the research was to collect information on the performance and importance of the parks to the capital city. One of the most important performance indicators for the new agency's management was the level of visitor satisfaction with the parks. But this question itself suggested others:

- How many people visited the parks?
- What sort of people were they (e.g. were they tourists or local people)?
- What did visitors think of the parks?

Gathering the information on visitor numbers was not a simple matter, since the parks are spread over different locations in London, and some of them are of substantial size, with multiple gates. Entrance is free, so there are no turnstiles or other day-to-day means of counting visitors.

CELTS devised a programme of primary research (Richards and Curson, 1993), 'sampling' the visitors to each park on eight days of the year. For each hour the researchers spent in a park, they spent forty-five minutes interviewing visitors using a questionnaire, and fifteen minutes counting the numbers travelling through the gates. Twenty thousand interviews were completed in the first year, the numbers being reduced in years two and three as knowledge of usage patterns enabled sampling to be better targeted.

The visitor counts enabled the researchers to build a rough 'model' of the numbers visiting each park, taking into account the relative use of different park gates by visitors, the day of the week, time of year and weather conditions. From this it was possible to estimate the annual number of visitors to each park (Centre for Leisure and Tourism Studies, 1995). The significance of the parks was much greater than had been realized, together receiving annually 30 million visits and 11 million visitors, one-fifth of them being overseas tourists.   *Case compiled by Tony Curson.*

An example of secondary research: the economic and social impact of the UK National Lottery

The UK National Lottery was established in 1994, considerably later than most of its counterparts in other countries. From the start, the Government ministry responsible for it, the Department of National Heritage (now the Department of Culture, Media and Sport) was keen to monitor research which might give an insight into the social and economic effects it had upon those who played it, upon the 'good causes' eligible for grants from the proceeds and more generally upon the life of the country. They therefore commissioned a 'study of studies', which would itself be published as a research digest and analysis. The contract was won by the Centre for Leisure and Tourism Studies (CELTS) at the University of North London, UK.

It was apparent that there would be a time-lag before the results of many of the UK studies were available; collecting literature upon lotteries overseas would therefore be especially important. Because of the proliferation of media commentary upon lotteries, it was recognized that it would be important to restrict collection to studies that offered original research or analysis of lottery impact.

The research team used a combination of methods to track down studies:

- Literature trawls were made using standard abstracts collections (in hard copy and on CD-ROM).

- Keyword searches of on-line sources were made.
- Calls were put out through electronic networks used by academics and through the CELTS World Wide Web page.
- Calls were placed in research journals.
- Correspondence was sent to all known state lotteries and lottery companies, 120 in all.

Once the research studies were located, abstracts were assembled on a relational (searchable) database. A classification was developed, fitting each research piece into one of eight topic themes. Experienced leisure scholars then wrote a literature review upon the resultant 'research map', highlighting the key findings and pointing out gaps in research-based knowledge. These were published in hard format (Centre for Leisure and Tourism Studies, 1996, 1997) and, in summary form, upon the CELTS Web pages (http://www.unl.ac. uk/celts/). The 'map' continues to grow as more people get to know about the new database and inform CELTS about their own work. The CELTS researchers are also learning of abstracts in languages other than English, and are continually reviewing and adjusting the classification categories to take in the greater range of subject matter which comes to their attention.

Case compiled by Dr Judy White.

Quantitative and qualitative research

One of the research issues about which there are many misconceptions is quantitative and qualitative research. Quantitative research involves the use of numerical data about a limited number of variables. Because the information about each variable is numerical a very large amount of it can be handled, and statistical methods may be used to verify the sampling and to discover relation-ships between variables. Of course, the use of computers has massively increased the researcher's ability to process large quantities of numeric data. In contrast, the information used in qualitative research is non-numerical; this means that only a limited amount of information about each variable can be handled but, and very importantly, a large and disparate set of variables can be considered.

There are several different types of quantitative and qualitative research. In many ways the differences between these types are more important than their designation as quantitative or qualitative. For example, econometric research in leisure (such as carried out in the UK by the Leisure Industries Research Centre and the Henley Centre) is very different from the visitor counts described in the Royal Parks case study, yet both would be described as quantitative. Qualitative research includes widely different methods such as participant observation (e.g. Buford, 1991) interviews with participants or policy-makers (e.g. Henry, 1993: 121), review of historical sources (e.g. Ousby, 1990), analysis of texts (e.g. Cohen, 1986), or image analysis (e.g. Edwards, 1996).

When investigating social phenomena, many of those new to research feel that it must be more 'scientific' to choose a quantitative method since it seems to rely less upon the researcher's own preconceptions and ability to select and interpret social phenomena. There is a 'security' in numerical data which the researchers feel will protect their research from criticism. Unfortunately such feelings are often without foundation! Quantitative research involves a selection of variables for study from a substantial number which exist in a social situation, any one of which might affect the issue under study. It frequently requires the construction of research instruments, such as questionnaires, from which it is extremely difficult to exclude the researcher's preconceptions and bias. Finally, interpreting the responses requires a good grasp of statistical mathematics, and even then the meaning of the findings can be difficult to establish.

However, there are also many potential problems with qualitative research. These are associated with the reliance upon the researcher for the direct generation of information. There may be more opportunity for the researcher to influence the phenomena under study in these circumstances, and thus to bias the results. The advantage of qualitative methods is the great number of factors or variables which can be considered; often information other than that anticipated as relevant at the research design stage can be captured as the research progresses. Nevertheless, these advantages imply that only a small number of cases or respondents can be investigated. Thus although the insight into each case or situation might be a deep one, it is much more difficult for a qualitative methodology to show that it is a typical one.

Because of the strengths and weaknesses of each research approach, wherever possible researchers tend to use a combination of methods.

An example of quantitative research: time diaries

One of the first developed techniques in leisure research was the use of time diaries. In this technique the respondents are asked to keep a log of activities they have participated in over a period of time. From these diaries it is possible for researchers to assess:

- the numbers involved, i.e. the proportion of people who participate in a particular leisure activity
- how often they do it, i.e. the frequency with which they take part
- how long they do it for, i.e. how many hours or minutes they spend on that activity in a week, month or year.

In the UK, a private sector research consultancy, the Henley Centre, makes extensive use of this technique. They use a sample of 1000 people tracking their use of time over a three-month period (i.e. 4000 people over one year). Researchers may find the results of these counts in the Henley Centre's journal *Leisure Futures*. The results are entirely numerical and can be expressed in a graphical manner. The sample size is large enough for some security about 'typicality'; on the other hand they provide no evidence as to the meanings of, or motivations behind, the activities reported.

An example of qualitative research: Thai women and Farang men

A notable example of the use of an ethnographic approach in tourism research, using both observation and interview techniques, has been Cohen's studies of the relationships between Thai women and Western men, taking place within the context of the Bangkok sex 'industry'. By living amongst the poor of the city over a period of two months, he was able to observe and interact with both the Thais and the Western tourists. This enabled him to gain a deep under-standing of what lay behind a pattern of usually fleeting relationships (Cohen, 1982). Considering the sensitive nature of the issues involved, as Ryan (1995: 103) notes: 'it is doubtful if more conventional empirically based quantitative methods could have generated such insights ...'. Cohen returned to Thailand in subsequent years, using similar qualitative techniques to build a picture of the implications of tourism for that country's social and cultural development.

An example of research using different approaches: satisfaction with leisure centres

Howat et al. (1996) wished to measure the satisfaction of customers with the service provided by public sector leisure centres in Australia. An objective of their work was to develop a means whereby managers of these centres could evaluate their own service, track service performance and make comparisons with other centres. They therefore adopted the customer questionnaire technique; the questionnaire consisted of a series of statements against which customers could indicate agreement/disagreement on a six-point scale. Analysis of the answers, using computer-based statistics, enabled them to identify underlying factors which influenced customer satisfaction. At first sight this appears a purely quantitative approach. However, the researchers followed a technique pioneered in the services field by Parasuraman, Zeithaml and Berry (1988, 1991) in generating the statements on the questionnaire from qualitative research. Customer focus groups and a panel of professionals were used to generate and refine the questionnaire statements. This qualitative element was the vital proving-ground for ensuring that they were asking about things which were important to customers.

Leisure and tourism research

So far in this chapter we have discussed research in general terms using leisure and tourism research to supply examples. It is important, however, not to uncritically accept the term 'leisure and tourism research'. It should not be taken to imply that there is one body of research knowledge which in some sense 'fits together'. This is very far from being the case and there are three main reasons why.

The first reason is that there is no agreement about what 'leisure' and 'tourism' are, and about how they should be defined. Hayward, Kew and Bramham (1994) identify four different definitions of leisure; the features of a research programme are likely to be greatly influenced by the definition used. It is also the case that many languages do not have a synonym for 'leisure', or that their political and professional discourse may have developed in another way in which 'leisure' is not the central concept (see, for example, Poujol, 1993).

International tourism organizations have worked to bring about a convergence in definitions of tourism to assist the compilation and interpretation of tourism statistics. However, researchers do not always find that these definitions fully reflect the aspects that they wish to investigate. Thus, the boundaries of research are much wider than the definitions would lead us to believe.

The second reason is that there is no general agreement that leisure and tourism have any particularly close relationship with one another. Leisure studies grew from attempts by sociologists and geographers in the 1960s and 1970s to understand the patterns and implications of the growth of leisure time in the developed countries. Gradually they evolved their own language and paradigms. Some leisure scholars treated tourism research as a subset of leisure research, assuming that concepts from, for example, leisure sociology could be applied to tourism (Lanfant, 1993). However, those researchers examining international tourism have generally found that leisure studies offers a programme of rather limited usefulness, and have developed their own programmes, drawing for example, upon anthropology and cultural studies. They have found the need for their own set of concepts (Burns and Holden, 1995; Dann, 1996). On the other hand, research upon domestic tourism within the developed regions, or upon inbound tourism to those developed regions, is often much more closely related to leisure research.

Our third reason is to do with the parameters set for the research. It can be very difficult, for example, to link up research conducted by different types of researchers, towards different ends even when they are about the same topic. As an example of this, Butler (1993) highlights the disparate characteristics of work assessing the impact of tourism by examining the implications of research conducted by government as part of policy formation, research conducted for a commercial concern in pursuance of tourism investment and work carried on by academics (see Table 1.1).

The parameters of research are also greatly influenced by the background of the researchers, particularly the academic discipline in which they have been

Table 1.1 Major characteristics of types of impact assessment studies

Characteristics	Public sector	Agent Private	Academic
Principal focus	Environmental	Economic	Social
Timing	Pre-development	Pre-development	Post-development
Tone	Neutral	Mostly positive	Mostly critical/negative
Breadth	Exhaustive in detail, focused in topic	Focused in topic, detailed	Broad in issues, less detailed
Context	Specific case study	Specific case study	Specific case study and general studies on themes or regions
Decision-making role	Major	Major	Minor
Dissemination	Rarely published, may be available to interested parties	Rarely published or disseminated except when required	Usually published and disseminated

Source: Butler (1993). Reproduced with kind permission of Routledge (redrawn).

trained. An economist's view of the impact of tourism is usually very different from an anthropologist's even though they are researching the 'same' phenomenon.

Keeping the above points in mind, we now move on to ask if there are any special features of research in leisure and tourism which make it special or different from other types of research.

Leisure and tourism research is new

Although the ways in which we experience them have changed and developed, leisure and tourism are not new phenomena. Research into them can be traced well back into the century, for example the Mass Observation study in Britain in the 1930s and 1940s (see Calder and Sheridan, 1984, or the work of US researchers such as Goffman, 1959; Whyte, 1955). However, with these and a small number of other interesting exceptions, their history as a subject for systematic research begins in the period following 1960. This reflects the greatly increased role of leisure time in the developed countries as working hours declined and incomes increased; it also reflects the development of global communications systems which have underpinned the growth of international mass tourism. There are several consequences of the youth of leisure and tourism research which it is helpful to examine.

Veal (1992) suggests that one of the reasons for the preponderance of descriptive research in leisure and tourism is the fact that it is so new. This must surely be the case. In spite of the best efforts of researchers, many aspects remain to be described; they must be 'mapped' before they can be 'modelled'.

When new subjects for research arise within the academy, they have to struggle for acceptance within the academic community, to generate a funding base for research and to prove their utility to the 'outside world'. Writing in the context of the development of the cross-disciplinary field of services management, Fisk, Brown and Bitner (1995) have proposed a three-stage metaphor for its evolution:

1 The 'Crawling Out' stage represents a time of risk-taking and discovery when the exponents of the embryonic subject have to justify and delineate it as a research area.
2 The 'Scurrying About' phase represents growing interest in the new field, represented by specialist conferences and the willingness of established journals to carry papers about it.

3   The 'Walking Erect' phase is characterized by an 'explosive growth' in the number of publications, more sophisticated research projects, acceptance of the subject by the wider academic community and the growth of specialist journals devoted to it.

If we apply this metaphor to leisure research and tourism research, it is probably true to say that, from following their different evolutionary paths, they have just started to 'Walk Erect'. The research base of both fields is expanding rapidly, and specialist research journals continue to be initiated. Research-based posts have been created in many universities, supporting the numerous undergraduate and postgraduate courses which are established in a number of countries, particularly in the English-speaking world. Throughout the world, doctoral students are choosing leisure and tourism topics for their research projects, promising a further expansion of research in the future.

It should be pointed out that the way this academic research is organized varies greatly between institutions. Some institutions specialize in leisure or tourism, but not both. Often the research takes place within a faculty or department which strongly influences the precise topics researched and the way research is undertaken. A business school, a school of hospitality studies, a cultural studies department or a geography faculty, for example, will all provide a different academic environment for leisure and tourism research. Prospective students and researchers need to take these factors into account when choosing an institution.

Outside the Higher Education sector the growth of research activity has been no less impressive. Many of the large management consultancies or business analysis companies employ leisure and tourism specialists. Some companies supply leisure and tourism information or intelligence on a commercial basis. Many small consultancies have been set up in recent years, able to undertake specialist research and to supply clients with professional expertise. Many larger leisure and tourism service organizations, such as airlines, employ specialist market research staff to provide them with customer feedback and, more generally, to monitor the changing market. Informal and formal networks link these activities to research based in the universities.

The relative newness of leisure and tourism research has arguably affected the balance between academic and client-based research. In several countries it has until quite recently been difficult for academics to obtain funds for 'pure' research. In consequence research performed under contract for clients within the leisure and tourism industries has played an important role. Although such research can often be 'spun-off' into more academic work, it is not always the best way to get to grips with fundamental research issues, since the client usually determines the parameters of the research so as to achieve a focus on the practical issues at hand.

The case study of the research on the Royal Parks in London (see above) illustrates this point. The academics conducting the research suggested that they should also complete some in-depth qualitative research to uncover more about park visitors' motivations for going to the parks, and their satisfaction with parks visits. But such work is time-consuming and therefore costly; in a time of tight budgets the client could not justify spending on research which went beyond quantitative format of the indicators by which the Government would assess the Royal Parks Agency's performance.

Cross-disciplinarity

Veal (1992) identifies the following academic disciplines as giving rise to leisure and tourism research:

- economics
- geography
- history
- philosophy
- political science
- psychology/social psychology
- sociology.

In his consideration of tourism research Przeclawski (1993) lists the above, but also includes:

- architecture
- anthropology
- biology
- ecology
- law
- marketing
- medicine
- pedagogics
- physical planning.

In fact even these lists are not exhaustive. One might, for example, put forward gender studies, sports science, hospitality management or management studies.

Like many academic disciplines these, too, are composite disciplines, there being a number of specialisms within them. Thus, there is room for many different perspectives within leisure and tourism research.

Most research problems in leisure and tourism will not fit simply into one of the established academic subjects, and ideally several of the above specialisms would be involved. This poses several questions for the researcher because the research may take him or her outside their particular research interest or expertise.

Przeclawski (1993) suggests that the best response to this issue is to conduct interdisciplinary research, in which a team of specialists from different disciplines interact to share perceptions and to develop a holistic view. In practice, this ideal has rarely, if ever, been achieved in primary research largely because the resources have not been available. Things are different in secondary research, since the growth in leisure and tourism studies is enabling scholars to search for relationships between studies and to devise new ways of describing phenomena. One of several possible examples is Burns and Holden's (1995) development of the term 'metatourism' to denote large-scale tourism dominated by the metropolitan centres, but taking place in the Third World. However, in spite of these advances, it is still generally the case that leisure and tourism research tends to be multidisciplinary, in the sense that many disciplines have an interest in it, but retain their own perspectives rather than achieving a new synthesis.

It is important for researchers to recognize that each academic discipline is highly specialized and has built up a body of existing research work which may be relevant to their own research area. This should not deter the researcher: there are still many basic and challenging issues in leisure and tourism studies about which little is known, and about which research is badly needed. However, it is unsound to conduct research that 'strays into' areas outside the researcher's own expertise without taking account of existing knowledge within them. Handling cross-disciplinary research is a major issue in itself which can be dealt with only briefly here. It is vital that the researcher has a strategy for dealing with the cross-disciplinary aspects of their own research.

First, it is important for the researcher to identify those aspects of the research which fall outside the area of his or her own competence. Second, he or she should consider how to address those aspects. Several options present themselves. It may be possible to seek specialist advice. In the case of student projects, students are likely to find that their supervisor or tutor is familiar with only some aspects of the work upon which they need to draw. Some guidance may be sought from academic staff whose specialism is closer to the discipline in question. In cases of more substantial research projects, researchers usually try to create access to other specialists in order to ensure that the expertise is on hand. Another option of course is for the researcher to become expert enough in a new area through identification and study of the major sources within it. The final option is to change the research objectives: consideration of what is involved may prompt the researcher to return to their research objectives and to draw them more tightly to their own field of expertise or interest. The third consequence of cross-disciplinarity is that it underscores the need to continually check progress of the research against the research objectives and plan. It is important that the plan can be adjusted in the course of the research so that it can respond to issues that arise during the research.

Concluding remarks

Let us reflect back on leisure and tourism research. It is a relatively new area of research endeavour which has generated many theoretical insights, and has suggested new approaches to countless practitioners and their organizations. However, the development of unifying research themes and methods is still in its early days; leisure and tourism research remains a loose collection of disparate academic and practical rationales. It is the responsibility of the researcher to understand this diversity and to choose an approach to their research which is appropriate to the subject matter and to the research objective. As the research proceeds, it will usually be increasingly difficult for the researcher to make alterations to the approach and methods initially selected. It is important therefore that time and care are spent on these initial phases of the research programme.

Thus it is vital to stress the need for a planned and timetabled approach to any research endeavour, whether large or small. However, students new to research projects have sometimes formed the impression that research proceeds through rigid adherence to a research schema gleaned from a research methods handbook. It is in fact rarely the case that research plans and programmes, once formulated, can be implemented without change; indeed, they sometimes require major revision.

So research in leisure and tourism is frequently a messy and unpredictable business in which things do not turn out as first planned. This is in part due to essentially methodological causes, such as the actual impracticability of a method which seemed plausible at the planning stage. As the body of research grows, so the experience of different methodologies grows too and this should help to reduce problems of methodological judgement.

In part, though, the unpredictability is due to the nature of research itself. Research is not simply about finding answers to questions, but of knowing *which* questions to ask. Yet that implies considerable knowledge about the subject under investigation or, to put it another way, that the researcher must already know many of the answers before he or she can know what the right questions are. Thus there is an iterative aspect to research, which accordingly proceeds by zigzags and loops rather than flying towards its target like an arrow. When the research is written up in journal papers or reports, the tendency is to present the research process with hindsight, stripped of the various branches which proved unproductive to the research goal. But, for the researcher, struggling through those branches is what forms the work, challenge, joy and excitement of leisure and tourism research.

Finally, a word of encouragement to those wondering whether to embark on a leisure or tourism research project. The leisure and tourism industries are of immense importance, critical to the economy of many countries, employing more people worldwide than any other, and having great consequences for our well-being as individuals, communities and societies. As we move into a more 'global' age, this significance can only grow. Research into these fields is a sort of crucible in which people with a multiplicity of research backgrounds and interests are gradually developing new ways of looking at people's lives and at the social worlds we inhabit. Although the amount of research undertaken is growing fast, and is daunting to those who try to keep abreast of it, it is actually rather small in relation to the size and importance of leisure and tourism activity. Your contribution therefore, as well as being interesting and enjoyable to undertake, has a good chance of being needed.

Acknowledgements

The author expresses his thanks to Tony Curson, Maureen Taylor and Judy White for their contribution of material for this chapter. The comments of Michael Hitchcock, Judy White and the anonymous reviewer on the manuscript are gratefully acknowledged.

Further reading on research methods

Clark, M., Riley, M., Wilkie, E. and Wood, R. (1998) *Researching and Writing Dissertations in Hospitality and Tourism.* London: International Thomson Business Press.

Gill, J. and Johnson, P. (1991) *Research Methods for Managers.* London: Paul Chapman.

Jankowicz, A. (1991) *Business Research Projects for Students.* London: Chapman and Hall.

Maykut, P. and Morehouse, R. (1994) *Beginning Qualitative Research.* London: The Falmer Press.

Preece, R. (1994) *Starting Research.* London: Pinter Publishers.

Robson, C. (1993) *Real World Research.* Oxford: Blackwell.

Ryan, C. (1995) *Researching Tourist Satisfaction.* London: Routledge.

Schwandt, T. (1997) *Qualitative Inquiry. A Dictionary of Terms.* London: Sage.

Veal, A. (1997) *Research Methods for Leisure and Tourism: A Practical Guide.* (2nd edn) London: Pitman/ILAM.

References

Archer, B. (1991) The value of multipliers and their policy implications. In *Managing Tourism* (S. Medlik, ed.) Butterworth-Heinemann, pp. 15–30.

Bernal, J. (1965) *Science in History*, (3rd edn). Pelican.

Buford, B. (1991) *Among the Thugs.* Secker and Warburg.

Burns, P. and Holden, A. (1995) *Tourism a New Perspective.* Prentice Hall.

Butler, R. (1993) Pre- and post-impact assessment of tourism development. In *Tourism Research: Critiques and Challenges* (D. Pearce and R. Butler, eds), pp. 135–55, Routledge.

Calder, A. and Sheridan, D. (1984) *Speak for Yourself: A Mass Observation Anthology, 1937–49.* Jonathan Cape.

Castels, M. (1989) *The Informational City.* Blackwell.

Centre for Leisure and Tourism Studies (1995) *Market Research Survey of People Using the Royal Parks.* University of North London Press.

Centre for Leisure and Tourism Studies (1996) *The Economic and Social Impact of the National Lottery: A Literature Review.* University of North London Press.

Centre for Leisure and Tourism Studies (1997) *The Economic and Social Impact of the National Lottery: A Research Digest – Vol. 1.* University of North London Press.

Cohen, E. (1982) Thai girls and *Farang* men: the edge of ambiguity. *Annals of Tourism Research*, **9**, 403–28.

Cohen, E. (1986) Lovelorn Farangs: the correspondence between foreign men and Thai girls. *Anthropological Quarterly*, **59** (3), 115–27.

Dann, G. (1996) *The Language of Tourism.* CAB International.

Edwards, E. (1996) Postcards: greetings from another world. In *The Tourist Image: Myths and Myth Making in Tourism* (T. Selwyn, ed.), pp. 197–222, Wiley.

Fisk, R., Brown, W. and Bitner, M. (1995) Services management literature overview: a rationale for interdisciplinary study. In *Understanding Services Management*, (W. Glynn and J. Barnes, eds) pp. 1–32, Wiley.

Foucault, M. (1970) *The Order of Things: An Archaeology of the Human Sciences.* Pantheon.

Giddens, A. (1976) *New Rules of Sociological Method*. Hutchinson.

Giddens, A. (1990) *The Consequences of Modernity*. Polity Press.

Goffman, E. (1959) *The Presentation of Self in Every Day Life*. Doubleday/Anchor.

Hargreaves, J. (1994) *Sporting Females: Critical Issues in the History and Sociology of Women's Sports*. Routledge.

Hall, C. (1994) *Tourism and Politics: Policy Power and Place*. Wiley.

Haywood, L., Kew, F. and Bramham, P. (1994) *Understanding Leisure*, (2nd edn). Stanley Thornes.

Henry, I. (1993) *The Politics of Leisure policy*. Macmillan.

Howat, G., Absher, J., Crilley, G. and Milne, I. (1996) Measuring customer quality in sports and leisure centres. *Managing Leisure: An International Journal*, **1**(2), 77–89.

Jarvie, G. and Maguire, J. (1995) *Sport and Leisure in Social Thought*. Routledge.

Josephson, M. (1961) *Edison: A Biography*. Eyre and Spottiswoode.

Kuhn, T. (1962) *The Structure of Scientific Revolutions*. University of Chicago Press.

Lanfant, M. (1993) Methodological and conceptual issues raised by the study of international tourism: a test for sociology. In *Tourism Research: Critiques and Challenges* (D. Pearce and R. Butler, eds) pp. 70–87, Routledge.

Lasch, C. (1980) *The Culture of Narcissism*. Sphere.

Lasch, C. (1985) *The Minimal Self*. Picador.

MacCannell, D. (1989) *The Tourist*, (2nd edn). Macmillan.

Morgan, G. (1986) *Images of Organization*. Sage.

Ousby, I. (1990) *The Englishman's England: Taste, Travel and the Rise of Tourism*. Cambridge University Press.

Oxford University Press (1992) *The Oxford Modern English Dictionary*. Clarendon Press.

Parasuraman, A., Zeithaml, V. and Berry, L. (1988) SERVQUAL: A multi-item scale for measuring consumer perceptions of service quality. *Journal of Retailing*, **64** (8), 12–40.

Parasuraman, A., Zeithaml, V. and Berry, L. (1991) Understanding customer perceptions of service. *Sloan Management Review*, **32** (3), 1–11.

Poujol, G. (1993) Leisure Politics and Policy in France. In *Leisure Policy in Europe* (P. Bramham et al., eds) pp. 13–39, CAB International.

Przeclawski, K. (1993) Tourism as a subject of interdisciplinary research. In *Tourism Research: Critiques and Challenges* (D. Pearce and R. Butler, eds) pp. 9–19, Routledge.

Richards, G. and Curson, T. (1993) *Market Research Methodology Study for the Royal Parks*. CELTS, University of North London.

Roberts, J. (1993) *History of the World*. BCA.

Ryan, C. (1995) *Researching Tourist Satisfaction*. Routledge.

Schön, D. (1991) *The Reflective Practitioner: How Professionals Think in Action*. Arena.

Senge, P. (1990) *The Fifth Discipline: The Art and Practice of the Learning Organization*. Doubleday/Currency.

Senge, P. et al. (1994) *The Fifth Discipline Fieldbook: Strategies and Tools for Building a Learning Organization*. Nicholas Brealey.

Storper, M. (1997) The city: centre of economic reflexivity. *The Service Industries Journal*, **17** (1), 1–17.

Urry, J. (1990) *The Tourist Gaze: Leisure and Travel in Contemporary Societies*. Sage.

Veal, A. (1992) *Research Methods for Leisure and Tourism*. Longman.

Whyte, W. (1955) *Street Corner Society*. Chicago University Press.

Wilson, D. (1993) Time and tides in the anthropology of tourism. In *Tourism in South East Asia* (M. Hitchcock, V. King and M. Parnwell, eds) pp. 32–47, Routledge.

2

An introduction to the Internet as an information source for sport, leisure and tourism research

Martin Scarrott

This chapter offers a general introduction to the methods by which the Internet can be used to access and exchange information in leisure and tourism research. It aims to give the researcher an understanding of its strengths and weaknesses as an information tool, and attempts to stimulate awareness of and enthusiasm for using the Internet to find information and communicate with other people. The intention is to provide just enough technical information to get you started and some selected examples of the kinds of information sources which can be found on the Internet free of charge. It will concentrate mainly upon one particular service available on the Internet, the World Wide Web, because it is currently the most dominant part of the Internet. There will also be an introduction to the use of electronic mail (e-mail) for communication. There are many books available which deal with the technical aspects of the Internet and the services which it provides. Browse the shelves in a bookshop or library to find something that suits your particular needs. Make sure that any book you use is recently published as Internet technology and services change rapidly and anything which is more than a year old is likely to contain information which is out of date. There are also numerous guides and tutorials to using the Internet, such as UK Index (1998), which can be accessed free of charge on the Internet itself. Further examples are given at appropriate points in this chapter.

The Internet defined

The Internet in simple terms is just a network (or, to be more precise, many smaller networks connected together) that connects millions of computers all over the world using the telecommunications network. This is achieved by using well-established methods of data exchange which are known as protocols. The World Wide Web protocol, called http, is the most dominant but as your experience of using the Internet develops you may encounter others such as file transfer protocol (ftp) and telnet. The Internet can be used to access information held on different computers. The Internet can also be used to communicate with other people on the Internet through electronic mail, usually known as e-mail. This facility is discussed later in this chapter.

How can the Internet help a researcher?

The Internet provides a means of accessing some substantive information resources in the fields of leisure and tourism. It also provides an effective channel of communication with other researchers in similar fields through e-mail. However, the Internet is not the answer to all your information needs. This chapter is concerned mainly with the methods that can be used to locate resources which are available free of charge, and subsequent chapters will introduce resources which are available at a cost. One of the major problems you will encounter in your use of the Internet will be trying to find information which is both relevant and of sufficient quality from the mass of information which is available.

Connecting to the Internet

The organization in which you work or study might already be connected to the Internet and you may be able to access it from your office or the library. It is also possible to connect to the Internet using a personal computer (PC) in your own home. To do this you will need to have an ordinary telephone line and a piece of equipment which enables the PC to send and receive data over the Internet. This piece of equipment is called a modem. Many PCs currently available on the market contain an internal modem as standard but if your PC does not you can buy a separate modem which will sit on your desktop. You will also need to use the services of a company which provides access to the Internet. Such a company is called an Internet service provider (ISP). Again, the organization in which you work or study may be able to provide this service for you, but if not you will have to use a commercial service. There are many companies offering such services, two of the major examples being Pipex and America Online. You simply access the services of the ISP using the normal telephone line. If you pay for telephone calls according to the location of the number you are dialling and the length of time you are connected then the location of the ISP's computer may be an important factor for you to consider. Furthermore, ISPs charge for their services in different ways, which may include the length of time you are connected to their service and/or a fixed monthly charge. Consequently you should seek advice from the computing support staff within your organization, a reputable computer dealer, friends and colleagues already using the Internet, or consult one of the many books available about the Internet before deciding which ISP to use.

The World Wide Web

The World Wide Web, usually referred to as 'the Web' or 'WWW', makes it possible to view documents that contain text and graphics on different computers. Such documents are known as hypertext documents. Sound and video pictures can also be delivered using the Web and documents containing these media are known as hypermedia. Documents on the Web are linked together and the user can switch seamlessly between documents held on different computers simply by pointing and clicking the mouse. Hence the word 'Web' was coined to describe the system. The documents on the Web are written in a code called hypertext markup language (HTML). In order to view these documents you will need a software package called a Web browser in addition to an Internet connection through a modem and an ISP.

Web browsers

Just as in the case of, for example, word processors or spreadsheets there are different Web browsers produced by different companies, which have slightly different functionality. Two of the most popular Web browsers are Netscape, produced by a company called Netscape Inc., and Microsoft's Internet Explorer. Many PCs currently on the market include a Web browser as standard but your Internet service provider may also provide you with one. Alternatively you could purchase a browser from a computer dealer or download one from the Web and

29

pay for it by credit card. If you work in education you may be able to download and use Netscape free of charge. Details are available from the Netscape Web pages http://home.netscape.com/ (The way in which Web pages can be accessed is explained below). At the time of writing Netscape was also making version four of its browser available free to anyone, so check before buying.

In general, most Web browsers enable the following main functions to be performed:

- Open, print and save to disc specific Web pages.
- Search the text of a Web page when it is displayed.
- Cut and paste information into other applications.
- Stop the current transfer of a Web page to your computer.
- Keep a record of Web pages you have found.

The computer support staff in your organization may be able to advise you about which browser to choose for your particular computer.

Accessing documents on the Web

Every document accessible via the Web has its own unique address which is called a universal resource locator (URL). Here is a typical example of the URL of a document available on the Web:

http://www.edinburgh.ac.uk

For the purposes of this introduction to the Web it is only necessary to note that URLs usually start with http:// which indicates that the document is in HTML format and therefore it is on the Web. When you have an accurate URL you can enter the details into your browser and access the document. Precisely how this is done depends upon the browser you are using, so check your browser's help facility or user manual for detailed information. Note that some (but not all) URLs are case sensitive. The URL above refers to the 'homepage' of Edinburgh University. An institution's or an individual's homepage has a similar function to the title and contents pages of a book. An individual document on the Web is usually referred to as a Web page and a collection of documents (or Web pages) kept on a particular computer is usually referred to as a website.

Recording the details of URLs for future use

Once you begin to search the Web you will soon discover URLs of documents that you will want to return to in the future. One very useful feature of most

Web browsers is the ability to store a URL in a special file. In most browsers this facility is called book marking but in some it is called a hot list or favourites. In Netscape, for example, you can organize this file, the bookmark file, into subject categories to suit your particular needs. The title of the Web page is also stored and there is a facility for adding a brief description to remind yourself of the content of a particular website. The websites can be revisited simply by opening the bookmark file and clicking on the required entry.

Some common problems

The Internet is not the answer to all your information needs and it is possible to waste hours 'surfing the net' finding little if anything of academic value. Perry (1995) questioned Internet users and quotes one user who stated that the Internet is 'extremely interesting but not the panacea proclaimed in the press'. Three years on from that survey there have been many developments in Internet technology but finding relevant information on the Internet is still far from easy. No single individual or organization is in overall control of it. It is only one medium for the delivery of information and it should be seen in the context of other information sources, such as printed books and periodicals, as well as other electronic media for the delivery of information which are discussed elsewhere in this book. It is important to note that anyone with the necessary computer hardware and software, and a basic knowledge of Internet technology, can publish material on the Internet and, consequently, the information on the Internet can be of poor quality and is sometimes inaccurate. Academic research published in books or academic journals by commercial publishers is subject to close scrutiny and verification before it is published. This however is not normally the case with much of the information published on the Internet. However, the Internet can give you access to some substantive information sources and improve your communication with other researchers.

There are also some common technical problems which can arise when using the Web which you should be aware of.

Slow response times

One of the most frustrating of these problems is the slow speed at which the Web sometimes works. This is usually attributed to problems on the network caused by heavy traffic, i.e. there are too many people using it. This could be caused by pressure of use on the local network within your organization, pressure on national or international links, or too many people trying to access the computer on which the Web pages you are trying to access are held. Unfortunately there's little you as an individual can do about it except to try connecting at a different time. For example, people in Europe often find that the response times when trying to access Web pages held on computers in North America are better in the morning because it is still night-time in North America and so the network traffic is less.

The URL quoted is inaccurate

Web pages and even entire computers can change their URLs or be discontinued. Sometimes you are automatically connected to the new URL but it is quite common to find a URL using a search engine (this process is described below) only to be faced with an error message such as 'document not located on this server' or 'this server does not have a DNS entry' or 'the server is not responding'. In each case check that you have entered the URL correctly. If it still does not work it may be worth trying again later as sometimes these error messages can be generated by other problems on the network.

Locating documents on the Web by subject

As has already been suggested the information held on the Internet is not particularly well organized and finding out what is available can be difficult. There are, however, ways of searching for information which is available on the Internet.

Internet search engines

Internet search engines are tools which enable you to search the Internet for information by subject. They can be accessed directly from your Web browser using the URL for the particular search engine you wish to use. There are many different search engines available and some examples are given below. All of the search engines work in slightly different ways and have different coverage so exactly the same search on two different search engines may give different results. The search engines work by using special software programmes known as 'robots' or 'crawlers' to search the Web and create catalogues of URLs which can then be searched. The major search engines are of North American origin although they are international in coverage. There are, however, an increasing number of national and regional search engines and some examples are given below. Many websites also have their own search engines which search for documents held on that website only.

When using a search engine remember to check the help facility to find out how best to perform a particular search. It is useful to have an understanding of some of the basic search concepts which can be used. The most important are the use of 'and', 'or' and 'not' to link search words together:

- And Use *and* when you want to find documents which contain all of the words you are searching for. For example tourism *and* government *and* Japan will find documents that have at least one occurrence of each of these three words. The more words you link together using *and* the fewer documents you will find. Hence this is a way of narrowing a search and making it more specific.
- Or Use *or* to find documents which contain at least one of the words you are searching for. For example leisure *or* recreation *or* sport. *Or* can also be used to find words of the same meaning, for example sea *or* ocean. Linking words with *or* will increase the number of documents found and broaden the search.
- Not Use *not* to exclude a particular word from a search. For example recreation *not* sport will find documents which have the word recreation in them but do not contain the word sport.

Searching for a phrase

Searches can often be narrowed by looking for a phrase. Many search engines allow you to do this by using inverted commas. For example '*leisure policy*' will find documents which contain the phrase leisure policy and is therefore more precise than linking the two words with *and* which would find documents where both words occur either as a phrase or separately.

Searching for part of a word

Searching on only part of a word can help to find words of similar meaning. Again, the way in which this is done varies between search engines but many use an asterisk. For example searching for *rail** would find railway, railways, railroad, railroads, and so on. This process is known as truncation.

Linking different concepts

On some search engines searches can be made more sophisticated by using brackets to link different concepts. For example, (sport *or* recreation) *and* government *and* Australia finds documents which contain both the words government and Australia and either sport or recreation.

Limiting a search

Some search engines also allow a search to be narrowed by limiting the search. For example, it may be possible to specify that you only want to search the titles of Web pages and not their text. It may also be possible to limit the search to a particular geographic area. Check the help facility of the search engine to see what (if any) methods it provides for limiting a search.

Some search engines simply ask you to enter your chosen search words into a box without making it clear how the search will be processed. Others give you certain options which might involve checking a box to select, say, *and* or it might involve you typing a particular character or characters (such as *and* + or *&*) between the search words. Remember to check the search engine's help facility to see exactly how you can refine the search.

Some examples of major search engines

General search engines

AltaVista: http://altavista.digital.com
Excite: http://www.excite.com
Infoseek: http://www2.infoseek.com
Inktomi: http://inktomi.berkeley.edu
Lycos: http://lycos.cs.cmu.edu
Open Text: http://index.opentext.net
Webcrawler: http://webcrawler.com

Geographic search engines

Australia

AAA World Matilda: http://www.aaa.com.au/matilda/
AltaVista Australia: http://www.altavista.yellowpages.com.au/

Europe

Altavista Europe: http://www.altavista.telia.com/
Euroferret: http://www.muscat.co.uk

Hong Kong

Channel Hong Kong: http://www.chkg.com/

New Zealand

AAA World Matilda: http://www.aaa.com.au/matilda/

South Africa

ANANZI: http://www.ananzi.co.za/

UK

GOD (Global Online Directory): http://www.god.co.uk
UK Web Library: http://www.scit.wlv.ac.uk/wwlib/

Further examples of search engines can be found at the following URL: http://www.dis.strath.ac.uk/business/engines.html For a more detailed discussion of search engines see Bradley (1998).

Subject trees

Subject trees (sometimes known as subject gateways or subject directories) are an attempt to organize the Web into subject categories. Documents are listed selectively, so only a small proportion of the total documents on the Web are included, but unlike documents found through search engines they have been examined and included in the subject tree for a particular reason. As with search engines subject trees work in slightly different ways. There are general subject trees and subject-specific subject trees. What follows is an indicative list of some general and subject specific subject trees.

General subject trees

Argus Clearing House: http://www.clearinghouse.net/
Compiled by North American librarians, this service gives websites a rating and lists them under broad subject categories.

Biz/ed: http://www.bized.ac.uk/
Biz/ed is a gateway to business and economics resources. It includes a section on travel and tourism.

Britannica Internet Guide: http://www.ebig.com/
This service claims to classify, rate and review over 65 000 Websites.

35

BUBL Information Service: http://bubl.ac.uk

BUBL is one of the key information gateways in the UK, providing access to many international Internet resources and services in the BUBL Link section. The BUBL 5:15 section includes a section called BUBL World Area Studies which lists at least five resources for every country.

Social Science Information Gateway (SOSIG): http://sosig.ac.uk

SOSIG is an on-line catalogue of thousands of high-quality Internet resources in the social sciences. Every resource has been selected by a librarian or subject specialist and a description is given in the database. Use the buttons at the top of each SOSIG page to search or browse the catalogue.

Scout Report Signpost: http://www.signpost.org/signpost/

This is a USA-based service which selects Internet resources and lists them under subject headings.

Yahoo: http://www.yahoo.com/

Yahoo is the largest subject tree available listing over 500 000 Web pages. The homepage lists a few broad subject categories which can be followed but there is also a search engine on this page. To perform a search simply type words into this box and click the search button. This results in the categories which match the search being displayed first, followed by a list of Web pages that have been indexed in Yahoo and match your search. There are local versions of Yahoo for the UK and Ireland (http://www.yahoo.co.uk/) and Australia and New Zealand (http://www.yahoo.com.au).

Leisure and tourism gateways

At the time of writing there were no comprehensive gateways to leisure and tourism resources. Many of the websites listed in the Appendix to this chapter contain links to other relevant websites. Here are some examples of websites which aim to list and provide links to websites in the fields of leisure and tourism:

Internet Hospitality Index: http://www.hospitalitynet.nl/hnindex.htm

This is a list of websites in the hospitality field arranged under very broad subject headings.

Leisure Studies Web Pages:
http://www.gu.edu.au/gwis/leis/services/lswp/index.htm

List of links to Web pages in the field of leisure studies.

René Waksberg's Tourism Research Index: http://www.tourism-montreal.org/tourism.htm
Extensive list of links to tourism research related Web resources arranged under broad subject categories.

Transport Research Web Links: http://www.its.leeds.ac.uk:8000/interesting-transport.html
Extensive listing of international websites for research in transport.

Yahoo Sports: http://www.yahoo.com/recreation/sports
A searchable list, including links, of specific sports, current sports stories and results, and trivia.

Yahoo Transportation: http://www.yahoo.com/Economy/Transportation/
The transport section of Yahoo with links to a wide range of resources arranged under subject categories.

Using electronic mail to communicate with other researchers

Electronic mail provides a means of sending a message from your computer to someone else's computer which is also connected to Internet. The process is normally quick although if you are sending a message to the other side of the world it can sometimes take a few hours to arrive. For the researcher e-mail provides a quick and efficient means of communication with other researchers all over the world. It has also meant that the results of research can be published and disseminated much more quickly than was previously possible.

In order to use e-mail you obviously need to be connected to the Internet. You also need to have an e-mail account, arranged for you by your Internet service provider and some e-mail software available on your PC. There are dozens of different e-mail software packages available and examples include Pine, Simeon and Eudora. Some of the Web browsers also have e-mail functionality so you may not need to have a separate e-mail package. Most ISPs will in any case provide some form of e-mail software as part of their service. An e-mail package should be able to perform the following functions as a minimum, in addition to sending and receiving messages:

* store messages received in directories created by the user for future reference
* send a file of text created previously

- print and delete messages
- forward a received message to someone else
- create a mailing list of people to whom you can send messages as a group
- include text from a message received in the reply to that message.

You can use e-mail to send a message of a few words or (assuming both you and the recipient have the appropriate software) you can send whole documents in word processed or other formats. One basic rule of e-mail is to put a useful word or phrase in the subject line which describes the subject content of the message you are sending.

E-mail addresses

E-mail addresses take the following form: person@placename. The person's name might be the name they use when they sign on to their computer (their login) and hence could be a mixture of numbers and letters, or it might be a meaningful name. For example, pt456@sheffield.ac.uk, or mark.smith@ united.com. As you become experienced in using e-mail you will learn that you can tell what sort of organization a person comes from by their e-mail address. In the examples above .ac.uk indicates an academic institution in the UK and .com indicates a commercial company.

Searching for e-mail addresses

Unfortunately there is no comprehensive global directory of e-mail addresses although there are directories you can use in a search for the e-mail address of a person or an organization. Those which list individual people are often described as 'white pages' whilst those that list organizations, usually commercial companies, are described as 'yellow pages'. These services tend to complement one another so you may have to search several to find an address. If you cannot find an address it does not necessarily mean that the person or organization you are looking for does not use e-mail, it might just be that their details have not been entered into the directories. The information contained in these directories can sometimes be out of date. Here are examples of e-mail directories, some of which allow you to enter your e-mail address into their database:

Bellsouth: http://www.yp.bellsouth.com/
Bigfoot: http://www.bigfoot.com/
Four 11: http://www.four11.com/
Infospace: http://www.infospace.com/

(This service contains a number of directories including white pages, yellow pages and a directory of American Government agencies.)

Who? Where?: http://www.whowhere.com/
World E-mail Directory: http://www.worlde-mail.com/index.shtml

(This service includes both white and yellow pages and claims to list over 18 million e-mail addresses.)

E-mail discussion lists

In addition to providing a means of contacting individuals, e-mail also offers the opportunity to engage in debate with groups of other researchers in your subject area through e-mail discussion lists. A message which is sent to an e-mail discussion list is forwarded to other people who are members of that list. Many of these lists are automated so when you send a message to the list it is broadcast (or posted) without being seen by a person. Some lists are edited by the person who operates the list, usually known as the 'list owner'. Such lists are known as moderated lists. Some lists are for anyone who has an interest in the topic of the list and they are referred to as 'open lists'. There are also lists for which membership is restricted to a particular group of people and these are referred to as 'closed lists'. There are many thousands of e-mail discussion lists and some examples which will be of interest to researchers in the leisure and tourism fields are listed here.

Green-Travel

Green-Travel is a moderated e-mail list. It is dedicated to sharing information about culturally and environmentally responsible, or sustainable, travel and tourism worldwide, including ecotourism and adventure travel. To join, send an e-mail to: majordomo@igc.apv.org and in the body of the message type only subscribe green-travel. Further information is available on the Green-Travel website at http://www.green-travel.com/

Hospitality-industries

This discussion group is aimed at those working in all areas of the hospitality industries, promoting research and academic networking. This includes all related aspects of business, management, finance, information technology, organizational behaviour and psychology. To join send an e-mail message to mailbase@mailbase.ac.uk and in the body of the message type only join hospitality-industries your first-name your last name; for example, join hospitality-industries Margot Hunter. Further information is available on the Mailbase website at http://www.mailbase.ac.uk/lists/hospitality-industries/

HOTEL-L

This is an open discussion list for people involved in hospitality education. To join, send an e-mail to LISTSERV@MIZZOU1.missouri.edu and in the body type subscribe HOTEL-L.

Infotec-Travel

Infotec-Travel is a moderated electronic mailing list. It is dedicated to the exchange of information about information technology in travel and tourism. To subscribe to this list send an e-mail to listserve@peach.ease.lsoft.com and in the body of the message type only subscribe infotec-travel your first-name your last name; for example, subscribe infotec-travel Mary Stein. This list has a Web page which explains its functions, how it can be used and an archive of the messages posted on it at http://www.infotec-travel.com/About

Leisurenet

Leisurenet is an unmoderated e-mail discussion list for researchers, scholars and professionals with interests in the field of leisure studies or recreation. Its members include people from professional associations, service providers (such as journal editors and publishers) in addition to academics. The list seeks to be international in scope and orientation. To subscribe to Leisurenet send an e-mail message to listproc@gu.edu.au and in the body of the message type only subscribe Leisurenet your first name your last name; for example, Subscribe Leisurenet John Smith. Further information is available on the following Web page: http://www.gu.edu.au/gwis/leis/services/lswp/index.htm

Small-tourism-firms

This open list is intended to provide a forum where researchers and lecturers in the area of small tourism and hospitality firms can exchange views and debate issues relevant to small tourism and hospitality firms. To join send an e-mail message to mailbase@mailbase.ac.uk with the message join Small-tourism-firms and give your first name and your last name. Further information is available on the Mailbase website at http://www.mailbase.ac.uk/lists/small-tourism-firms/

Tourism

Tourism is an unmoderated open list which runs on the Mailbase system. It is intended for academics and researchers in tourism. To join send an e-mail message to mailbase@mailbase.ac.uk with the message join tourism and give your first and last names. Further information is available on the Mailbase Website at http://www.mailbase.ac.uk/lists/tourism/

TRINET

TRINET is a closed mailing list for academics in the tourism field. For further information send an e-mail message to TRINET@uhmtravel.tim.hawaii.edu

Locating further e-mail discussion lists

There are also several directory services which can be used to locate e-mail discussion lists. Examples include the following:

Directory of Scholarly and Professional E-conferences
http://n2h2.com/KOVACS/
List of Lists http://catalog.com/vivian/interest-group-search.html
Mailbase http://www.mailbase.ac.uk/
(Mailbase provides over 1800 lists for the UK academic community.)
Publically Accessible Mailing lists http://www.NeoSoft.com/internet/paml/

For a more detailed explanation of electronic mailing lists sess Kirkwood (1997).

Conclusion

This chapter has presented a basic introduction to the use of the Internet in leisure and tourism research and in doing so has concentrated on the use of the World Wide Web and electronic mail. It has been concerned primarily with the methods by which information available on the Internet free of charge can be located. However, it is now possible for the organizations which deliver information over the Internet to make a charge for it. Subsequent chapters of this book will introduce various services which are charged for on the Internet and which you will only be able to access if your organization, usually through its library, has paid a subscription to them.

Appendix: Some examples of relevant websites

This is a very selective list giving examples of some resources which are relevant to researchers in the fields of leisure and tourism. Only websites which have some value to researchers have been included. Many of the websites listed contain links to further resources.

General

Hospitality Net: http://www.hospitalitynet.nl/
This website is aimed mainly at people working in the hospitality sector. It includes a 'news' section and it also has an index, with links, to other websites in the hospitality area.

Hospitality and tourism indexes, abstracts and bibliographies:
http://info.lib.uh.edu/indexes/hosp.htm
Links to free indexing services available on the Web.

Reference lists: http://playlab.uconn.edu/frl.htm
An extensive list of bibliographies on various leisure and tourism related topics.

Company information

One of the many uses of the Internet, and in particular the Web, is for marketing. Consequently many organizations use it to promote the services they offer and some sell their services, such as flights or package holidays, on the Web. See, for example, Murphy, et al. (1996) on the use of the Web in the marketing of hotels, Murphy, Forrest and Wotring (1996) on marketing applications in the restaurant sector and Bedard (1995) on marketing applications in the tourism sector. The Web is often a good source for locating information about a particular company, although the quality of websites can vary tremendously in terms of content and presentation. For example, some company websites may contain copies of the company's annual reports and accounts and other information of value to the researcher, whilst others contain nothing more than advertising for the company. If you are interested in the activities of a particular company try using the Yahoo companies directory at http://www.yahoo.com/Business_and_Economy/Companies/ or one of the major search engines listed above to see if it has any Web pages.

There are many companies that specialize in providing information and data about companies, including their share prices, financial statements and position within their particular sector of the economy. Much of this is expensive to obtain and although it is available on the Internet you will only be able to access it if you or your organization is willing to pay for it. Your library should be able to advise about any such services which it may be able to access on your behalf. However, some limited financial data about companies is available free on the Web. Here are a few examples.

General

Business Information Sources on the Internet:
http://www.dis.strath.ac.uk/business/financials.html
This website has dozens of links, with descriptions, to Websites providing company and financial information.

Financial Times: http://www.ft.com/
This website gives the closing day's share prices for the UK and other major world stock markets. You will have to register to use the service and this is easily done through the website.

Australia

Australian Stock Exchange: http://www.asx.com.au
Daily share prices and daily market reports.

Europe

CAROL: http://www.carol.co.uk/
CAROL is a service offering one point access to European company annual reports.

USA

American Stock Exchange: http://www.amex.com
Listings of share prices by company name

Hoover Online: http://hoovers.com/
Basic details of over 10 000 companies plus links to over 4000 company websites.

NASDAQ Stock Market: http://www.nasdaq.com
Current day's high and low share prices plus the previous day's close and net change.

Leisure studies

The Academy of Leisure Sciences: http://www.geog.ualberta.ca/als/als1.html
The Academy of Leisure Sciences is based at the University of Alberta in
Canada. Its website includes access to a series of working papers in full text
called 'White Papers'. Topics covered include the benefits of leisure, tourism,
leisure and the economy and leisure and health.

**Australian Council for Health, Physical Education and Recreation
(ACHPER): http://www.achper.org.au/**
The ACHPER is a national professional association representing people who
work in the areas of health education, physical education, recreation, sport,
dance, community fitness or movement sciences. Its website includes information about the organization and a list of its publications which are available in
printed form only.

Countryside Recreation Network: http://www.sosig.ac.uk/crn/
The Countryside Recreation Network aims to exchange and spread information to develop best policy and practice in countryside recreation. Its website
includes a directory of its research projects and the full text of its newsletter,
Countryside Recreation Network News.

Leisure Information Network: http://www.lin.ca/
The Leisure Information Network is a website aimed mainly at people working
in the Canadian leisure industry.

Parks Canada: http://parkscanada.pch.gc.ca/
Parks Canada is the Canadian Government agency which is responsible for
Canadian Parks. The Library section of this website provides access to the full
text of a number of its publications.

**Working Papers in Sport and Leisure Commerce:
http://www.hmse.memphis.edu/WPSLC/wpmain.htm**
This website provides access to the full text of Working Papers in Sport and
Leisure Commerce, which is an occasional working paper series. At the time
of writing the papers available were: Avenues of contestation: football hooli-
gans running and ruling urban spaces by Richard Giulianotti and Gary
Armstrong; Women and leisure: a qualitative analysis of constraints and opportunities by D. Dowling, R. P. Potrac and R. Jones and P.L.A.Y., Nike and
Michael Jordan: national fantasy and the racialization of crime and punishment
by Cheryl L. Cole.

World Leisure and Recreation Association: http://www.worldleisure.org/
The WLRA is a worldwide, non-governmental organization, dedicated to discovering and fostering those conditions best permitting leisure to serve as a force for human growth, development and well-being. This website includes information about the organization and details about its publications which are available in printed form.

Sport

International Association for Sports Information:
http://www.sirc.ca/iasi/iasi.html
The aims of the International Association for Sport Information (IASI) are to stimulate support and develop activities in the field of international documentation and information for physical education and sport. The website includes information about IASI and the full text of its newsletters.

Subject Index to Selected Sports Web Pages:
http://www.umist.ac.uk/UMIST_Sport//sport2.html

Australia

Australian Sports Commission (ASC): http://www.ausport.gov.au/ascmain.html
This website contains extensive information about Australian sport and the role of the ASC. Follow the link to the National Sports Information Centre for access to factsheets on various topics designed specifically for students. There is also an e-mail enquiry facility.

Canada

Sports Information and Research Centre (SIRC): http://www.sportsquest.ca/
SIRC is the largest sports library and information service in the world and this website contains much information of value to the sports researcher.

New Zealand

Hillary Commission for Sport Fitness and Leisure:
http://www.hillarysport.org.nz/
The Hillary Commission for Sport Fitness and Leisure is responsible for promoting these activities in New Zealand. The website has extensive information about the organization as well as some basic facts about sport in New Zealand.

UK

English Sports Council: http://www.english.sports.gov.uk/eschome.htm
The English Sports Council is the UK Government agency which aims to lead the development of sport in England. The website includes extensive details about the organization and some details about its publications.

USA

Gender Equity in Sports: http://www.arcade.uiowa.edu/proj/ge/About.html
Gender Equity in Sports is a research project designed to serve as a resource for any individual investigating the state of affairs in interscholastic or inter-collegiate sport. The website contains extensive information about the project and its findings.

**International Institute for Sport and Human Performance:
http://darkwing.uoregon.edu/~iishp/index.html**
The International Institute for Sport and Human Performance is based at the University of Oregon. Its website includes the full text of some research papers which are listed in the Publications section.

Tourism

Government tourism organizations

The national tourism organizations of many countries have websites. Very often these are of little value to the researcher as they contain little more than tourist information. However, an increasing number publish details of their research on the Web for the tourist industry and this can often include tourism statistics. Some examples are included here to indicate the type of information which can be located. If you know of the existence of a tourism organization, try performing a search for it on one or more of the search engines.

World Tourism Organization: http://www.world-tourism.org/
This website contains information about the World Tourism Organization, its work, services, and publications. The statistics service is only available on a subscription basis. It also contains links to many of the official tourism organizations around the world at http://www.world-tourism.org/TOURWORL.HTM This is a very good place to search for the websites of government tourism organizations.

Australia

Office of National Tourism (Australia):
http://www.dist.gov.au/tourism/index.html
The Office of National Tourism is responsible for developing and implementing the Australian Government's tourism policy. In addition to providing information about the department and its work, this website contains a large amount of information about Australian tourism. There are articles on a broad range of topics such as where to find Australian tourism data, cultural tourism, ecotourism and the backpacker market. A large amount of statistical data is also provided and there are links to a number of online publications in the Bookshop section.

Canada

Canadian Tourism Information Network:
http://206.191.33.50/tourism/tindu.html
This is the site of the Canadian Tourism Commission (CTC), the Canadian Government's tourism agency. It contains information about the CTC's programmes and services, and provides access to Canadian travel and tourism related sites on the Internet. The Canadian Tourism Information Network (CTIN) provides a gateway to travel and tourism information on the Internet in Canada. It was created to meet the needs of two main audiences: travellers seeking information on Canadian destinations and activities; and Canadian tourism businesses seeking information to assist in decision-making. The CTC has a comprehensive library and information service called the Tourism Reference and Documentation Centre. A list of its recent acquisitions is available on this website and some information about the services which the centre provides. The CTIN also provides access to some recent Canadian Tourism statistics. These pages are available in both English and French.

New Zealand

New Zealand Tourism Board: http://www.nztb.govt.nz/
This website contains some details about the role of the New Zealand Tourism Board, its structure, goals and policies.

Tourism Policy Group: http://203.97.170.9/tpg/
This website includes the full text of a number of research reports and summaries of many others which are available in paper form. The Tourism Policy Group is a policy unit within the Ministry of Commerce. It has a staff

of seven in Wellington and two officers at Wairakei and Taupo. They advise the New Zealand Government on the development of New Zealand tourism policy and represent the Government's tourism interests to other governments, intergovernmental organizations and fora, and monitor overseas trends to assess their relevance to New Zealand. The Tourism Policy Group promotes the objective that long-term tourism development must be environmentally, socially and economically sustainable.

UK

British Tourist Authority: http://www.visitbritain.com/toc/toc.htm
The British Tourist Authority's website is, at the time of writing, limited almost exclusively to tourist information and contains little of use to the academic researcher.

Wales Tourist Board: http://www.tourism.wales.gov.uk/index.html
This website contains some reasonably detailed visitor statistics.

USA

Federal government
In the USA there are two notable Federal Government websites for tourism research:

Tourism Industries Network (TINET): http://www.tinet.ita.doc.gov/
US inbound and outbound tourist statistics, forecasts for international travel to the USA and international trade receipts and payments are included on this website.

Tourism Policy Council: http://tpcnet.doc.gov/
The Tourism Policy Council aims to 'ensure that the United States' national interest in tourism is fully considered in Federal decision making.' The website includes links to relevant statistical sources.

State government
At state level most of the material seems to be limited to tourist information, although here are two examples of State websites of value to researchers:

Hawaii Tourism Office: http://www.hawaii.gov/tourism/
This website contains extensive information about tourism policy and development in Hawaii. It includes comprehensive statistics and some research reports.

Community Travel Research Database (Texas):
http://research.travel.state.tx.us/home.htm/home1.htm
Includes domestic and international tourist statistics and a number of tourism research reports.

Tourism trade organizations

Association of British Travel Agents (ABTA): http://www.abtanet.com/
ABTA claims to be 'the UK's Premier Trade Association for Tour Operators and Travel Agents'. Its website includes a directory of its members and links to related resources on the Web. Some of the material is accessible by ABTA members only.

Association of National Tourist Offices: http://www.tourist-offices.org.uk/
This website has names and postal addresses of the major national tourist organizations and in some cases links to their websites.

ECoNETT: http://www.wttc.org/
ECoNETT is a joint project between the World Travel and Tourism Council and the European Commission to develop an information network for tourism and the environment. ECoNETT aims to increase overall awareness of sustainable travel and tourism and, in turn, stimulate changes in management practices, destinations and corporations to achieve sustainable travel and tourism development. Full-text searching of the site is possible and links to related sites are provided. Some information is given in Spanish and French.

Pacific Asia Travel Association (PATA):
http://www.dnai.com/~patanet/psto.html
PATA promotes tourism and travel in the Pacific Asia region. Its website includes the full text of its monthly publication *Issues and Trends, Pacific Asia Travel.*

Travel Industry Association of America (TIAA): http://www.tia.org/
The TIAA describes itself as the 'national, non-profit association that serves as the unifying organization for all components of the US travel industry'. Its website contains some basic statistical data about the US travel industry, although the full database is accessible to members only. The association's press releases are also available.

World Travel and Tourism Council: http://www.wttc.org/
The World Travel and Tourism Council (WTTC) is a global coalition of 100 Chief Executive Officers from all sectors of the travel and tourism industry,

including accommodation, catering, cruises, entertainment, recreation, transportation and travel-related services. The site gives information about the organization, its members, services, publications and activities.

References and further resources

Bedard F. (1995) Tourism and information technologies. *Teoros Revue-de-Recherche-en-Tourisme*, **14** (3), 6.

Boutell, T. (1998) World Wide Web FAQ. http://info.ox.ac.uk/help/wwwfaq/ (accessed 20 July 1998).

Bradley, P. (1998) Search Engines. http://www.philb.com/compare.htm (accessed 17 July 1998).

Branscomb, H. (1998) *Casting Your Net: A Student's Guide to Research on the Internet.* Allyn & Bacon.

Kirkwood, R. S. M. (1997) Electronic Mail Discussion Lists. Loughborough University, http://www.lboro.ac.uk/info/training/general/e-mail_lists.htm (accessed 17 July 1998).

Murphy J. et al. (1996) Hotel management and marketing on the Internet: an analysis of sites and features. *Cornell Hotel and Restaurant Administration Quarterly*, **37** (3), 70–8.

Murphy, J., Forrest, E. and Wotring, C. (1996) Restaurant marketing on the World Wide Web. *Cornell Hotel and Restaurant Administration Quarterly*, **37** (1), 61–7.

Netscape Inc. (1998) Netscape Handbook. http://home.netscape.com/eng/mozilla/1.1/handbook/ (accessed 20 July 1998).

Perry, C. (1995) Travellers on the Internet. *Online*, **19** (2), 29–34.

UK Index Ltd (1998) The UK Index Beginners Guide. http://www.ukindex.co.uk/begin0.html (accessed 17 July 1998).

Webber, S. (1998) Reviews of Search Engines. http://www.dis.strath.ac.uk/business/search.html (accessed 20 July 1998).

Winship, I. and McNab, A. (1996) *The Student's Guide to the Internet.* Library Association.

3

Using libraries for sport, leisure and tourism research

Karen King and Martin Scarrott

This short chapter aims to provide guidance on using libraries as a source of information and data for conducting research in the fields of leisure and tourism. It will show that libraries are an important source of information, and are adapting to changes in the ways in which information is transmitted and stored. Secondary research is particularly reliant upon the use of libraries and their resources, but much primary research also involves examining research which has already been completed and which can often be accessed through libraries. In order to discover what research has been done in a particular area, and what has been published, it is essential to conduct a systematic search for published literature. This process is often described as a literature search and will be outlined in this chapter. This chapter also presents a summary of how to record references to literature that you find during the search.

Libraries exist to make data and information in all forms available to their users. Traditionally this meant providing collections of printed material, mainly in the form of books and periodicals. However, libraries are much larger and much more sophisticated than even the largest bookstores. They do more than just make information and data available, they organize knowledge. Most libraries arrange printed material on their shelves in subject order.

There are many such subject classification schemes in operation but basically they all attempt to organize knowledge in a relative and logical way. When using a library it is important that you learn how to use its resources efficiently and effectively and that you take advantage of any facilities available to help you. Many academic libraries, for example, run courses to help people to use the resources they make available. This might include, for example, training sessions on using the Internet in general or on the use of a particular electronic database.

Today it may appear to be the case that with more and more information becoming available over the Internet the library is increasingly irrelevant or out of date for the purposes of research. However, libraries are increasingly providing access to electronic data along with the more traditional information sources and, in the case of many academic libraries, they have actually led the way within their organizations in the use of information technology (IT). There has been much debate about the future of the printed book and the future of libraries. Print on paper still provides the best means to read (Crawford and Gorman, 1995, ch. 2). Books will be with us for many years to come although they are, and will continue to be, supplemented by electronic media. Many, but not all, libraries will therefore be offering printed and electronic sources in a mixed system. Increasingly, service will be delivered outside the walls of the library (and its parent organization) using communications technology. Librarians will have a number of roles in supporting information provision and use which will include: collecting, managing and developing resources in printed and electronic formats; resource discovery, which will include tracking developments in scholarly communication; developing mechanisms for access to databases at local, national and international levels; teaching library users how to find, use and manage information and carrying out secondary research on behalf of members of their organization or clients.

So, information exists in many different forms and in many different places and libraries and librarians are there to help you to find information for your research. Many surveys conducted over recent years indicate that libraries are seen by the public as 'a good thing'. This said, libraries are expensive to set up and run, and need a strong reason for their existence. This reason will vary depending upon the type of library concerned. There are various kinds of library offering different kinds of services and meeting different aims and objectives. Libraries are generally regarded as falling into one of the following categories:

- public libraries
- academic libraries
- special libraries
- national libraries.

Libraries which are most likely to be relevant for the purposes of leisure and tourism research will tend to fall into one of the first three categories, although the British Library in the UK has a special role in respect of interlibrary loans (ILL), which will be discussed later in this chapter.

Public libraries

Public libraries are run and funded by local government. Their services are usually free, although a charge may be raised in some cases, for example for reserving books, borrowing audiovisual materials or accessing the Internet in those libraries equipped to offer this service. In addition, many larger libraries now provide business information services and resources such as company annual reports, and market research reports such as those produced by Mintel and Keynote. Charges are more likely to be raised for services in this area, for example printouts of company details or research undertaken by library staff on behalf of customers. A charge is also likely to be made for faxing information out to customers.

Academic libraries

This term encompasses all libraries which are part of an academic institution, whether it be the Oxbridge or Harvard universities or the local secondary or high school. Stock held in these libraries and the services provided by them is intended primarily for the use of students of the institution, to support course work or to facilitate research, hence it is not usually possible to borrow items from these libraries unless you are studying there. However, many (but by no means all) academic libraries will permit access to their collections for on-site research. Access to sources of information held electronically is less likely to be available to people from outside the institution. Access to such systems is often controlled by a personal ID code or password, which must be input to allow the user onto the system. Most academic libraries in institutions running tourism and leisure courses will hold good collections of material on the subject. There is often a member of staff dedicated to collecting and developing resources and services in particular subject areas which may include leisure and/or tourism. This person may be able to offer advice about available resources and search strategies.

There are numerous directories available which list courses in universities and other institutions of higher education and they can be used to identify institutions which offer courses in the fields of sport, leisure and tourism. Your local library should have at least one such directory relevant to your country. Ask the library staff for advice. There are also lists of institutions offering courses in leisure and tourism available on the World Wide Web. For example Reni Waksberg's Tourism Research Index (Waksberg, 1998) lists institutions offering tourism courses under the Schools section. The Leisure Studies Education Web Page (Coleman, 1997) lists institutions worldwide which offer courses in leisure studies. Some selected examples of academic libraries at institutions which offer leisure and tourism related courses are included in the Appendix to this chapter.

Special libraries

This term is used to refer to libraries which are part of industrial or commercial organizations, government departments or special interest organizations. The collections will vary depending on the focus of the organization. For example it is unlikely that a collection held by ICI would be of much interest for leisure and tourism research, whereas that held by the Countryside Commission, (UK) would.

The Countryside Commission library in Cheltenham, Gloucestershire, is open to visitors, but a visit must be booked in advance through the librarian. Only one visitor at a time is invited, but in addition to access to the collection, a library tour is given. Photocopying facilities are available, for which there is a small charge.

Another special library in the UK which is of exceptional value to leisure and tourism researchers is the British Tourist Authority/English Tourist Board (BTA/ETB) library in London. The resources span virtually all subjects pertaining to the tourism industry in the UK. Subjects covered include economic, social and historical aspects of tourism, forecasts, and marketing and development. Visitors are again invited to make an appointment, and there is a charge raised for use of the resources. The library also offers an information brokerage service, whereby the staff will conduct your research and supply the results by post or fax. The charge for this service is calculated per twenty minutes of staff time. A special information pack for students is available from the BTA/ETB Mail Order service. The address is given in the Appendix to this chapter.

In Canada, the Canadian Tourism Commission(CTC) has a large library called the Tourism Reference and Documentation Centre (TRDC) which is open to the public. Opening hours are 8.30 a.m. to 4.30 p.m. Monday to Friday. A list of their journal titles and their new acquisitions is available on the CTC Website. (Canadian Tourism Commission, 1998). The TRDC staff respond to information requests for tourism industry intelligence and research documentation received by mail, phone, fax, e-mail or walk-in visitors to the centre. Electronic databases, tourism-related CD-ROMs and economic and statistical information, such as Statistics Canada's tourism-related publications, are available to those who use the centre.

In London, the English Sports Council has an information service which includes one of the largest sports libraries in the UK. However, it only offers a limited service to people outside the English Sports Council and only postgraduate students and academics are admitted to the library. Its information service does, however, have a telephone enquiry service and it will send out information packs, which include an extensive range of bibliographies, to members of the public. The address and telephone number can be found in the Appendix to this chapter.

As illustrated by the above examples, access arrangements vary from library to library, and in most cases it is advisable to telephone the organization and enquire whether they will allow you to use their service. Many special libraries will undertake detailed secondary research for employees of their parent organization. If you work in a commercial organization which has a library or information service it is worth checking to see what facilities and services it offers. It is probably much more than just a collection of books.

There are directories available which list the names and addresses of libraries. They can be used to locate useful libraries. Your local library will almost certainly have at least one directory which lists libraries in your country or area. Examples include *The Aslib Directory of Information Sources in the United Kingdom* (ASLIB, 1994), *American Library Directory* (1997) and *Directory of Special Libraries in Australia* (Fuller, 1995). Ask the library staff for advice about an appropriate directory to use as there are numerous directories available for each country.

A list of important special libraries for leisure and tourism research, along with their contact details, is given in the Appendix to this chapter.

Using libraries for research

A literature search is something you may need to do for several reasons. Perhaps you need background information on an area, or tourism statistics.

You may need to find out what sort of people live within easy driving distance of a location, how much they earn on average, do they have children? This kind of information and much more can be obtained from published literature available in one library or another. This literature could be in a variety of forms such as books, individual chapters in multi-authored books, articles in journals, documents on the World Wide Web and so on. Depending upon the nature of the work you are undertaking the literature search and subsequent review may form the whole basis of the research or it may be used to inform your own primary research. Veal (1997) lists six 'roles' of literature in research:

1 The entire basis of the research.
2 A source of ideas.
3 A means of discovering what research has been done by others.
4 A source of methodologies or theories.
5 A means of comparing your research with that of others.
6 To provide specific information or data to support a particular theory.

So, in what specific ways can libraries assist in this process?

Library catalogues

The first place to look for literature in most libraries is the library catalogue, a comprehensive list of all the items held in a library. Although originally these were collections of small cards held in special cabinets, most are now in electronic format, called Online Public Access Catalogues, or OPACs. These catalogues make it relatively simple to see if the library has the particular item you require, where it is located within the library, how many copies there are and which, if any, are already out on loan.

It may also be possible to access the catalogues of other libraries from here. If you have difficulty in using the catalogue, the library staff will help you to get started, or in some cases will perform the search for you. You will also be able to search for material on a particular subject, and this usually means thinking of certain words which describe the subject in which you are interested. You may be able to narrow or broaden the terms of your search during the process to help you to find just what you need, but results will only tell you the general contents of a book, not whether it contains a specific picture or table. In addition, the catalogue will not list details of articles in journals. Articles in journals can be traced by subject by using one of the many abstracting and indexing tools which are described in Chapter 5.

The catalogues of many academic, and some public, libraries can be accessed on the World Wide Web. There are numerous gateways on the Web which list library catalogues and provide an easy way to identify and access an appropriate library catalogue. One of the most comprehensive international gateways to library catalogues available on the Web is Webcats (Scott and Macdonald). A comprehensive list of university library catalogues available on the Web in the UK is provided by the NISS Gateway (NISS, 1998).

So, the library catalogue lists the items held in the library and is a general subject index. It enables you to discover what books are available. Books can be a good source of general ideas and there are many books published in the leisure and tourism fields. It is possible to discover further sources by using the bibliographies which are included in many academic books. Bibliographies are simply lists of documents, but there are other tools which can be used.

The Internet

The Internet was introduced in Chapter 2 which concentrated mainly upon the methods for locating, free of charge, information resources that are available on the World Wide Web. Libraries make extensive use of the Internet and librarians are actively involved in both providing information on the Internet and attempting to impose some kind of order on to the information available through, for example, the construction of subject gateways (see Chapter 2).

Libraries also make available the services of commercial information providers via the Internet to their users. In some cases the library pays a subscription for a service so that its users can access it on an unlimited basis, either through computers in the library, elsewhere in the organization or from their own homes via a dial-up connection using a modem. In other cases the library can access commercial services using the Internet on behalf of its users which are charged for by a combination of the amount of time connected to the service and the amount of information which is accessed. The user does not have direct access to the service but may be present whilst a librarian carries out a search. Such a service is often referred to as a mediated on-line search.

Abstracts, indexes and bibliographies

These allow a search to be extended beyond the bounds of one particular library. A bibliography is simply a list of documents. These could be published books or articles in journals or literature in any other form. Basically they allow the researcher to search for literature by subject. They are commercial services so, unlike library catalogues, they list documents which are not necessarily available in the library that you happen to be using. Increasingly they are in electronic rather than printed form. Many such tools may be available in a large library for the researcher to use. However, in some cases a more appropriate tool can be accessed by the library staff through an on-line search as described above. Always seek advice from the library staff about which tools to use to search for the information that you are looking for. Abstracts, indexes and bibliographies are described in detail in Chapter 5.

Statistics

How many people play soccer? From which country do most inbound tourists to the USA come? Statistical publications can be an interesting and informative source of information and can be used to argue for or against a particular viewpoint. Methods for tracing statistical sources are examined in detail in Chapter 6. These sources do, however, have to be used with caution. Statistics can be interpreted in different ways and the methods used to collect data can vary making comparison difficult. For more detail about using statistical sources see Veal (1997: ch. 6).

Theses and dissertations

A thesis is a statement of the findings of research and the conclusions drawn from it which is presented for the award of a degree at a university or other institution of higher education. In the UK the term 'thesis' is used in relation to work completed at PhD level only and the term 'dissertation' is used to describe an in-depth piece of work completed to satisfy the requirements for a degree below that level (such as a BSc or MA). However, in North America the term 'dissertation' is used to describe work at PhD level and the term 'thesis' to describe work below that level. (Lyons and Wilson, 1997). There are several tools available for discovering what theses and dissertations have been completed on a particular subject. Three specific examples are listed here but many of the tools listed in Chapter 5 can also be used to trace theses and dissertations.

Australia

University of Tasmania. *Union List of Degree Theses in Australian Libraries.* University of Tasmania Library.

New Zealand

New Zealand Library and Information Association (1993) *Union List of Higher Degree Theses in New Zealand Libraries*. Wellington.

North America

University Microforms International. *Dissertation Abstracts International*. Ann Arbor, Michigan.
This publication indexes mainly North American doctoral (i.e. PhD) theses. The number of leisure and tourism dissertations is relatively small.

UK and Ireland

Aslib. *Index to Theses Accepted for Higher Degrees by the Universities of Great Britain and Ireland*. London: Aslib.
This is an index to British and Irish theses and it includes summaries (abstracts). The number of leisure and tourism theses is small but is increasing.

Ask for advice in your library about tracing and obtaining access to theses. In order to obtain a thesis it is necessary to have accurate details including the name of the institution to which the thesis was submitted in addition to its author, title and date. Theses can often be obtained through document delivery or interlibrary loan services as described below.

Document delivery services

Many libraries can obtain documents which have been traced during the course of a literature search on behalf of the researcher. Such a service is often described as interlibrary loan or document delivery. There are many national and regional interlending schemes in existence. In some cases the library may be able to obtain the documents over the Internet from a commercial information provider. Such document delivery services vary greatly so it is advisable to ask the library staff what kind of service is available to you.

Sometimes charges are made for such services. The British Library Document Supply Centre (BLDSC) in the UK provides an international document delivery service. It can supply books on loan and photocopies of articles from journals to other libraries around the world on your behalf. In North America there are many regional interlibrary loans schemes in existence which libraries can use to borrow or obtain photocopies of material on behalf of their readers. In order to use such services you need to have an accurate reference to the item you require, but you do not need to provide the details of a library which holds it.

Recording references

Once you have found material which is going to be useful for your work, it is vital to remember to keep an accurate record of it and to give due credit to the person or organization that produced the original material which you may have quoted or paraphrased in your own work. This is evidence of your own scholarship and demonstrates that your research is based upon an established body of knowledge. It is important to provide this information so that someone who reads your work can identify the item you have used, so they can obtain a copy for themselves if they believe it would be useful to them. It is also important to keep accurate records of material you have discovered in case it is necessary to use a document delivery service, as described above, to obtain the material and also to enable you to easily refer back to an item you have consulted should the need arise. These descriptions of documents are known as bibliographic citations or bibliographic references.

If you are doing the work for a course at a Higher Education institution it will probably be worth checking with your lecturers to see if they have any preferences regarding the method of recording references; many will do, and you may lose marks if you disregard this.

How to compile bibliographic references

Lists of bibliographic references can be compiled using one of two styles, the Harvard method and the Numeric method.

It is important to make sure your references are correct, complete and consistent. The reference should give the author, or authors, first. If there are more than three authors, then list the name of the first author only, followed by 'et al', which means 'and others'.

For a book, when using the Harvard method, you should then give the date the book was published immediately after the author's name, then the title of the book in italics using a colon to separate the title from the subtitle, if the book has one, then the place the book was published, followed by a colon and the name of the publisher. The date, place and publisher details can be found in the front of the book. If using the Numeric method put the date the book was published at the end of the reference. Hence, the only difference between these two methods is that in Harvard the date appears after the author's name, but with Numeric it appears later in the reference.

An example of a bibliographic reference to a book using the Harvard method:

MacCannell, D. (1976) *The Tourist: A New Theory of the Leisure Class*. London: Macmillan.

An example of a bibliographic reference to a book using the Numeric method:

MacCannell, D. *The Tourist: A New Theory of the Leisure Class*. London: Macmillan, 1976.

For an article, the dates will be presented in different ways, depending on whether you are using the Harvard or the Numeric method. The author of the article should be given followed by the date if the Harvard method is being used, then the title of the article, followed by the title of the journal in which the article appeared, in italics. The volume number of the journal appears next, followed by the part number in brackets, e.g. 16 (5), and the year of publication if the Numeric method is being used. Finally the numbers of the pages on which the article appears, e.g. 118–125 are given.

An example of a bibliographic reference to an article in a journal using the Harvard method:

Rimmington, M. and Kozak, M. (1997) Developments in information technology. *Anatolla* 8 (3), 59–80.

An example of a bibliographic reference to an article in a journal using the Numeric method:

Rimmington, M. and Kozak, M. Developments in information technology. *Anatolla* 8 (3), 1997, 59–80.

Citing bibliographic references in your own work

As indicated above it is important to acknowledge your use of other people's work and ideas in your own research by acknowledging it in your text. Again, the Harvard and Numeric methods are slightly different.

Harvard

This method uses the name of the author and the date of the work when paraphrasing or directly quoting a work in your own research. For example, Tourism is very important to the nation's economy, (Allott, 1997); similarly for a direct quote '65% of the population take too little exercise' (Shaw, 1992). At the end of your work, you list these references in alphabetical order by the surname of the author, and subdivide them, if you need to, by year and letter. For example, if you have two quotes from Allott from different publications but both from 1997, the first should be listed as:

Allott, D (1997a) Canada for tourism. *Tourism Society Journal*, 48, (6), 29–30.

and the second as:

Allott, D. (1997b) *The Canadian Tourist Board*. Toronto: Free Press.

in the list of references, and similarly as Allott (1997a) etc. in the text of your work. Although the initials of the author are given in the list of references, only the surname is used in the text. In both the Harvard and Numeric methods, where a direct quote is used in the text, the page number from which the quote is taken is usually given too, for example (Allott, 1997: 26).

Numeric

Using this method, each mention of someone's work, or each quote, is followed by a number in brackets, beginning with (1). The list of references is then shown in numerical order at the end of your work. For example, Richards (2) argues that the signs are good for an increase in Australian cultural tourism. This would then be listed as:

2. Richards, S. *The Future for Australian Tourism*. New York: McGraw-Hill, 1996.

Under the Numeric system you would normally have a numerical list of references at the end of your work. These are known as endnotes. However, it is also possible to give these references at the bottom of the page where they occur. These are known as footnotes. In addition to the references you might also have a separate bibliography which is a list of material which you have used but not directly quoted from or referred to. It can also contain material which the author suggests readers might like to refer to (suggested reading).

With regard to the citation and referencing of electronic materials, particularly websites, the latest rules seem to be that you should provide the Internet address for the item, e.g. http://www.lmu.ac.uk/ etc., the name of the person who created the site, if possible, and the date on which you looked at the site. The guidance on how to cite and reference these items is constantly being updated, and details about Internet addresses and this type of resource are given in Chapter 2.

There are many books available which describe how to cite references, and documents on this topic can also be found on the World Wide Web. See for example, Veal (1997: ch. 5), Bosworth (1992), Cross and Towle (1997) and Canterbury and Christchurch College (1997).

Conclusion

To conclude, this chapter has attempted to illustrate some of the ways in which libraries and librarians can assist in the research process. It has indicated the general methods by which literature in leisure and tourism can be traced. Some of the search tools introduced here are discussed in more detail in subsequent chapters of this book. The services and resources provided by libraries vary greatly so you should always ask for specific advice on your information problem. The tools that you use and the way in which you use them will vary not only according to the nature of your research but also according to the particular library that you are using.

Appendix: Some libraries for leisure and tourism research

Australia

Australian International Hotel School
PO Box E243
Queen Victoria Terrace
Barton, ACT 2600
Tel: 06 234 4455
E-mail: aihs@slim.slnsw.gov.au

Australian Sports Commission
National Sport Information Centre
PO Box 176
Belconnen, ACT 2616
Tel: 06 252 1369
E-mail: nsic@ausport.telememo.au
Website: http://www.ausport.gov.au/nsic/nsicspin.html

Central Queensland University
Rockhampton MC
Queensland 4702
Website: http://www.library.cqu.edu.au/limshome.htm

Department of Environment, Sport and Territories Library
PO Box 787
Canberra
ACT 2601
Tel: 61 2 6274 1209
Fax: 61 2 6274 1215
E-mail library@dest.erin.gov.au
Website: http://environment.gov.au/portfolio/library/library.html

Department of Transport (WA)
136 Stirling Highway
Nedlands
WA 6009
Tel: 09 389 0669

Griffith University
Queensland, 4111
Tel: 7 38 757 111
Website: http://medea.itc.gu.edu.au/lils/coord/search.htm

Hunter Valley Research Foundation
PO Box 23
Tighes Hill
NSW 2297
Tel: 049 69 4566
Website: http://www.Newcastle.edu.au/hvrf/

Monash University
Wellington Road
Clayton
Victoria, 3168
Tel: 61 3 990 52665
E-mail: library@monash.edu.au
Website: http://www.lib.monash.edu.au/

Office of Tourism
PO Box 1545
Canberra ACT 2601
Tel: 06 279 7224
Website: http://www.dist.gov.au/tourism/

Queensland Department of Tourism, Sport and Racing
GPO Box 354
Brisbane
QLD 4001
Tel: 07 237 1282

Ryde College – Northern Sydney Institute of TAFE
The Library
250 Blaxland Road
Ryde
NSW 2112
Tel: 02 808 8326

SA Sports Institute
Coaching Resource Centre
PO Box 219
Brooklyn Park
SA 5032
Tel: 08 416 6631
E-mail: di.forgan@ausport.telememo.au

University of Canberra
The Library
PO Box 1
Belconnen ACT 2616
Tel: 06 201 5068
Website: http://www.canberra.edu.au/new/services/library.html

University of Technology, Sydney
PO Box 123
Broadway
Sydney
NSW 2007
Tel: 2 330 1990
Website: http://www.lib.uts.edu.au/library-catalogues.html

Canada

Canadian Tourism Commission
Tourism Reference and Documentation Centre (TRDC)
235 Queen Street, 400D
Ottawa, Ontario K1A 0H6
Tel: 613 954 3943
Website: http://206.191.33.50/tourism/trdc.html

Pacific Rim Institute of Tourism
Suite 930
555 West Hasting
Vancouver, British Columbia V6B 4N6
Tel: 604 682 8000
E-mail: nancy_brenner@mindlink.bc.ca
E-mail: donna_green@mindlink.ba.ca

Sport Information and Research Centre
107-1600 James Naismith Drive
Gloucester, Ontario K1B 5N4
Tel: 1 800 665 6413 (North America), 1 613 748 5658 (worldwide)
Fax: 1-613-748-5701
E-mail: moreinfo@sirc.ca
Website: http://www.sirc.ca/

Tourism Industry Resource Centre
PO Box 2703
Whitehorse
Yukon Y1A 2C6
Tel: 867 667 5449
E-mail: tirc@yknet.yk.ca
Website: http://www.yukonweb.com/government/tourism/tirc

University of Calgary Libraries
Calgary, Alberta
T2N 1N4
Tel: 403220 8895
Website: http://www.acs.ucalgary.ca/UofC/departments/INFO/library/

University of Northern British Columbia
University Library
3333 University Way
Prince George, BC
V2N 4Z9
Website: http://library.unbc.edu/

University of Victoria
MacPherson Library
McPherson Building
Ring Road
PO Box 1800, STN CSC
Victoria, BC, V8W 3H5
Tel: 250 7218274
Website: http://gateway.uvic.ca/

New Zealand

Hillary Commission for Sport, Fitness and Leisure
PO Box 2251
Wellington
Tel: 64 4 472 8058
E-mail: rwhite@hillarysport.org.nz

Lincoln University Library
POB 84
Canterbury
New Zealand.
Tel: 64 3 325 2811
Website: http://www.lincoln.ac.nz/libr/default.htm

The University of Waikato Library
Private Bag 3105
Hamilton
Tel: 64 7 856 2889
Website: http://www.waikato.ac.nz/library/

Victoria University of Wellington Library
PO Box 3438
Wellington
Tel: 64 4 472 1000
E-mail: library@vuw.ac.nz
Website: http://www.vuw.ac.nz/library/

UK

The British Library for Development Studies
Institute of Development Studies
Brighton BN1 9RE
Tel 01273 606261
Fax: 01273 621202/691647
E-mail: blds@sussex.ac.uk
Website: http://www.ids.ac.uk/blds/blds.html

British Tourist Authority Library
Thames Tower
Backs Road
London W6 9EL
Tel: 0181 565 3011

British Library of Political and Economic Science
10 Portugal Street
London WC2A 2HD
Tel: 0171 955 7229
Website: http://blpes.lse.ac.uk

Countryside Commission
John Dower House
Crescent Place
Cheltenham GL50 3RA
Tel: 01242 521381
E-mail: info@countryside.gov.uk
Website: http://www.countryside.gov.uk/

English Sports Council
Information services
16 Upper Woburn Place
London WC1H 0QP
Tel: 0171 273 1500
E-mail: info@english.sports.gov.uk
Website: http://www.english.sports.gov.uk/

Glasgow Caledonian University
Cowcaddens Road
Glasgow G4 0BA
Tel: 0141 331 3000
Website: http://www.gcal.ac.uk/library/index.html

Hotel, Catering and Institutional Management Association
Information Service
191 Trinity Road
London SW17 7HN
Tel: 0181 672 4251
E-mail: library@hcima.org.uk
Website: http://hcima.org.uk/its/geninfo.htm

Institute of Leisure and Amenity Management
ILAM House
Lower Basildon
Reading RG8 9NE
Tel: 01491 874800
Website: http://www.ilam.co.uk/

Leeds Metropolitan University Library
Calverley Street
Leeds LS1 3HE
Tel: 0113 2835958
Website: http://www.lmu.ac.uk/lis/

National Coaching Foundation Information Centre
114 Cardigan Road
Leeds LS6 38J
Tel: 0532-744802

Oxford Brookes University Library
Headington
Oxford OX3 0BP
Tel: 01865 741111
Website: http://www.brookes.ac.uk/services/library/

School of Oriental and African Studies Library
Russell Square
London WC1H 0XG
Tel: 0171 323 6109
Fax: 0171 636 2834
E-mail libenquiry@soas.ac.uk.
Website: http://www.soas.ac.uk/Library/HOME.HTML

Scottish Sports Council
Information Centre
Caledonia House
South Gyle
Edinburgh EH12 9DQ
Tel: 0131 317 7200

Sheffield Hallam University
Pond Street
Sheffield S1 1WB
Tel: 0114 2255555
Website: http://www.shu.ac.uk/services/lc/

South Bank University
Borough Road
London SE1 0AA
Tel: 0171 928 8989
Website: http://www.sbu.ac.uk/lis/

Sports Council for Wales
Information Centre
Sophia Gardens
Cardiff CF1 9SW
Tel: 01222 391571 200

Sports Library
Main Library
Surrey Street
Sheffield S1 1AS
Tel: 0114 2735929
E-mail: sports.library@dial.pipex.com

University of North London
236–250 Holloway Road
London N7 6PP
Tel: 0171 6072789
Website: http://opac.unl.ac.uk

University of Luton
Park Square
Luton LU1 3JU
Tel.: 01582 734111
Website: http://www.luton.ac.uk/LearningResources/index.html

University of Surrey
Guildford
Surrey GU2 5XH
Tel: 01483 300800
Website: http://www.surrey.ac.uk/Library/

USA

Amateur Athletic Foundation of Los Angeles
2141 W. Adams Blvd
Los Angeles
CA 90018
Tel: 213 730 9696
E-mail: aafla@class.org

American Hotel and Motel Association
Information Center
1201 New York Avenue, NW
Washington
DC 20005-3931
Tel: 202 289 3100
E-mail: infoctr@ahma.com
Website: http://www.ahma.com/pubs.htm

Arizona State University
University Libraries
PO Box 871006
Tempe
AZ 85287
Tel: 602 965 9011
Website: http://www.asu.edu/lib/

Indiana University
Health, Physical Education and Recreation Library
HPER Building 031
Bloomington
IN 47401
Tel: 812 855 4420
E-mail: Heynse@ucs.indiana.edu
Website: http://www.indiana.edu/~libhper/index.html

National Transportation Library
400 7th St, SW
Room 2200
Washington
DC 20590
Tel: 202 366 0746
Website: http://isweb.tasc.dot.gov/library/library.htm

New York University
The Elmer Holmes Bobst Library
70 Washington Square South
New York
NY 10012
Tel: 212 998 2505
Website: http://www.sce.nyu.edu/chtta/html/h1cht.html

PATA Center
Pacific Asia Travel Association
1 Montgomery Street
West Tower, Suite 1750
San Francisco
CA 94104
Tel: 415 986 4646
E-mail: pata@class.org

Sporting News
PO Box 56
St Louis
MO 63166
Tel: 314 993 7787

State University of New York
College at Cortland – Memorial Library
Box 2000
Cortland
NY 13045
Tel: 607 753 2221
Fax: 607 756 2499

University of California at Los Angeles
University Research Library
05 Hilgard Avenue
Los Angeles
CA 90024-1575
Tel: 310 825 4879

University of Colorado
Boulder
CO 80309
Tel: 303 492 1411
Website: http://www-libraries.colorado.edu/ucb/libraries.htm

University of Illinois
Tourism Research Laboratory
1206 South Fourth Street
Champaign
IL 61820
Tel: 217 333 4410
E-mail: drfez@uiuc.edu

University of Texas
Todd-McLean Physical Culture Collection
Department of Kinesiology
217 Gregory Gymnasium
Austin
TX 78712
Tel: 512 471 4890

United States Sports Academy
1 Academy Drive
Daphne
AL 36526
Tel: 205 626 3303
E-mail: library@ussa-sport.ussa.edu
Website: http://www.sport.ussa.edu/library.htm

US Travel Data Center
1100 New York Avenue, NW
Suite 450
Washington
DC 20005-3934
Tel: 202 408 1832
E-mail: scook@tia.org

Washington State Department of Transportation Library
PO Box 47425
310 Maple Park Ave SE
Olympia
WA 98504-7425
Tel: 360 705 7750
E-mail: library@wsdot.wa.gov
Website: http://www.wsdot.wa.gov/hq/library/default.htm

WTO Research and Education Center
Gelman Library, Room 104
George Washington University
Washington
DC 20052
Tel: 202 994 6049
E-mail: data:shm@gwuvm.gwu.edu

References and further reading

American Library Directory (1997) Bowker.

Arnzen, M. (1996) Cyber citations: documenting Internet sources presents some thorny problems. *Internet World*, **7,** 9. http://www.internetworld.com/print/monthly/1996/09/cybercitations.html (accessed 20 July 1998).

ASLIB. (1994) *The Aslib Directory of Information Sources in the United Kingdom*, 8th edn. Aslib.

Banks, A. (1998) A Guide for Writing Research Papers Based on Modern Language Association (MLA) Documentation. http://webster.commnet.edu/mla.htm (accessed 20 July 1998).

Bell, J. (1993) *Doing your Research Project: A Guide For First Time Researchers in Education and Social Science*. Open University Press.

Bosworth, D. (1992) *Citing your References: A Guide for Authors of Journal Articles and Students Writing Theses or Dissertations*. Underhill Press.

British Standards Institute (1990) *Recommendations for Citing and Referencing Published Material: Guidlines for Authors and Editors*. British Standards Institute (BS 5605).

Canadian Tourism Commission (1998) Tourism Reference and Documentation Centre. http://206.191.33.50/tourism/trdc.html (accessed 17 July 1998).

Canterbury and Christchurch College (1997) Recording References, Harvard System. http://www.cant.ac.uk/LIST/organise/or_s2f.htm (accessed 17 July 1998).

Coleman, D. (1997) Leisure Studies Education. Australian and New Zealand Association for Leisure Studies, http://www.gu.edu.au/gwis/leis/services/lswp/index.htm (accessed 17 July 1998).

Crawford, W. and Gorman, M. (1995) *Future Libraries*. American Library Association.

Cross, P. and Towle, K. (1996) A Guide to Citing Internet Resources. University of Bournemouth, http://www.bournemouth.ac.uk/service-depts/lis/LIS_Pub/harvardsystint.html (accessed 17 July 1998).

Fuller, J. (ed.) (1995) *Directory of Special Libraries in Australia*. 9th edn. Australian Library and Information Association Special Libraries Section.

Gibaldi, J. (ed.) (1998) *MLA Style Manual and Guide to Scholarly Publishing*, 2nd edn. Modern Language Association of America.

Holderness, M. (1992). Time to shelve the library. *New Scientist*, December.

Lyons, F. and Wilson, C. (1997) How to formulate a student project or dissertation. In *The Student's Companion to Sociology* (C. Ballard, J. Gubbay and C. Middleton, eds). Blackwell.

NISS (1998) Library OPACs in HE. http://www.niss.ac.uk/reference/opacs.html (accessed 6 April 1998).

Nurcombe, V. (ed.) (1994) *Environment and Leisure: Proceedings of Two One Day Seminars. Who Publishes Official Information On the British National Heritage and Who Publishes Official Information on the Environment*. Library Association Information Services Group.

Scarrott, M. (1997) Information and data sources. In *The Student's Companion to Sociology* (C. Ballard, J. Gubbay and C. Middleton, eds). Blackwell.

Scott, P. and Macdonald, D. Webcats: Library Catalogues on the Web. University of Saskatchewan Libraries, http://www.lights.com/webcats/ (accessed 17 July 1998).

Smith, D. (1994) *Bibliographic Citation: A Guide*. Leeds Metropolitan University.

Sport and Recreation Information Group (1996) *SPRIG Directory of Periodicals in Sport and Recreation*. 3rd edn, SPRIG. (This directory includes library holdings of key sports journals in the UK.)

Turabian, K. (1996) *A Manual for Writers of Term Papers, Theses, and Dissertations*, 6th edn. University of Chicago Press.

Veal, A. J. (1997) *Research Methods for Leisure and Tourism*, 2nd edn. Pitman.

Waksberg, R. (1998). Reni Waksberg's Tourism Research Index. http://www.tourism-montreal.org/tourism.htm (accessed 17 July 1998).

Walker, J. (1997) Columbia Online Style: MLA Style Citations of Electronic Resources. http://www.cas.usf.edu/english/walker/mla.html (accessed 21 July 1998).

4

Journals as sources of information in sport, leisure and tourism

David Airey, Geoff Cole and Ruth Mitchell

Background

For any researcher, journals, whether in paper or electronic form, invariably represent the key source for a review of the literature and past research. Books may provide the basis for understanding the subject matter and getting to grips with the concepts. They will also usually give the starting point for further references and sources. But it is the journals that are the jumping-off point for new research and insights. While there are some overlaps between the two, the basic distinctions are that books are not published regularly, they normally appear on a one-off basis and, except for edited collections, they usually have just one or two authors. They provide an overview of their subject area and to a greater or lesser extent they cater for a range of readers from students to researchers. As a result the information contained in books is normally more generalized and is likely to be more dated. Journals and periodicals, on the other hand, appear regularly, they concentrate on providing topical information, from research outputs to news, they usually contain the work of more than one writer and they are designed to cater for a fairly specific readership. In brief, while books provide the overview, journals set out the current 'state of the art'. It is this latter feature which makes them so important for researchers.

The title 'journal' or 'periodical' can embrace a number of different types of publications with frequencies that range from daily or weekly to annual. Within these, the most important for the researcher is what are called 'academic journals'. For this reason, while the first part of this chapter provides an overview of a range of different types of publications, the latter part concentrates mainly on the academic journals and the listing in Appendix 1 at the end of this chapter consists mainly of such publications.

Academic journals typically appear quarterly, sometimes more frequently and occasionally as an annual review. The key contents of academic journals are normally articles and reports of ongoing or completed research. Most also contain other items such as editorial-type comments on topical issues, conference reports and book reviews. Academic journals are also normally refereed. This means that the articles and reports are subject to comment and approval, not only by the journal editor but, perhaps more importantly, by referees who may be drawn from an editorial board listed in the journal or from elsewhere. The referees are usually specialists in the field who, among other things, will be able to comment on the scholarship, the accuracy, relevance and presentation of the work being considered for publication. Typically academic journals operate a double blind refereeing system which means that at the time of refereeing the identity of the author is unknown to the referee and vice versa. In order to avoid individual bias and to take the widest view of the research community in the field, most journals use more than one referee; some three or more. The importance of academic journals is that they contain up-to-date material that has been subject to scrutiny by academic peers. For these reasons they provide a crucial and generally sound basis for further study.

In line with the growth of leisure and tourism as areas of academic study and research, there has been a substantial increase in the number of academic journals serving these areas. The earliest in the field, although not originally refereed, was the *Tourist Review* which first appeared in 1946. This is now the journal of the Swiss-based international organization International Association of Scientific Experts in Tourism or Association Internationale d'Experts Scientifiques du Tourisme (AIEST). Other early arrivals on the scene were from the USA, the *Journal of Travel Research*, first published as the *Travel Research Bulletin,* in 1962, the *Annals of Tourism Research* in 1973, and *Leisure Sciences* in 1977, and from Canada *Loisir et Société/Society and Leisure* in 1978. The first of these is the journal of the American based Travel and Tourism Research Association (TTRA). From the UK, *Tourism Management* (originally the *International Journal of Tourism Management*) first appeared in 1980 and *Leisure Studies*, which is the journal of the Leisure Studies Association, appeared in 1982. There are currently upward of forty academic journals published in English dealing with leisure and tourism or sixty if the field is

broadened to include hospitality. In addition to these, given the multidiscpli-
nary nature of leisure and tourism studies, the content of journals covering
other fields often also have a direct relevance for researchers. For example,
journals dealing with management, planning or the environment often contain
material with an immediate bearing on leisure and tourism.

In areas of study such as leisure and tourism that are associated with a
specific sector of the economy or with a particular profession, academic journals
are often complemented by professional journals. It is sometimes difficult to
maintain a distinction between the two. Not only are some academic journals
also house publications of professional bodies, but some of the papers in academic journals have a clear professional orientation. Perhaps the most important
dividing line is that, except for those that specifically aim at the academic
community, the articles appearing in professional journals are not usually
subject to external peer review or refereeing. Professional journals may be
divided into two types. The first are the house journals of professional associations. In this respect the *Tourist Review*, the *Journal of Travel Research* and
Leisure Studies, referred to above as academic journals, may also be considered
professional journals. Also falling into this category are *Tourism*, the journal
of the Tourism Society, which is a UK-based professional body, and *Hospitality*, which describes itself as the management magazine of the UK-based Hotel
and Catering International Management Association (HCIMA). Such publications usually contain serious articles alongside news and information relevant
to members. The second type are journals that carry serious, usually lengthy,
articles that are of direct interest to professionals working in the field rather
than being specifically for academics and researchers. Such articles may include,
for example, country reports and forecasts such as those that appear in the
International Tourism Reports, published by Travel and Tourism Intelligence
in London, or sector analyses and forecasts such as those of the *Travel and
Tourism Analyst* and *Travel Industry Monitor* from the same publisher.

Trade periodicals usually appear weekly or monthly in the form of newspapers or magazines. They contain news items and technical information and may
also sometimes contain reports which can provide important information for
the researcher, at least to keep abreast of current issues. In recognition of the
fact that there are many different groups of interests within leisure and tourism,
there are many different trade journals. These include, in the UK, for example,
publications such as *Travel Trade Gazette UK and Ireland* and *Travel Weekly
UK* which cover the work of travel agents and tour operators, *Caterer and
Hotelkeeper* for the hospitality sector and *Leisure Management* for those
involved in the management of sports centres, visitor attractions and other

components of leisure. Similar publications in the USA include *Hotel and Motel Management* and *Park and Grounds Management*. Alongside the trade publications there is also a very wide range of consumer magazines such as *AAA Going Places* or *Executive Travel*. Some of these contain information of relevance to researchers.

General newspapers and magazines also contain information of direct relevance to researchers, including those focusing on hospitality and leisure. They not only contain news stories, but also carry investigative articles and analyses which are essential reading for anyone aiming to keep up-to-date in their field. In this respect, serious newspapers and magazines, such as the *Economist*, can play an important part in the researcher's work.

In addition to the above there are a number of other periodicals that contain important information for researchers. These include, for example, regular or irregular bulletins and reports of international agencies, such as *IATA Review* from the International Air Transport Association, *WTO News* from the World Tourism Organization or the reports of the International Civil Aviation Organization.

The academic journals

In two important ways, leisure and tourism represent very broad fields of enquiry which pose particular problems for the researcher in identifying relevant literature. First, as has been noted, they draw upon a wide range of other disciplines and areas of study. For this reason, depending on the research topic, the researcher needs to be alert to the literature in fields as diverse as marketing, psychology, health, management or economics, each of which has its own specialist journals and other publications. Secondly, within leisure and tourism themselves, there are a number of very different fields of enquiry and, again, each supports specialist literature. This is not the place to set out all the disciplines and fields that are contained within leisure and tourism but it is appropriate to delineate the main fields that may provide a starting point for a review of the relevant literature. One way of doing this is by clustering the academic journals of the field. These broadly fall into six groups:

- leisure, recreation and sport
- tourism
- hospitality management
- travel and transport

- attractions and heritage
- other.

Each of these groups contains journals that have articles related to leisure and tourism. But most also contain material that falls outside these fields. The initial task of the researcher is to identify their field of enquiry as a basis not only for identifying the relevant journals but also for establishing how far to go into the fields covered by the journals.

Leisure, recreation and sport

Journals in this area include those that take a broad approach to leisure as a field of study as well as more narrowly focused publications. Examples of the former type include *Leisure Studies*, *Leisure Sciences*, *Loisir et Société/Society and Leisure*, the *Journal of Leisure Research* and the *Journal of Applied Recreation Research*. These were all started between the late 1960s and early 1980s as 'leisure' emerged as a distinct field of academic enquiry and they have played an important role in establishing the field. They all cover a range of different types of leisure activities and from a range of different social science perspectives: economic, social and psychological. These broad based journals contrast with the many highly focused publications that deal with a particular type or aspect of leisure, recreation and sport. Included in the latter are, for example, the *Sport Science Review* and *Sport History Review* as well as publications relating to particular sports and activities and sport medicine. The latter include, for example, the *British Journal of Sports Medicine,* the *American Journal of Sports Medicine*, the *Therapeutic Recreation Journal* and the *Journal of Applied Sport Psychology*. Reflecting the development of scholarship and research in these areas, such journals were established rather earlier than those concerned with leisure as a whole.

Tourism

As a relatively recent arrival on the academic scene, there has been a rapid growth in journals devoted to tourism. The early journals, such as *Annals of Tourism Research* and *Tourism Management*, took a relatively broad view and contained articles dealing with many different sectors and aspects of tourism, although in the case of *Annals of Tourism Research* the emphasis is strongly on social sciences. These have been joined by journals with a similarly broad approach such as *Tourism Analysis* and *Progress in Tourism and Hospitality Research*. The latter originally appeared as an annual publication called *Progress in Tourism, Recreation and Hospitality Management* but from 1995 has appeared quarterly. More recently, as the field of enquiry has developed and research contributions have grown, so the opportunities for more specialist journals have multiplied. These include, for example, journals which focus on particular aspects such as the *Journal of Sustainable Tourism*, *Tourism Economics* and the *Journal of Travel and Tourism Marketing*. They also include those that deal with particular regions of the world such as the *Pacific Tourism Review*.

Hospitality management

Although hospitality operations and management are key components of tourism, their study has tended to develop as a separate field of enquiry. As such they are supported by their own journals. However, many of these carry articles specifically concerned with tourism, just as tourism journals contain pieces devoted to hospitality. This overlap is reflected in some of the titles such as the *Journal of International Hospitality, Leisure and Tourism Management*. The early leading journal in the field was the *Cornell Hotel and Restaurant Administration Quarterly*, which first appeared in 1960. This was developed at the university of that name which had one of the earliest hotel management programmes in the USA. Its emphasis was on providing material of direct relevance to practising hotel and catering managers as well as academics. A journal devoted to hotel and catering management, *HCIMA Review*, was established in the UK in 1974 but at the time the field was insufficiently developed to sustain its continuation and it ceased publication in 1978. Subsequently, as the area has developed, a number of journals have been established such as the *International Journal of Hospitality Management* and the *International Journal of Contemporary Hospitality Management* (initially called the *Journal of Contemporary Hospitality Management*) in the UK and the *Journal of Restaurant and Foodservice Marketing* in the USA. Also more specialist publications have emerged dealing with particular aspects of the business such as the *Journal of Gambling Studies* or the *Journal of Hospitality and Leisure Marketing*. Although individual emphases vary, one of the strong themes of the hospitality journals is the extent to which they concentrate on issues related to management and organizational behaviour.

Travel and transport

There are two kinds of journals dealing with travel and transport. They either deal with a particular mode of transport or they deal with transport or an aspect of transport as a whole. Included in the former are titles such as, for example, the *Journal of Air Transport Management*, the *Railway and Canal Historical Society Journal* and *Maritime Policy and Management*. Within these, some of the contributions, particularly in the field of air transport, relate specifically to the transportation of tourists. Many of the more general publications focus on management and policy aspects of transport. These include, for example, *Transport Management* which is the house journal of the Institute of Transport Administration, the *Journal of Transport Economics and Policy* and *Transport Policy*. They also include titles like *Transportation Science* and the *Journal of Transport History*. Given the wide range of transport issues covered in these journals, many of which have little to do directly with tourism or leisure travel, the researcher needs a carefully developed research strategy to identify relevant key journals and content in this field.

Attractions and heritage

Visitor attractions represent a relatively new area of academic study in leisure and tourism. As such, journals devoted specifically to attractions and their management from the perspective of leisure and tourism are fairly recent arrivals. An example is *Festival Management and Event Tourism*. However, some of the component sectors that make up visitor attractions have journals that have been established for far longer. For example, *Museum International* dates back to 1948 and it has subsequently been joined by a range of other publications devoted to museums such as *Museum Practice* and *Museum Management and Curatorship*. Similarly other fields such as the theatre have long established titles like *Theatre Studies* and natural and heritage attractions are covered in publications such as the *International Journal of Heritage Studies* or the many publications contained within planning and geography (see below).

Other

It is impossible to identify here all the many other fields which support journals whose contents relate in some way to leisure and tourism. Indeed, they may quite properly appear in the contents of almost the full span of journals from anthropology to zoology. However, within this span there are a few fields in which leisure and tourism appear to figure more regularly than in others. These include the study of the service industries which is itself a relatively recent arrival. The *Service Industries Journal* and the *International Journal of Service Industry Management* include papers specifically on leisure and tourism. Similarly the planning journals, such as the *Town Planning Review*, and the many journals concerned with human geography, such as *Environment and Planning A*, *Environment and Planning D: Society and Space*, *Progress in Human Geography* and *Area* include contributions relevant to leisure and tourism. The third group are the journals devoted to business, management and organization behaviour where leisure and tourism organizations are sometimes the focus for case studies and other enquiries. These include, for example, journals such as *Managerial and Decision Economics* and *Long Range Planning*.

New developments

This brief review suggests that the researcher in leisure and tourism is faced with an almost bewildering range of journal titles. As relatively new fields of enquiry, new journals devoted to leisure and tourism are being established and these are increasingly focusing on particular sectors and aspects. At the same time the journals serving the longer-established fields of enquiry, such as geography, management, museums and transport, contain material that relate to the growing areas of leisure and tourism that increasingly impact upon their work. As a result, from a dearth of academic literature devoted to leisure and tourism twenty years ago, we have moved to a situation where the researcher must be highly selective in searching the literature.

At the same time as the literature has been developing, the forms of distribution have been changing. In the past, journals have typically been quarterly publications delivered in printed paper form. The key development for the future is electronic distribution. So far relatively few journals are available in their entirety in electronic form. However, at this stage, many have contents lists on the World Wide Web. Given the volume and range of literature this clearly represents a major resource for today's and tomorrow's researchers.

Using journals

Identifying relevant journal articles

Literature searching is discussed in more detail in Chapter 2. You will need to decide, at the outset, whether a comprehensive search of the literature is required. You may decide, for a variety of reasons, that you will limit your search, knowing that you only need to trace references to a representative number of journal articles. Your search of the literature will take some or all of the following factors into account:

- The period of time to be covered: just very recent journal articles, articles published during the last five or perhaps ten years, or everything that has ever been published.

- The geographical area to be covered: just the UK, the USA, or worldwide.
- The language of publication: whether to limit the search to publications in English or any other language.
- Access to journals: whether to concentrate on one library which is easy for you to use.

Browsing

Browsing through recent issues of relevant journals is one way of discovering what has been written on a particular topic. However, this can be time-consuming and inevitably limits your search to those journals to which you have easy access. This approach may be best suited to the kind of search where a few representative articles are needed, where some recent information is required but not a comprehensive literature search, such as for a short essay.

Contents page services, both printed and electronic, are a useful way of finding out what has been published in particular journals. Printed services include the Current Contents series, of which the *Social and Behavioral Sciences* title is the most relevant for leisure and tourism. Electronic services can be accessed in a variety of ways:

- Subscription to an electronic mailing list (usually free of charge), such as ContentsDirect from Elsevier.
- Subscription to an on-line service (not necessarily free of charge), such as UnCover or British Library Inside Information. Your Librarian will be able to provide guidelines and instructions on how to use these.
- Membership of e-mail discussion lists, such as TRINET and Leisurenet, which often list the contents pages of recent academic journals.
- Accessing World Wide Web sites set up by individual publishers, such as *Journal of Tourism Studies* and *Leisure Studies*.

Current awareness bulletins, such as *Articles in Hospitality and Tourism* and *Sports Documentation Monthly Bulletin*, are also useful sources of information about the contents of recent journals.

Abstracts and indexes

The most effective and efficient way of searching the journal literature for articles on particular topics, perhaps for a comprehensive search of the literature for a dissertation, is to use indexing and abstracting publications (which are discussed in more depth in Chapter 5). They provide lists of journal articles arranged by topic, making it much easier and quicker to compile relevant references. Also, indexes and abstracts will cover a much wider range of journals than you would normally have access to and will identify other journals to which you do have access but which you had not considered.

Abstracting publications, such as *Leisure, Recreation and Tourism Abstracts*, have the added bonus of providing you with a short summary (or abstract) of the article in question. This can be very useful as a way of discovering what the article is about, particularly if your local library does not hold the original. The abstract will give you enough information to help you decide whether to get hold of the full text of the original article.

Abstracting and indexing publications are available in a range of formats: printed, CD-ROM and on-line. You would normally be expected to use the printed and CD-ROM versions yourself, but your librarian may be able to search an on-line database for you and may pass the cost on to you.

If you require very recent, up-to-the-minute information, abstracting and indexing publications will not be suitable sources, as they have a built-in delay before references are published. In this case, browsing through recent issues of key journals, magazines and, perhaps, general newspapers will be the best solution.

Further references

The bibliography at the end of an academic journal article is a vital way of expanding the literature search by suggesting other potentially relevant published material. If you are doing a comprehensive literature search, you will want to follow up these suggestions and, unless you are very disciplined, you may soon be inundated with too much rather than not enough information.

If you have discovered a useful reference, you can trace more recent articles that refer to it by using citation indexes, such as the *Social Sciences Citation Index*.

Understanding references

It is important to be able to recognize and understand references to journals in the literature, particularly how they differ from references to books. A reference will include enough information to enable you to trace the original article for yourself. A reference to a journal article will have volume and issue numbers, two titles, the article title and journal title, and would typically look like this:

Author(s) of article:	Go, F. M.
Title of article:	A conceptual framework for managing global tourism and hospitality marketing
Title of journal:	*Tourism Recreation Research*
Volume and issue numbers:	21(2)
Date of publication:	1996
Page numbers:	37–43

Obtaining journal articles

Having carried out a literature search using indexing and abstracting publications, created a list of journal articles relevant to the topic in question and decided which ones are to be read, the next step is trace where those journals can be found.

Your own library

The first step will be to use the catalogue at your local library. If you are a student at a college or university which specializes in tourism and leisure studies, you can expect to find a fair number of the journals to which your search has led you. If, however, you are working in the industry, you may be able to use a local college or university library for reference. Your local public authority library is unlikely to hold many, if any, of the journals you wish to consult.

Other libraries

Unless your local library holds a significant number of the journals you wish to consult, you will need to consider other ways of satisfying your requirements. There may be other academic or specialist libraries within your region or further afield which would allow you to consult their journal collection for reference purposes.

An increasing number of libraries are making their catalogues, sometimes referred to as OPACs or Online Public Access Catalogues, available on the Internet and they can usually be accessed through the parent institution's home page. Your own library may have included links from their homepage to other library catalogues.

Interlibrary loan and document supply

All academic libraries and most public libraries operate some kind of inter-library loan service, whereby particular journal articles can be requested, usually on payment of a fee, from another library.

You may also consider using one of the growing number of electronic document supply services, such as UnCover and ISI Document Solution, which supply copies, on payment of a fee (usually by credit card), of the journal articles traced through them. Or you could try using HOSTLINE which is a fee-based service, specializing in hospitality and tourism, run by the Nestlé Library at Cornell University in the USA.

Electronic journals

A growing number of journals are being published in electronic format. Some printed journals have an electronic equivalent, while other journals are available only electronically. Electronic journals may be produced on floppy disk or CD-ROM or they may be made available via the Internet. Chapter 2 discusses the Internet in more detail.

It is usually necessary to take out a subscription to use electronic journals, whether on disk or via the Internet. This will require payment of a fee, in return for which a password will be allocated. Your local library may have paid this fee to enable you to use them.

Referring to journal articles

Recording references

At the outset of undertaking research you must decide how to record and keep track of the references you have found and used. There is nothing more frustrating than discovering at the writing-up stage that you have made extensive use of a particular publication and have forgotten to make a note of where you found it.

A simple card filing system is recommended, in which details of each publication consulted are recorded on a small card. The cards can be filed for later use, alphabetically by author, article title, journal title, or topic. It is also worth adding a short summary of the content of the article to remind you what it was about, and perhaps a note of the library where you consulted it.

There are also a number of database management software packages, such as Microsoft Access, and bibliographic software packages, such as ProCite and Reference Manager, which allow you to record details of journal references in a database. In addition you can sort and use the data to produce a bibliography.

Referring to sources in a bibliography

At the end of every piece of work, whether it is a short report or a major literature review, you should include a list of all the articles that you refer to or have used.

This enables other people to follow up your findings for themselves. You must also acknowledge the contribution of other people to your work. It is unfair to claim for yourself insights and discoveries which in fact other people have made. Academic institutions often have a policy regarding plagiarism, or the unacknowledged use of someone else's work, and may impose penalties on students who contravene the rules.

There are conventions for the production of a bibliography at the end of your work. Shields and Walton (1996) of the University of Northumbria at Newcastle and the Academic Services Group (1996) at Bournemouth University have produced useful guides that are accessible via the Internet.

In summary, the elements required for citing journal articles are as follows:

author(s) of article, title of article, title of journal, volume number, issue number, page numbers and date.

The journal title is often underlined or italicized in order to distinguish it from the article title, which is sometimes enclosed in quotation marks. This convention is not necessary, but may be followed for aesthetic reasons.

As long as your references are comprehensive, i.e. include all the elements needed for someone else to trace the original document, and consistent, i.e. elements are included in the same style and order, it does not really matter which convention you choose. However, there are two major conventions that are universally used and recognized:

- *Harvard, or author-date, method.* This method has the elements for citing journal articles in the following order: author(s) of article, date, title of article, title of journal, volume number, issue number, and page numbers. A journal reference using the Harvard method would look like this:

Powe, N. and Willis, K. (1996) Benefits received by visitors to heritage sites: a case study of Warkworth Castle. *Leisure Studies*, 15(4), 259–275.

- *Vancouver, or numerical, method.* This method has the elements in the same order except for the date which has a lower priority. A journal reference using the Vancouver method would look like this:

  Powe, N. and Willis, K. Benefits received by visitors to heritage sites: a case study of Warkworth Castle. *Leisure Studies*, 15(4), 1996, 259–275.

There is, as yet, no universally agreed convention for citing electronic journal sources, but Cross and Towle (1996) of Bournemouth University have produced a useful guide that is accessible via the Internet.

Referring to sources in the text

Within your essay or dissertation you will often wish to refer to someone else's work, because the findings and insights of someone else have influenced your thinking to a certain extent. Sources of direct quotations and references to other people's work should always be acknowledged in essays and dissertations. A quotation should be exactly as it appears in the source and any omission from the source quotation should be indicated by ellipses. The way you refer to sources within the text will depend on which method for citing your references you have chosen.

- *Harvard method.* The Harvard (author-date) method of referencing requires that the author and date of the cited text are included, in brackets, within the text. The items referred to are then listed at the end of the essay or dissertation in one alphabetical sequence by author. The reference within the text would look like this: 'Research over the last three decades, beginning with Lucas (1964), has shown clearly that key factors which affect the quality of the experience for the user include the number and type of other users encountered, as well as the expectations and experience of the users themselves.' The bibliography would look like this:

  Boyd, S. W. and Butler, R. W. (1996) Managing ecotourism: an opportunity spectrum approach. *Tourism Management*, 17(8), 557–566.
  Lucas, R. C. (1964) Wilderness perception and use: the example of Boundary Waters Canoe Area. *Natural Resources*, 3(3), 394–411.
  Morrison, A. M. et al. (1996) A profile of the casino resort vacationer. *Journal of Travel Research*, 35(2), 55–61.

- *Vancouver method.* The Vancouver (numerical) method uses superscript numbers (or numbers in brackets) within the text which refer you to the item in the bibliography. Each item is then listed at the end of the essay or dissertation in numerical order, using the same numbers as appear in the text. The reference within the text would look like this: 'Research over the last three decades, beginning with Lucas (21), has shown clearly that key factors which affect the quality of the experience for the user include the number and type of other users encountered, as well as the expectations and experience of the users themselves.' The bibliography would look like this: 20. Peterson, R. T. A content analysis of the depiction of seniors in restaurant television commercials. *Journal of Hospitality and Leisure Marketing*, 3(4), 1996, 49–65.
21. Lucas, R. C. Wilderness perception and use: the example of the Boundary Waters Canoe Area. *Natural Resources*, 3(3), 1964, 394–411.
22. Mathur, A. and Moschis, G. P. Use of credit cards by older Americans. *Journal of Services Marketing*, 8(1), 1994, 27–36.

Appendix 1: List of journals

This is a selection of English language journals currently published worldwide in the fields of leisure and tourism. They are mostly academic journals, but some professional and trade journals are also included. For each one, the title, frequency of publication, date of first publication, publisher, country of publication, type of journal, subject coverage, and World Wide Web address if appropriate, are listed. Further details of these and other journals can be found in directories such as *Ulrich's International Periodicals Directory*.

AAA Going Places
Six per annum
1982
Automobile Association of America
USA
Consumer
Travel

Acta Turistica
Two per annum
1989
Faculty of Economics, University of Zagreb
Croatia
Academic
Tourism

American Journal of Sports Medicine
Six per annum
1972
American Orthopaedic Society for Sports Medicine
USA
Academic
Sports medicine
http://www.sportsmed.org/j/j.htm
(tables of contents) (accessed 17 July 1998)

Anatolia: an International Journal of Tourism and Hospitality Research
Quarterly
1997
Anatolia Dergisi
Turkey
Academic
Hospitality and Tourism
http://members.tripod.com/~anatoliajournal/
(tables of contents, abstracts, and instructions to authors) (accessed 17 July 1998)

Annals of Leisure Research
1998
Australian and New Zealand Association for Leisure Studies
New Zealand
Academic
Leisure
http://www.gu.edu.au/gwis/leis/services/anzals/anzjour.htm
(instructions to authors) (accessed 30 April 1998)

Annals of Tourism Research
Quarterly
1973
Elsevier Science Ltd
UK
Academic
Tourism
http://www.elsevier.nl:80/inca/publications/store/6/8/9/
(tables of contents, and instructions to authors) (accessed 17 July 1998)

Area
Quarterly
1969
Institute of British Geographers
UK
Academic
Geography

Asia Pacific Journal of Tourism Research
Two per annum
1996
Asia Pacific Tourism Association
Korea
Academic
Tourism
http://bubl.ac.uk/journals/bus/apjotr/
(tables of contents, and abstracts) (accessed 17 July 1998)
http://www.hotel-online.com/Neo/Trends/AsiaPacificJournal/index.html
(instructions to authors) (accessed 17 July 1998)

Asia Travel Trade
Monthly
1969
Interasia Publications Ltd
Singapore
Trade
Travel trade in Asia

Asian Hotel and Catering Times
Monthly
1976
Thomson Press Hong Kong Ltd
Hong Kong
Trade
Hospitality

Australian Hotelier
Monthly
1984
National Publishing Group Pty Ltd
Australia
Trade
Hospitality
http://www.abp.com.au/
(general information) (accessed 17 July 1998)

Australian Journal of Hospitality Management
Two per annum
1994
University of Queensland
Australia
Academic
Hospitality

Australian Leisure Management
Six per annum
1997
Asia-Pacific Leisure
Australia
Professional
Leisure
http://www.spin.net.au/~leisure/
(tables of contents, and full text of selected articles) (accessed 17 July 1998)

Bottomline
8 per annum
1986
International Association of Hospitality Accountants
USA
Professional
Hospitality accounting and finance
http://www.iaha.org/BottomLine/current/index.htm
(full text of selected articles) (accessed 17 July 1998)

British Journal of Sports Medicine
Quarterly
1968
British Association of Sport and Medicine
UK
Academic
Sports medicine
http://www.bmjpg.com/data/jsm.htm
(tables of contents, and instructions to authors) (accessed 17 July 1998)

Caterer and Hotelkeeper
Weekly
1878
Reed Business Publishing
UK
Trade
Hospitality

Contours
Quarterly
1982
Ecumenical Coalition on Third World Tourism
Thailand
Professional
Tourism in developing countries

Cornell Hotel and Restaurant Administration Quarterly
Six per annum
1960
Elsevier Science Inc. for Cornell University School of Hotel Administration
USA
Academic
Hospitality
http://www.elsevier.nl:80/inca/publications/store/5/2/3/0/4/0/
(tables of contents) (accessed 17 July 1998)

Current Issues in Tourism
Two per annum
1998-
Channel View Publications
UK
Academic
Tourism

Economist
Weekly
1843
Economist Newspaper Limited
UK
Newspaper
Current affairs
http://www.economist.co.uk/
(full text of selected articles) (accessed 17 July 1998)

Environment and Planning A
Monthly
1974
Pion Ltd
UK
Academic
Urban and regional planning
http://www.pion.co.uk/ep/indexa.html
(tables of contents, and instructions to authors) (accessed 17 July 1998)

Environment and Planning D: Society and Space
Six per annum
1983
Pion Ltd
UK
Academic
Human geography and social theory
http://www.pion.co.uk/ep/indexd.html
(tables of contents, and instructions to authors) (accessed 17 July1998)

Executive Travel
Monthly
1979
Reed Travel Group
UK
Trade
Travel

Festival Management and Event Tourism
Quarterly
1993
Cognizant Communication Corporation
USA
Academic
Tourism
http://www.als.uiuc.edu/leist/fmet/home.html
(tables of contents, and instructions to authors) (accessed 17 July 1998)

FIU Hospitality Review
Two per annum
1983
Florida International University
USA
Academic
Hospitality

Hospitality
Monthly
1972
Hotel and Catering International Management Association
UK
Professional
Hospitality
http://hcima.org.uk/general/hospit.htm
(tables of contents) (accessed 17 July 1998)

Hotel and Motel Management
21 per annum
1875
Advanstar Communications Inc.
USA
Trade
Hospitality
http://www.innvest.com/misc/hmm/index.htm
(general information) (accessed 17 July 1998)

Hotels: the Magazine of the Worldwide Hotel Industry
Monthly
1967
Cahners Publishing

USA
Trade
Hospitality
http://www.cahners.com/mainmag/hot.htm
(general information) (accessed 17 July 1998)
IATA Review
Quarterly
1985
International Air Transport Association
Switzerland
Professional
Air transport

In Focus
Quarterly
1990
Tourism Concern
UK
Professional
Tourism
http://www.oneworld.org/tourconcern/infocus.htm
(general information) (accessed 17 July 1998)

Information Technology and Tourism
Quarterly
1998
Cognizant Communication Corporation
USA
Academic
Tourism

International Journal of Contemporary Hospitality Management
7 per annum
1990
MCB University Press Ltd
UK
Academic
Hospitality and tourism
http://www.mcb.co.uk/cgi-bin/journal1/ijchm
(tables of contents, abstracts, and instructions to authors) (full text articles available to subscribers) (accessed 17 July 1998)

International Journal of Heritage Studies
Quarterly
1995
Intellect
UK
Academic
Heritage
http://www.intellect-net.com/journals/ijhs.htm
(abstracts, and instructions to authors) (accessed 17 July 1998)

International Journal of Hospitality Management
Quarterly
1982
Elsevier Science Ltd.
UK
Academic
Hospitality and tourism
http://www.elsevier.nl/inca/publications/store/6/5/9/
(tables of contents, and instructions to authors) (accessed 17 July 1997)

International Journal of Service Industry Management
Three per annum
1990
MCB University Press Ltd
UK
Academic
Service industries
http://www.mcb.co.uk/cgi-bin/journal1/ijsim
(tables of contents, and instructions to authors) (full text articles available to subscribers) (accessed 17 July 1998)

International Tourism Reports
Quarterly
1971
Travel and Tourism Intelligence
UK
Professional
Tourism
http://www.t-ti.com/pub_inttourrep.htm
(general information) (accessed 17 July 1998)

International Travel Law Journal
Quarterly
1994
University of Northumbria at Newcastle
UK
Professional
Travel law
http://www.unn.ac.uk/academic/ss/law/lsu/trvmenu.htm
(instructions to authors) (accessed 17 July 1998)

Journal of Air Transport Management
Quarterly
1994
Elsevier Science Ltd
UK
Academic
Air transport
http://www.elsevier.nl/inca/publications/store/3/0/4/3/8/
(tables of contents, and instructions to authors) (accessed 17 July 1998)

Journal of Applied Recreation Research
Quarterly
1971
Wilfrid Laurier University Press
Canada
Academic
Recreation
http://info.wlu.ca/~wwwpress/jrls/jarr.html
(general information) (accessed 17 July 1998)

Journal of Applied Sport Psychology
Two per annum
1989
Association for the Advancement of Applied Sport Psychology
USA
Academic
Sport psychology
http://spot.colorado.edu/~aaasp/pubs.html
(general information) (accessed 17 July 1998)

Journal of Gambling Studies
Quarterly
1985
National Council on Problem Gambling
USA
Academic
Gambling
http://www.plenum.com/cgi/getarec?ple20000130
(general information) (accessed 17 July 1998)

Journal of Hospitality and Leisure Marketing
Quarterly
1992
Haworth Press Inc.
USA
Academic
Hospitality, leisure and tourism

Journal of Hospitality and Tourism Education
Quarterly
1997
Council on Hotel, Restaurant and Institutional Education
USA
Academic
Hospitality and tourism
http://chrie.org/pubeduca_new.html
(general information) (accessed 17 July 1998)

Journal of Hospitality and Tourism Research
Three per annum
1997
Council on Hotel, Restaurant and Institutional Education
USA
Academic
Hospitality and tourism
http://chrie.org/pubresea_new.html
(general information) (accessed 17 July 1998)

Journal of International Hospitality, Leisure and Tourism Management
Quarterly
1997
Haworth Press Inc.
USA
Academic
Hospitality, leisure and tourism

Journal of Leisurability
Quarterly
1974
Leisurability Publications Inc.
Canada
Academic
Leisure

Journal of Leisure Research
Quarterly
1968
National Recreation and Park Association
USA
Academic
Leisure

Journal of Park and Recreation Administration
Quarterly
1986
Sagamore Publishing
USA
Academic
Leisure
http://wwwrpts.tamu.edu/AARPA/journal.html
(abstracts, and instructions to authors) (accessed 17 July 1998)

Journal of Restaurant and Foodservice Marketing
Quarterly
1994
Haworth Press Inc.
USA
Academic
Hospitality

Journal of Sport and Social Issues
Quarterly
1977
Sage
USA
Academic
Sport

Journal of Sport Tourism
Quarterly
1993
Sports Tourism International Council
Canada
Academic
Sport and tourism
http://www.mcb.co.uk/journals/jst/welcome.htm
(full text articles) (accessed 17 July 1998)

Journal of Sustainable Tourism
Quarterly
1993
Multilingual Matters Ltd.
UK
Academic
Tourism
http://www.multi.demon.co.uk/journals.htm JOST
(general information) (accessed 17 July 1998)

Journal of Tourism Studies
Two per annum
1990
James Cook University
Australia
Academic
Tourism
http://www.jcu.edu.au/dept/Tourism/JTS/jts.htm
(tables of contents, abstracts, and instructions to authors) (accessed 17 July 1998)

Journal of Transport Economics and Policy
Three per annum
1967
London School of Economics and Political Science
UK
Academic
Transport

Journal of Transport Geography
Quarterly
1993
Elsevier Science Ltd
UK
Academic
Transport
http://www.elsevier.nl:80/inca/publications/store/3/0/4/4/8/
(tables of contents, and instructions to authors) (accessed 17 July 1998)

Journal of Transport History
Two per annum
1953
Manchester University Press
UK
Academic
History of transport
http://www.man.ac.uk/mup/
(general information) (accessed 17 July 1998)

Journal of Travel Research
Quarterly
1972
University of Colorado at Boulder
USA
Academic
Tourism
http://bus.colorado.edu/BRD/JTR.htm
(general information) (accessed 17 July 1997)

Journal of Travel and Tourism Marketing
Quarterly
1992
Haworth Press Inc.
USA
Academic
Tourism
http://www.ins.gu.edu.au/bhm/journal/jttm.htm
(tables of contents, and instructions to authors) (accessed 17 July 1998)

Journal of Vacation Marketing
Quarterly
1995
Henry Stewart Publications
UK
Academic
Tourism

Leisure Futures
Quarterly
1982
Henley Centre for Forecasting
UK
Professional
Leisure, sport and tourism
http://www.textor.com/cms/dHCLF.html
(general information) (accessed 17 July 1998)

Leisure Intelligence
Quarterly
1983
Mintel International Group Ltd
UK
Trade
Leisure
http://www.mintel.co.uk
(full text reports available to subscribers) (accessed July 1998)

Leisure Management
Monthly
1981
Leisure Media Company Ltd
UK
Trade
Leisure

Leisure Manager
Six per annum
1983
Institute of Leisure and Amenity Management
UK
Trade
Leisure

Leisure Sciences
Quarterly
1977
Taylor and Francis Inc.
USA
Academic
Leisure
http://www.tandfdc.com/JNLS/lsc.htm
(tables of contents, and instructions to authors) (accessed 17 July 1998)

Leisure Studies
Quarterly
1982
Routledge
UK
Academic
Leisure
http://journals.routledge.com/ls.html
(tables of contents, abstracts, full text of selected articles, and instructions to
authors) (full text articles available to subscribers) (accessed 17 July 1998)

Leisure Travel News
Weekly
Miller Freeman Inc.
USA
Electronic
Travel
http://www.ttgweb.com/homepage.htm
(full text articles) (accessed 17 July 1998)

Lodging
Monthly
1975
American Hotel Association Directory Corp.
USA
Trade
Hospitality
http://www.ei-ahma.org/webs/lodging/index.html
(full text of selected articles) (accessed 17 July 1998)

Lodging Hospitality
Monthly
1949
Penton Publishing Co.
USA
Trade
Hospitality

Loisir et Société/Society and Leisure
Two per annum
1978
Presses de l'Université du Québec
Canada
Academic
Leisure
http://www.uqtr.uquebec.ca/loisir/Documentation/LetS/ls.html
(instructions to authors) (accessed 17 July 1998)

Long Range Planning
Six per annum
1968
Elsevier Science Ltd
UK
Academic
Business planning
http://www.elsevier.nl/inca/publications/store/3/5/8/
(tables of contents, and instructions to authors) (accessed 17 July 1998)

Managerial and Decision Economics
Six per annum
1980
Wiley
UK
Academic
Management economics
http://www.interscience.wiley.com/jpages/0143-6570/
(instructions to authors) (accessed 17 July 1998)

Managing Leisure
Quarterly
1996
Routledge
UK
Academic
Leisure
http://journals.routledge.com/ml.html
(tables of contents, abstracts, full text of selected articles, and instructions to
authors) (full text articles available to subscribers) (accessed 17 July 1998)

Maritime Policy and Management
Quarterly
1973
Taylor and Francis
UK
Academic
Shipping
http://www.tandf.co.uk/jnls/mpm.htm
(instructions to authors) (accessed 17 July 1998)

Museum International
Quarterly
1948
Blackwell Publishers
UK
Professional
Museums
http://www.blackwellpublishers.co.uk/scripts/webjrn1.idc?issn=13500775
(tables of contents, and instructions to authors) (accessed 17 July 1998)

Museum Management and Curatorship
Quarterly
1982
Elsevier Science Ltd
UK
Academic
Museums
http://www.elsevier.nl/inca/publications/store/3/0/4/5/8/
(tables of contents, and instructions to authors) (accessed 17 July 1998)

Museum Practice
Three per annum
1996
Museums Association
UK
Professional
Museums
http://www.city.ac.uk/artspol/mus-prac.html
(general information) (accessed 17 July 1998)

Pacific Tourism Review
Quarterly
1997
Cognizant Communication Corporation
USA
Academic
Tourism
http://www.ins.gu.edu.au/bhm/journal/ptr.htm
(tables of contents, and instructions to authors) (accessed 17 July 1998)

Park and Grounds Management
Monthly
1948
Madisen Publishing
USA
Trade
Management of outdoor open spaces

Progress in Human Geography
Quarterly
1977
Arnold
UK
Academic
Geography

Progress in Tourism and Hospitality Research
Quarterly
1995
John Wiley and Sons, Ltd
UK
Academic
Hospitality and tourism
http://www.wiley.com/wileychi/journals/documents/pth/
(instructions to authors) (accessed 17 July 1998)

Railway and Canal Historical Society Journal
Three per annum
1954
Railway and Canal Historical Society
UK
Academic
History of railways and canals

Revue de Tourisme
See *Tourist Review*

Service Industries Journal
Quarterly
1981
Frank Cass
UK
Academic
Hospitality, leisure and tourism
http://www.frankcass.com/jnls/sij.htm
(tables of contents, and instructions to authors) (accessed 17 July 1998)

Shipping and Tourism
Annual
1991
Electra Press
Greece
Trade
Shipping

Ski Area Management
Six per annum
1962
Beardsley Publishing Corp.
USA
Trade
Skiing

Society and Leisure
See *Loisir et Société*

Sociology of Sport Journal
Quarterly
1984
Human Kinetics Publishers
USA
Academic
Sport and society
http://www.humankinetics.com/infok/journals/ssj/intro.htm
(tables of contents, and instructions to authors) (accessed 17 July 1998)

Sport History Review
Two per annum
1970
University of Windsor
Canada
Academic
History of sport

Sport Science Review
Two per annum
1992
Human Kinetics Publishers
USA
Academic
Sport science
http://www.humankinetics.com/infok/journals/ssr/intro.htm
(tables of contents) (accessed 17 July1998)

Theatre Studies
Annual
1955
Ohio State University
USA
Academic
Theatre

Therapeutic Recreation Journal
Quarterly
1967
National Therapeutic Recreation Society
USA
Academic
Leisure and recreation

Tour and Travel News: Travel Trade Gazette North America
Weekly
1985
Miller Freeman Inc.
USA
Trade
Travel

Tourism
Quarterly
1978
Tourism Society
UK
Professional
Tourism

Tourism Analysis
Quarterly
1996
Cognizant Communication Corporation
USA
Academic
Tourism

Tourism, Culture and Communication
Quarterly
1997
Victoria University
Australia
Academic
Tourism
http://westgate.vut.edu.au/tour_hosp/research/tour_cult_com.html
(general information) (accessed 17 July 1998)

Tourism Economics
Quarterly
1995
In Print Publishing Ltd
UK
Academic
Tourism

Tourism Geographies: An International Journal of Tourism Space, Place and Environment
Quarterly
1999
Routledge
UK
Academic

Tourism
http://www.for.nau.edu/geography/tg/index.html
(instructions to authors) (accessed 17 July 1998)

Tourism and Hospitality Management
Two per annum
1995
WIFI Osterreich Wirtschaftsforderungsinstitut der Bundeskammer der gewerblichen Wirtschaft, Vienna, Austria and University of Rijeka Faculty of Hotel Management, Opatija, Croatia
Austria and Croatia
Academic
Tourism and hospitality

Tourism and Hospitality Review
1996
George Washington University
USA
Electronic
Tourism and hospitality
http://gwis.circ.gwu.edu/~iits/journal/ej.htm
(full text articles) (accessed 17 July 1998)

Tourism Intelligence Quarterly
Quarterly
1980
British Tourist Authority
UK
Statistics
Tourism
http://www.visitbritain.com/shop/research.htm
(general information) (accessed 17 July 1998)

Tourism Management
Eight per annum
1980
Elsevier Science Ltd
UK
Academic
Tourism
http://www.elsevier.nl:80/inca/publications/store/3/0/4/7/2/
(tables of contents, and instructions to authors) (accessed 17 July 1998)

Tourism Policy and International Tourism in OECD Member Countries
Annual
1961
Organization for Economic Co-operation and Development
France
Statistics
Tourism
http://www.oecd.org/publications/catalog/78/78_95_01_1.html
(general information) (accessed 17 July 1998)

Tourism Recreation Research
Two per annum
1976
Centre for Tourism Research and Development
India
Academic
Tourism

Tourist Review/Revue de Tourisme/Zeitschrift für Fremdenverkehr
Quarterly
1946
International Association of Scientific Experts in Tourism
Switzerland
Academic
Tourism

Town Planning Review
Quarterly
1910
Liverpool University Press
UK
Academic
Town planning

Transport Management
Six per annum
1944
Institute of Transport Administration
UK
Newsletter
Transport

Transport Policy
Quarterly
1994
Elsevier Science Ltd
UK
Academic
Transport
http://www.elsevier.nl/inca/publications/store/3/0/4/7/3
(tables of contents, and instructions to authors) (accessed 17 July 1998)

Transportation Science
Quarterly
1967
Centre de Recherche sur les Transports, University of Montreal
Canada
Academic
Transport

Travel Industry Monitor
Monthly
1990
Travel and Tourism Intelligence
UK
Trade
Tourism
http://www.t-ti.com/pub_travindmon.htm
(general information) (accessed 17 July 1998)

Travel and Tourism Analyst
Six per annum
1986
Travel and Tourism Intelligence
UK
Professional
Tourism
http://www.t-ti.com/pub_travtouranal.htm
(general information) (accessed 17 July 1998)

Travel Trade Gazette Asia
Weekly
1974
Miller Freeman Pte. Ltd
Singapore

Trade
Travel
http://www.ttg.com.sg/home.html
(full text articles) (accessed 17 July 1998)

Travel Trade Gazette Europa
Fortnightly
1968
Miller Freeman Technical Ltd
UK
Trade
Travel

Travel Trade Gazette UK and Ireland
Weekly
1953
Miller Freeman Technical Ltd
UK
Trade
Travel

Travel Weekly
Two per week
1958
Reed Travel Group
USA
Trade
Travel
http://www.oag.com/catalog/travagnt.htm
(general information) (accessed 17 July 1998)

Travel Weekly UK
Weekly
1969
Reed Travel Group
UK
Trade
Travel
http://www.oag.com/catalog/travagnt.htm
(general information) (accessed 17 July 1998)

Visions in Leisure and Business
Quarterly

1982
Appalachian Associates
USA
Academic
Leisure and tourism

World Leisure and Recreation
Quarterly
1958
World Leisure and Recreation Association
Canada
Academic
Leisure and recreation
http://www.uleth.ca/~wlra/journal.html
(tables of contents) (accessed 17 July 1998)

WTO News
Six per annum
1989
World Tourism Organization
Spain
Professional
Tourism
http://www.world-tourism.org/newshead.htm
(full text articles) (accessed 17 July 1998)

Zeitschrift für Fremdenverkehr
See *Tourist Review*

Appendix 2

The following organizations, services, databases and software packages have
been mentioned in this chapter. More information can be found by contacting
them as indicated.

British Library Inside Information, http://lister.bids.ac.uk/blii.html (accessed 17 July 1998).
ContentsDirect,
    http://www.elsevier.nl:80/inca/homepage/about/contentsdirect/Menu.shtml (accessed 17
    July 1998).
HOSTLINE, http://www.nestlelib.cornell.edu/hostline/ (accessed 17 July 1998).
International Civil Aviation Organization, http://www.icao.int (accessed 17 July 1998).
ISI Document Solution, http://www.isinet.com/prodserv/tga/tgadoc.html (accessed 17 July
    1998).

Leisurenet. Send an electronic mail message from your usual computer to listproc@gu.edu.au with no subject heading and no automatic signature, saying on a single line: subscribe leisurenet your first name your last name.

Microsoft Access. Produced by Microsoft Corporation, http://www.microsoft.com/products/prodref/3_ov.htm (accessed 17 July 1998).

ProCite, produced by Research Information Systems, http://www.risinc.com/pc/ (accessed 17 July 1998).

Reference Manager, produced by Research Information Systems, http://www.risinc.com/rm/rmmain.html (accessed 17 July 1998).

TRINET. Send an electronic mail message to TRINET@uhmtravel.tim.hawaii.edu requesting further information.

UnCover, http://uncweb.carl.org/ (accessed 17 July 1998).

References

The following sources have been mentioned in this chapter but not included in the list of journals in Appendix 1 above.

Academic Services Group (1996) Harvard System. Bournemouth University, http://www.bournemouth.ac.uk/service-depts/lis/LIS_Pub/harvardsyst.html (accessed 17 July 1998).

Articles in Hospitality and Tourism. University of Surrey, http://www.lib.surrey.ac.uk/AHT2/ (accessed 17 July 1998).

Cross, P. and Towle, K. (1996) A Guide to Citing Internet Sources. Bournemouth University, http://www.bournemouth.ac.uk/service-depts/lis/LIS_Pub/harvardsystint.html (accessed 17 July 1998).

Current Contents: Social and Behavioral Sciences. Institute for Scientific Information, http://www.isinet.com/prodserv/cc/cchp.html (accessed 17 July 1998).

HCIMA Review (1974–78) Hotel Catering and Institutional Management Association.

International Journal of Tourism Management (1980–81) IPC Science and Technology Press.

Journal of Contemporary Hospitality Management (1989) MCB University Press.

Leisure Recreation and Tourism Abstracts. CAB International, http://www.cabi.org/catalog/journals/absjour/3r.htm (accessed 17 July 1998).

Progress in Tourism, Recreation and Hospitality Management (1989–94) Belhaven Press.

Shields, G. and Walton, G. (1996) Cite Them Right: How to Organize Bibliographical References. University of Northumbria at Newcastle, http://www.unn.ac.uk/central/isd/cite (accessed 17 July 1998).

Social Sciences Citation Index. Institute for Scientific Information, http://www.isinet.com/prodserv/citation/citindhp.html (accessed 17 July 1998).

Sports Documentation Monthly Bulletin. University of Birmingham Centre for Sports Science and History.

Travel Research Bulletin (1962–71) University of Colorado.

Ulrich's International Periodicals Directory. Bowker.

5

A guide to using bibliographies, abstracts and indexes

Denise Harrison

Introduction

Over the last two decades we have seen a considerable increase in the amount of literature which has been published. Leisure and tourism is an area which has seen major growth. A number of factors have contributed to this and they include the demand for academics to raise their research profile, external competition and new legislation. Literature appears in many different forms – as books, journal articles, annual reports, government material, conference proceedings, dissertations and theses. Keeping up to date with what has been published and when is a difficult task. There are, however, a variety of ways of doing this. The aim of this chapter is to introduce you to abstracting and indexing journals and bibliographies, the use of which will enable you to do just this – keep up to date with published information quickly and efficiently.

Indexing and abstracting journals and bibliographies bring together similar documents and list them in a variety of ways so that you can look through using a known author's name, a title, a journal title or a topic you are interested in. You are then provided with full details of the document such as author, title, place of publication, publisher and ISBN to help you trace the item either in a library or via a bookseller. These details are known as the document's bibliographic details. Bibliographies may be published once only, annually, or at regular intervals so that you can check them whenever a new issue is produced. Some group a variety of materials together such as books, journals, book reviews, government material, all of which relate to a specific topic. Others confine themselves to one type of material, for example books. Whatever their compilation and subject content, if you check relevant bibliographies regularly you will keep up to date with the latest documents that have been published. Some bibliographies are called indexes, especially if they include references to articles from journals. In some cases there will be an abstract, a résumé of what the article or document is about; these are called abstracting journals. Abstracting journals are probably the most useful. A document's title can be misleading but an abstract attempts to give a clear account of what the document is about. You will then have to decide whether it is worth obtaining a copy of the original document. Indexes, bibliographies and abstracting journals are all databases – they are essentially searchable collections of data – which can be used to help you conduct your literature search.

This chapter will provide a list of the most useful and important indexing and abstracting journals and bibliographies which you should try to look at if you are doing research into a leisure- or tourism-related issue. The majority of these databases were originally produced as printed publications. Now, however, almost all are produced in electronic form. Indeed, the same publication may be available in a variety of different electronic formats. Take, for example, the Social Science Citation Index which is an index to the core journals in the social sciences. This database is available not only in printed form but also in different electronic formats. It is available on a computer disk, called a CD-ROM. In some libraries you may have to obtain this disk from the library staff and use it at a dedicated computer. In other libraries you may be able to use it on a number of different machines without actually handling the disk if it has been networked. In most university libraries in the UK this database can be accessed on the World Wide Web through a gateway known as BIDS (Bath Information and Data Services). Some libraries which have neither the CD-ROM, the printed version or access to the BIDS gateway may be able to access the Social Science Citation Index on the Internet. The data which is accessed is essentially the same whichever media is used to access it. You will need to ask for advice about the availability of a particular database in the library which you are using.

Some guidance for using electronic databases

The advent of electronic databases has made literature searching much simpler and quicker than wading through volumes of paper publications. Several years can be scanned at once. You can sit at a computer and enter keywords for a topic you are interested in. The computer will look through all the references in the database and provide you with a list of possible documents that you might like to consult. Always read carefully any documentation which is provided with a database. Although the basic concepts for using databases are the same the commands used vary.

There are a number of basic techniques which can be used to refine a search using an electronic database.

Using 'and' between the keywords

If you retrieve too many references you can add additional keywords using 'and' to find references which contain both or all of the keywords you are using. For example, leisure *and* government *and* policy will find references which have all of these three keywords in them. Adding more keywords connected using *and* reduces the number of references retrieved.

Searching for a phrase

If you retrieve too many references you may be able to reduce the number and produce a more accurate result by searching for a specific phrase. The way in which you search for a phrase varies between databases but the concept is simple. For example, searching for the keywords 'local *and* government' will retrieve references which contain both the words 'local' and 'government' anywhere in them, whether they occur as a phrase or not. However, searching for the phrase 'local government' will only find that phrase and will reduce the number of irrelevant references retrieved.

Using 'or' between the keywords

On the other hand your search might reveal very few items of interest. You will then need to think of another way to describe the topic which broadens the search. One way of broadening a search is to link the keywords using 'or'. For example, 'developing countries *or* third world' would find references with either the phrase 'developing countries' or the phrase 'third world'.

Searching on the stem of a keyword

Another way to broaden the results of a search is to search on the stem of a word. Again, the exact way this is done varies between different databases.

Very often an asterisk is used. For example, 'hotel*' would find references containing the words:

- hotel
- hotels
- hotelier
- hoteliers, and so on.

This technique is often known as truncation.

Constructing a more sophisticated search

It is possible to combine the techniques described above to make the results of a search more accurate. Again, the exact way this is done will vary depending upon the database being used. For example, '(United Kingdom *or* Great Britain) and sustainable tourism' would find references which contained the phrase 'sustainable tourism' and either the term 'United Kingdom' or 'Great Britain'. Some indexes identify different search terms which may be used. Such an index is known as a thesaurus. It will indicate terms which are both narrower and broader as well as terms which have a similar meaning.

Once you have got your list of references you can go through and select the ones you think are most useful. Remember, the indexes and bibliographies only provide you with references to material, they do not provide the full text of the document. If you do decide you would like to see the original you can check to see if it is available from your local library; if not, see if they offer an inter-library loans service. More details later in the chapter.

The number of abstracting and indexing journals and bibliographies which are now available, has, like the number of publications, grown considerably over the years and continues to do so. What I have tried to do is to list those that I and colleagues have found most useful for tourism and leisure research. Wherever possible I have given a brief description for each entry.

Indexing and abstracting journals

Anbar

Publisher: MCB University Press, Bradford, UK.
This database indexes over 400 management journals including about fifteen in the area of tourism and hospitality management. It covers many management-related

disciplines, such as marketing and human resource management, which may be of interest to the leisure and tourism researcher. It is available on a CD-ROM and on the Web, but note that the Web version can only be accessed if you, your organization or the library that you are using has paid for a subscription to it.

Articles in Hospitality and Tourism

Available from 1985. Monthly. Publisher: University of Surrey and Oxford Brookes University, UK.
Available in printed form and on the World Wide Web. Note that you will only be able to access the Web version if you, your library or your organization has paid for a subscription to it.

The database indexes over 100 international academic and trade journals. It provides a very short abstract (usually just one or two sentences) for each article indexed.

Arts and Humanities Citation Index

Available from 1976. Three per year including an annual cumulation. Publisher: Institute for Scientific Information.
Available in printed form, as a CD-ROM and on the Web via Bath Information and Data Services (BIDS) in most UK universities.

This covers all subject areas for the arts and humanities, including dance, film, radio and television, language, music and literature. It provides a unique facility called citation searching. Once you have identified a key paper you can discover subsequent papers which have cited it. You can trace how research has developed and identify other material on similar topics.

ASSIA (Applied Social Sciences Index and Abstracts)

Available from 1987. Bimonthly plus annual cumulations. Publisher: Bowker-Saur Limited.
This is available in printed form and electronically as a CD-ROM. It contains a lot of useful material on sociological and leisure related issues, with a British bias.

Australian Education Index

Available from 1957. Three per year plus annual cumulations. Publisher: Australian Council for Educational Research.

Available in printed form and electronically as part of the CD-ROM International ERIC.

This indexes Australian education reports and journal literature and like the British and Canadian equivalents covers physical education and educational topics of special interest to teachers and coaches of sport.

Australian Government Index of Publications

Publisher: Australian Government Publishing Service.

Available free of charge on the Web at the following address: http://www.agps.gov.au/products/agip.htm

This lists Australian Government Publication Service (AGPS) published titles, other works produced by AGPS (where AGPS acts as printer, producer and/or distributor rather than publisher) works sold by AGPS, including titles for which AGPS is acting as an agent for another publisher (government or non-government) and works of other Commonwealth agencies reported to AGPS.

Australian Tourism Index

Publisher: Department of Hospitality Tourism and Marketing, Victoria University.

This database indexes material on Australian tourism, including all of the publications of the Pacific Asia Travel Association. Abstracts are included and the database goes back to 1982. It is available in both printed and electronic forms.

Bibliographie Touristique

Available from 1971 Publisher: Centre des Hautes Etudes Touristiques, Aix-en-Provence, France.

This is an extensive index, available in printed form only, to the literature of tourism held in the library of the Centre des Hautes Etudes Touristiques in Aix-en-Provence, France. The text is in French with some English.

British Education Index

Available from 1961. Four quarterly issues with annual cumulations in the fourth issue. Publisher: Brotherton Library, University of Leeds.

Available in printed form, as part of the CD-ROM International ERIC and on the Web via Bath Information and Data Services (BIDS) in most UK universities.

This consists of an author list and a subject list; abstracts are available for a growing number of entries. There is extensive coverage of topics such as physical education. Its strength lies in its wide coverage of educational topics. It is of special interest to teachers and coaches working in schools or with children.

British Humanities Index

Available from 1915. Quarterly with annual cumulations. Publisher: Bowker-Saur Limited.
Available in printed form and electronically as a CD-ROM.
This indexes and abstracts humanities-related articles published by British newspapers and journals and is the only source for some British social science journals before 1987. Material is arranged by subject headings and includes current topics of interest, personal names and general subjects. It also has a thesaurus which refers you to related headings to enable you to broaden your search if necessary.

Canadian Education Index

Available from 1965. Quarterly (4th issue annual cumulation). Text in English or French. Publisher: Micromedia Limited.
Available in printed form and electronically as part of the CD-ROM International ERIC.

This indexes Canadian education report and journal literature and, like the British and Australian equivalents, covers physical education and educational topics of special interest to teachers and coaches of sport.

Current Contents (Social and Behavioural Sciences)

Available from 1969. Weekly. Publisher: Institute for Scientific Information.
This is available in printed form and reproduces the tables of contents of over 1340 journals in the social and behavioural sciences. It has book reviews and the address of a wide range of publishers.

Education Index

Available from 1929. Monthly September to June, plus quarterly and annual cumulations. Publisher: H. W. Wilson.
This is the USA's equivalent of the British Education Index. It is available in printed form and on a CD-ROM. Coverage of sport is divided into several

subheadings and in addition a list of more specific individual terms is offered. A special feature of the printed version of the Education Index is a separate section at the end of each issue devoted to listing published book reviews, which enables readers to check press opinion of newly published material.

European Business ASAP

Publisher: Information Access Company.
This database is available on a CD-ROM and on the Web. It contains the actual text of just over 100 general business and management journals, many of which have articles on tourism from time to time. Despite its title many of the journals included are North American. Note that you will only be able to access the Web version if you, your organization or the library that you are using has paid for a subscription to it.

Geographical Abstracts: Human Geography

Available from 1966. Monthly. Publisher: Elsevier.
Available in printed form and on a CD-ROM called Geo Abstracts.
This is an international abstracting service for human, social and historical geographers and planners. There is also a physical geography index. It is useful for sociological topics too.

Hospitality Index

See International Hospitality and Tourism Database

Index New Zealand

Available from 1987. Publisher: National Library of New Zealand.
Index New Zealand contains abstracts of selected New Zealand publications including newspapers, nearly 300 New Zealand journals, reports, conferences, theses, education resources and other publications about New Zealand and the Pacific. The subjects covered include sport and leisure. This database is available electronically in many libraries in New Zealand.

Inside Information

This service is under development with the British Library. Previously available via Bath Information and Data Services (BIDS) it will in the future be provided by the British Library Document Supply Centre (BLDSC). It will provide details from the contents pages of the most heavily requested journals at BLDSC. Users will be able to order whole documents for delivery to their own computer but there will be a charge for the service.

International Bibliography of the Social Sciences

Available from 1951. Annual. Publisher: British Library of Political and Economic Science.

This is an annual publication produced in four volumes which indexes 100 000 articles from 2500 journals and 20 000 books. It does not contain abstracts. Most UK universities provide access to the Web version of this database via Bath Information and Data Services (BIDS). This database indexes the social sciences in the broadest sense.

International ERIC

This database, available on CD-ROM comprises the British Education Index and its American equivalent ERIC, the Australian Education Index and the Canadian Education Index.

The American section of ERIC covers two databases Current Index to Journals in Education (CIJE) and Resources in Education (RIE). The indexes are produced by sixteen clearing houses and are the most comprehensive source for education-related issues. Over 750 journals are indexed along with books, research and conference papers. All the indexes on the CD-ROM have a thesaurus which will alert you to a wide range of subject terms to help you with your search.

International Hospitality and Tourism Database CD-ROM: the guide to industry and academic resources

Available from 1996. Annual plus quarterly updates. Publisher: Wiley and Sons. This CD-ROM publication replaced the printed Hospitality Index, which ceased in 1995. The database indexes over eighty hospitality and tourism journals.

Leisure Recreation and Tourism Abstracts

Available from 1976. Quarterly. Publisher: CAB International, UK.
Available in a number of formats: in printed form with annual cumulations, as a floppy disk, as a CD-ROM called TourCD and as part of the CD-ROM CAB Abstracts.

This is one of the major abstracting sources and is indispensable for researchers. It covers a whole range of leisure-related topics including the strategic development of leisure, recreation, sport, tourism and hospitality activities, facilities, products and services. Books, journal articles, conference papers, working papers, monographs and theses are all included. Abstracts are also included for most of the documents indexed.

Monthly Catalog of United States Government Publications

Publisher: Government Printing Office, USA.
The Monthly Catalog of United States Government publications is an index of US Government publications. It can now be accessed free of charge on the Web, back to 1994, at http://www.access.gpo.gov/su_docs/dpos/adpos400.html Data prior to 1994 is available in printed form and electronically on a CD-ROM.

Museum Abstracts

Available from 1985 to 1997 (ceased publication 1997). Was monthly. Publisher: Scottish Museums Council.
This was available only in printed form and covered museums and museum management, heritage interpretation, exhibit design and display, tourism conservation and the arts.

Physical Education Index

Available from 1978. Quarterly. Publisher: Ben Oak Publishing.
This deals only with English language materials but covers a wide spread of subjects: dance, health, physical education, recreation, sports, sports medicine, coaching, fitness and various academic aspects of the subject area. It is arranged alphabetically by subject and at the end of each issue is a useful separate section on reviews of new books.

Psychological Abstracts

Available from 1927. Monthly. Publisher: American Psychological Association.
Available as a printed publication and electronically as the CD-ROM PsycLit. This provides abstracts from over 1400 international journals in psychology and related fields from 1974 to the present. A feature of this database is that it contains an index of books from 1987.

SCAN: selected new publications and articles

1980. Irregular but usually four issues per year with an index produced at irregular intervals. Publisher: English Sports Council.

This is a printed publication produced by the English Sports Council. It provides abstracts for material contained in their information unit and includes details of monographs, journal articles, government body handbooks, annual reports, yearbooks, new publications, forthcoming conferences. The layout is in three parts: periodical articles are cited alphabetically by the title of the journal in which they appear; handbooks, annual reports and yearbooks are then listed in alphabetical order; the third section gives details of new publications arranged alphabetically by author's name. Each entry has a unique number and a brief abstract is given to indicate the contents of each item.

Social Sciences Citation Index (SSCI)

Available from 1966. Annual. Publisher: Institute for Scientific Information.

Available in printed form as four volumes, including a subject index and on the Web via Bath Information and Data Services (BIDS) in most UK universities. This indexes around 4700 journals in sociology and related disciplines. It includes conference proceedings and book reviews. Like the Arts and Humanities Citation Index it provides the unique facility of citation searching. Once you have identified a key paper you can discover subsequent papers which have cited it. You can trace how research has developed and identify other material on similar topics.

Social Sciences Index

Available from 1974. Quarterly plus annual cumulations. Publisher: H. W.Wilson.

This is available in printed form and provides an author and subject index to periodicals in the fields of anthropology, community health and medicine, economics, geography, sociology and social work. It is also available on CD-ROM.

Sociological Abstracts

Available from 1953. Bimonthly. Publisher: Sociological Abstracts Inc., US.

Available in printed form and as a CD-ROM called Sociofile.

This is an important source for references in social geography, gender studies, demography, social research and methodology. It contains non-evaluative abstracts of journal articles and conference proceedings and provides an index to book reviews.

SportDiscus

1975. Quarterly updates. Publisher: Sport Information Resource Centre.
SportDiscus is a CD-ROM formed from the database Sport. Although it is a general sports database, coverage of sociological and leisure related issues is good. It lists journal articles, conference papers, book chapters, audiovisual items and dissertations and theses. It also includes a database of French language articles on sport.

Sports Documentation Monthly Bulletin

Available from 1971. Monthly. Publisher: University of Birmingham, UK.
This was formerly the Sports Information Bulletin. It abstracts and indexes conference papers, reports and journal articles under author and subject with cumulative annual indexes. It covers a wide range of material in sport, physical education and recreation. English language and foreign material is included, with a translated title for the latter. The bulletin is divided into broad subject headings and relevant topics can be located from the contents pages and from the author index and subject index both of which appear in each issue and are cumulated annually. Cross-references are given to assist in locating the best search terms to use. From 1987 the bulletin gives an abstract of each item, which now makes this publication a very useful and important source. Each issue carries about 300 items and a full list of the journals covered and of conference proceedings indexed is given at the end of the issue.

Sportsearch: contents of current journals

Available from 1974. Monthly. Publisher: SIRC, Canada (text in English and French).
This updates the Sport Data Base in the printed form and was formerly Sport and Recreation Index until 1977. It is also available as a CD-ROM. It covers nearly 300 sports and physical education journals as well as books, conference proceedings and dissertations from all parts of the world, but mainly in the English language.

TourCD

See Leisure Recreation and Tourism Abstracts.

United Kingdom Official Publications Index (UKOP)

Available from 1980. Quarterly. Publisher: Chadwick Healey.
This CD-ROM covers all British official government publications and important international ones published by HMSO and government departments. Publications from organizations such as UNESCO, OECD and the World Health Organization are also included.

UnCover

This is an independent journals index service and includes 18 000 journal titles and over 15 million articles. It also offers a document delivery service at a cost. There is a one to two week delay between a journal being published and it appearing in UnCover and the average cost of an article is about $20. UnCover Express covers approximately 20 per cent of the database and offers a one-hour service. In the UK it is accessible on the Web via Bath Information and Data Services (BIDS).

Urbadisc

Publisher: London Research Centre.
Urbadisc is available electronically and contains a number of different European databases which index literature relating to urban affairs. The English language databases are Accompline and Urbaline. They index pressure group literature, British newspapers and specialist trade journals in addition to books and articles in academic journals.

Weekly Checklist Catalogue

Publisher: Government of Canada, Depository Services Programme.
The Weekly Checklist is a list of Canadian Federal Government publications. A printed list is produced each week. The Weekly Checklist Catalogue is available on the Web free of charge and goes back to January 1993. The URL is http://dsp-psd.pwgsc.gc.ca/search_form-e.html

World Hospitality and Tourism Trends (WHATT)

Publisher: Hotel and Catering Institutional Management Association.
This database is available on a CD-ROM. It indexes over sixty hospitality management periodicals and it includes short abstracts. The CD-ROM also contains a database of research which lists some major research projects in hospitality management.

Conference proceedings

Conference proceedings can be published in a variety of forms: as separate publications, as whole issues of a periodical or as part of a periodical. The main source for tracking down and obtaining conference proceedings is detailed below.

Index of Conference Proceedings

Available from 1964. Monthly with annual cumulations. Publisher: British Library.

This covers all types of conference proceedings received by the British Library and immediately available on interlibrary loan. It is available in printed form and as the CD-ROM Boston Spa Conferences on CD-ROM. The paper copy is arranged by subject keyword and in chronological order within that. There are a large number of conferences and seminars held on sport and leisure topics and indexed in this publication.

Report literature

British reports, translations and theses

Available from 1971. Monthly. Publisher: British Library Document Supply Centre (BLDSC).

This records all the relevant documents that have been added to the British Library. The list is organized in subject order and all items are available on interlibrary loan. From January 1998 it will be known as the British National Bibliography for Report Literature (BNBRL).

Government Reports Announcements and Index

Available from 1984. Publisher: National Technical Information Service, Washington, DC.

This publication provides abstracts for US government-sponsored research and also includes some non US technical report literature.

Resources in Education

Available from 1966. Monthly. Publisher: US Department of Education.

Available in printed form, as part of one of the two CD-ROMs ERIC or International ERIC and electronically via Bath Information and Data Services (BIDS).

This provides up-to-date information about education-related research and resources. There is a strong US/Canadian bias but British issues have adequate coverage in the education/leisure related field.

Theses and dissertations

Before starting research for a postgraduate dissertation or thesis you need to be aware of what research has already been done in the field and what research is currently in progress. This can provide invaluable links either via the bibliography at the end of a dissertation or thesis or by providing contacts at other institutions.

Bibliography of Education Theses in Australia

Available from 1982. Annual. Publisher: Australian Council for Educational Research.
This is available in printed form and electronically as part of the CD-ROM International ERIC.

Current Research in Britain: Social Sciences

Available from 1980. Annual. Publisher: Longman Cartermill Ltd.
Available as a paper copy or as a CD-ROM.
This is a national register of current research being carried out at UK universities and colleges. It can help you to identify new research topics or enable you to pinpoint names and addresses of others carrying out similar research.

Dissertations Abstracts

Available from 1966. Quarterly. Publisher: UMI.
American dissertations can be found in Dissertation Abstracts which is available in paper form for the years 1939–90 and in CD-ROM format from 1982. Since 1988 theses from European institutions have been included. All titles can be obtained on microfilm from the British Library Document Supply Centre (BLDSC) in the UK and from University Microforms Inc. (UMI) in the USA.

Index to Theses Accepted for Higher Degrees in the Universities of Great Britain and Ireland

Available from 1950. Semi-annual. Publisher: Aslib Association for Information Management.

All British higher degree theses are listed here. It is still available in print form and also as a CD-ROM. The paper copy has a detailed subject index. Both provide abstracts of the titles included most recently. The listing is about eighteen months behind British Reports, Translations and Theses, now the British National Bibliography for Report Literature (BNBRL).

Sport and Leisure Research on Disc

Available from 1998. Annual. Publisher: University of Sheffield.
This is a database which covers dissertation and thesis material at MA, MSc, MEd, MPhil, PhD level. Contributions are from fifteen UK universities. The titles are already included in the SportDiscus CD-ROM but the advantage of this database is that vital information of accessibility is included.

Bibliographies

You might want to check the bibliographies of some of the world's leading research libraries. The most important include the following.

British National Bibliography

Available from 1950. Weekly. Publisher: British Library.
Available in printed form as well as a CD-ROM.

This is a listing of all British publications and is available from 1950 onwards. It is arranged by classmark with subject and author indexes.

The Catalogue of the British Library

This is available in printed form as the British Library General catalogue of printed books to 1975 with supplements on microfiche. It is also available as a CD-ROM covering material up to 1975. The British Library OPAC (Online Public Access Catalogue) is also available over the Internet. Consult their Web site at http://portico.bl.uk/

National Union Catalogue

This is the American equivalent of the British National Bibliography. It was produced in paper form but is available on microfiche from 1980 and is also available as the Library of Congress OPAC over the Internet: http://lcweb.loc.gov/

National Library of Australia

The catalogue of the National Library of Australia can be consulted on the Web at http://ilms.nla.gov.au/webpac/.

National Library of New Zealand

The catalogue of the National Library of New Zealand can be consulted free of charge on the Internet. It can be accessed from the following Web page http://www.natlib.govt.nz/online/ils/.

Checking publication details

You may wish to see if relevant material you have come across is still in print. For this you will need to check the following.

Australian Books in Print

Publisher: R. R. Bowker.
This printed publication lists in print books which are about, or have been published in, Australia.

Bookseller (UK)

Available from 1858. Weekly. Publisher: Whitaker and Sons Ltd.
This is the most up-to-date listing of new books appearing each week. There is a 'Publications of the Week' section in each issue. It forms the basis of Whitaker's Books in Print on microfiche and the CD-ROM Bookbank. It is particularly useful for the large number of official publications that are included.

Books in Print (USA)

Available from 1947. Annual. Publisher: Bowker.
Available in print, on microfiche and as a CD-ROM.
This is a similar publication to Whitaker's Books in Print but covers North American literature.

Cumulative Book Index

Available from 1898. Monthly with annual cumulations. Publisher: H. W. Wilson.

Available in print form and on CD-ROM.

This presents a world list of books published in the English language for a given year and has an American bias.

New Zealand Bibliographic Network (NZBN)

NZBN is a network linking most public, university, government and other libraries in New Zealand. It can be accessed from within many libraries in New Zealand and on the Internet. For further details see the following Web page: http://www.natlib.govt.nz/online/nzbn/

New Zealand Books in Print

Publisher: R. R. Bowker.

This printed publication lists over 20 000 books which were published in New Zealand and the Pacific Islands and are in print.

Whitaker's Books in Print (UK)

Available from 1874. Annual. Publisher: Whitaker and Sons Ltd.

Available in printed form, on microfiche and as a CD-ROM.

This lists over 850 000 titles from some 30 000 publishers and distributors in the UK. Books are listed in one alphabetical sequence of authors, titles and subjects. It covers British books and English language titles published internationally but available in the UK.

Obtaining material

This is a somewhat daunting list of titles and it would be impossible to try and consult them all. Select the ones you feel are most relevant and look through them using keywords or subject terms you have thought of or that they suggest. When you have searched through them and drawn up a list of articles and documents that you want to get hold of ask a librarian for help. If you cannot get the material from your own local or university library they will be able to advise you about obtaining it from another source. Members of academic institutions sometimes have free access to interlibrary loan or other document delivery services; public libraries often charge a small fee. Whatever service you use always leave plenty of time. Photocopies of journal articles might arrive in a matter of days but books, theses and reports can take much longer.

Conclusion

Checking abstracting and indexing journals is a time-consuming task. If you select wisely from the list provided and are organized and systematic in your search for information, then you will find that the time spent will be worth while. You will be assured that you are kept aware of the latest documents which have been published and so be kept abreast of new developments in your field, and any research you undertake will not be duplicated elsewhere.

Further reading

Bell, J. (1993) *Doing your Research Project: A Guide for First-time Researchers in Education,* 2nd edn. Open University Press.

Gubbay, J. and Middleton, C. (1997) *The Student's Companion to Sociology.* Blackwell.

Lambert, C. M. (1987) *Sources of Information on Sport and Recreation,* 2nd edn. Department of the Environment.

Myhill, M. (1994) *The World at your Fingertips: A Guide to Electronic Information Sources Relevant in Education.* LISE.

Prytherch, R. (1988) *Sports and Fitness: An Information Guide.* Gower.

Shoebridge, M. (ed.) (1992) *Information Sources in Sport and Leisure.* Bowker-Saur.

Smeaton, R. (1993) *Researching Education: Reference Tools and Networks.* LISE.

6

Finding out about statistics and market research

Sarah Ward and Wendy Luker

Introduction

This chapter aims to give an overview of the availability of statistics and market research in the areas of leisure, sport and tourism. We will describe sound methods for tracing statistics and market research, and also indicate how these sources should best be used. We will explain how various sources may (and may not) be used to draw comparisons, and also give advice on basic techniques for exploiting this kind of data – skills which can be carried over to help in the use of other kinds of materials. We will then go on to describe some of the major sources of statistical and market research information in these subject areas, both in hard copy (i.e. books, journals etc.) and also electronic sources (CD-ROMs, World Wide Web sites etc.)

Using statistics and market research

Statistics

Statistics are collections of numerical data, usually presented in a table. They may have been collected from a simple count of some process or activity (for example, the number of people passing through a turnstile to visit a museum), or they may be the results of a survey or questionnaire (the number of people responding 'yes' to a question – have you visited a museum in the last twelve months?). They can play an important part in any research you do as they can be used to prove or support an argument you are making – for example, if you were trying to illustrate an increase in leisure spending, it would strengthen the argument to supply statistics showing increases in attendance at sporting fixtures.

One of the first things you will have to do is make sure you understand the way that the data has been gathered and also the way it is being expressed and presented. For example, at the most basic level, are the figures you are looking at percentages or totals? Are the figures expressing thousands, millions or are they the actual amounts? In some cases, an index is used (with a particular year being taken as the base year having a value of 100) and subsequent years' values are expressed as a percentage change to that figure. Every few years, however, the base is reset to 100, which restricts the number of years across which you can draw a direct comparison with those which are working from the same 100 base. A familiar example of this is the retail price index. You should also check any abbreviations that are in use to make sure that you understand what is meant by them.

You will need to understand the source of the data you are looking at. This would be significant if you were comparing statistics that had been gathered by two different organizations (e.g. national statistical organizations from two different countries). Are the bases that have been used to gather the data comparable, therefore allowing you to draw contrasts between the resultant data? For example, if you were collating numbers of tourists visiting a range of countries for specific years, you will find that figures are not available in the same format for every country, and for some countries the data may not be available at all. So, in some instances you may be able to find numbers of tourists visiting the country, but in other instances the number of foreign visitors arriving at the frontiers of the country is the only figure recorded, and this may include visitors arriving for purposes other than tourism, e.g. business travellers. Sometimes the only figures available may be the numbers of tourists staying in registered accommodation – but these figures will not include any tourists who stay with family members, and are certainly not directly comparable with numbers of foreign visitors arriving at frontiers.

Statistics may be collated by official (government) bodies, which obviously stamps them with the authority of that source, for example the British Tourist Authority (BTA). Whilst a range of tourism and related statistics can be assembled from a range of government publications, the BTA publish comprehensive, subject-specific statistics with accompanying analysis, and this is also true for some non-governmental industry bodies. One of the factors you will have to understand when searching for statistics is that the collation of reliable and comprehensive collections of this type of data is an expensive and time-consuming process. Great Britain is well served by authoritative statistical organizations, but this is not necessarily the case internationally.

Market research

Market research is carried out to assist and improve marketing decisions; it can include many types of information, but the most usual focus is information about the market. In competitive markets where marketing decisions may entail a major financial commitment, and where costs of failure are high, the data upon which decisions are being taken needs to be rigorous and reliable.

The most important category of market research within leisure, sport and tourism is consumer market research (other market research categories are business to business, and industrial). Consumer markets can be further divided into fast-moving consumer goods (foods, drink, frequent purchases), and other markets (consumer durables and services such as leisure and travel). Marketing is often global, but consumer market research reports may only cover the UK perspective or the UK market.

Consumer market research reports may include: profiles of consumer spending, preferences and lifestyle; profiles of companies; and economic indicators. There is a strong overlap with statistical sources as most market research publications contain statistical data. Care must be taken in using this data for comparison or analysis, particularly if you are using data from different sources. The reliability of the data depends on the sample size, and also on the way the sample has been selected. Quality standards are assured for reports produced by organizations who are members of the Association of Market Survey Organizations, or the Association of British Market Research Companies.

Using indexes and contents lists

A first and basic rule for using collections of statistics and/or market research is one that applies to the use of many different types of information tools, and that is the use of contents lists and indexes which are supplied with the material, whether this be in hard copy format (e.g. book/pamphlet/journal) or in electronic format (e.g. CD-ROM, World Wide Web site). Using contents and indexes can give you the most efficient access to the material contained in the items you have traced.

Contents lists

Because you are most likely to be using collections of statistics which cover a wider subject area than your particular research topic, it is important to establish as quickly as possible if the item you are looking at is likely to hold a significant amount of relevant material. This is particularly pertinent for the subject areas which this book covers, as each of the topics has a number of related areas from which you will also need to draw material. For example, when looking for sports statistics, you may well find relevant material under headings as diverse as health, recreation, pastimes, outdoor activities, injuries statistics, and many others, depending on the emphasis of your research.

Taking the useful *Key Data* (Office for National Statistics, annual a) as an example; this is a quick reference tool produced in the UK by the Office for National Statistics (in New Zealand, *Key Statistics* [Statistics New Zealand, monthly] performs a similar function; for Australia, *Australia at a Glance* [Australian Bureau of Statistics, annual a] covers the same level of detail; in the USA, there is a similar publication titled *USA Statistics in Brief*). It does not give depth of detail for any of the topics that it covers, but does supply useful 'snapshot' statistics across a range of subject areas and, usefully, refers to the more detailed statistical resources from which these details have been taken – leading you on to further information should you need it. With a publication which covers such a wide range of subject areas, a quick glance at the contents pages will show you how the book is structured and organized, and also which chapters are most likely to be of use to you. So, in the case of *Key Data* the contents pages show us that the book is divided into clearly defined subject-specific chapters, (e.g. 'Population and vital statistics', 'UK finance', 'Lifestyles and tourism') of which a number may be of interest. The subject groupings are quite wide, and there is no specific chapter entitled, for example, 'Sport'. Under the major chapter heading 'Lifestyles and tourism', however, is the subheading 'Participation in leisure activities'. On turning to this chapter, you will find tables of data which are of relevance to sport, one indicating participation in activities away from the home, including visits to spectator sports events, and one giving percentages of males and females participating in the most popular sports, games and physical activities. Whilst *Key Data* represents by no means as complicated a set of data as you may need to come to terms with on a detailed search for in-depth statistics, this kind of example should indicate to you the need to maintain a flexible and open-minded approach to identifying useful material.

Using indexes

As can be seen from the previous section, whilst contents lists will give you a clear idea of the structure and layout of a publication, whatever its format, a well-constructed index can give you the most precise access to the content. Again, a flexible approach is essential to get the most fruitful results. A key element in the successful searching of any collection of material is to have a number of synonymous search terms thought out in advance – you may have a fixed idea of what you want to find, but this may not necessarily match up either with the way in which the data is presented in the publication you have to hand, or with the way the authors/editors of that text have chosen to describe it. So, if the initial set of terms you have decided to look up gives you no results, you should be able to search the index from an alternative approach.

Taking the *Annual Abstract of Statistics* (Office for National Statistics, annual b) as an example, this is another collection of statistics widely available in UK libraries as it provides a broad spectrum of statistics on aspects of economic, social and industrial life in Britain, drawn from a range of government departments and other organizations (similar coverage is given by the *Statistical Abstract of the United States* [National Technical Information Service, annual] the *Year Book Australia* [Australian Bureau of Statistics, annual b], the *New Zealand Official Yearbook* [Statistics New Zealand, annual] and the *Canada Year Book* [Statistics Canada, biennial]). Using the contents pages will give you an indication of the structure of the volume, but in this case, the long lists of tables listed under each chapter heading mean that it would be inefficient to trawl through these to find the precise information that you need. If we use the example of tourism statistics, looking up the stem 'touris' in the index gives us the entry 'Tourists – expenditure in the United Kingdom'. Thinking around the subject to find related headings, however, we can also find 'Passenger movement' and 'Transport' – with a number of subheadings.

Sources of statistics

Tracing statistics

The reference collections of larger public libraries, and those of college and university libraries will have some kind of statistics collection. In some cases, this may well be just some copies of the more general statistical publications but, as has already been described, these do at least list the source of their material, giving you an idea of the publications you need to trace to get the level of detail you need. College and university libraries are likely to have statistics to support the courses in which they specialize; so, for example, you would not necessarily find a depth of leisure statistics in the library of a college or university where no leisure courses are taught (university libraries will have the most comprehensive collections of statistics in their specialist areas, as well as good general subject coverage). However, there are several major tools that you can use to trace statistics, which you should be able to find if you have access to a reasonable reference collection. If you are unable to find any of the items listed here, it is well worth asking the staff at the library you use most if they know where these items may be available in your area

In the United Kingdom, the Office for National Statistics produces the *Guide to Official Statistics* (Office for National Statistics, 1996). This appears approximately every five years, and enables you to trace statistics produced by the Government Statistical Service and other official bodies. A brief description of the source publication is given, plus publication details. The guide is divided into twelve chapters, covering broad subject areas – the chapter on 'Transport' covers travel and trade; leisure and travel are covered within the chapter on 'Social statistics'. The *Guide* also has an excellent index.

To trace international statistics, it is worth investigating whether the national statistical organization of the country in which you are interested has a World Wide Web site. If so, this can be the quickest way of accessing the most up-to-date information about the range of statistics available for that country in your subject area. In some cases, summary statistics are available free on the website, and these may well contain sufficient detail for your needs. It is a characteristic of the World Wide Web that sites change and are moved on a regular basis, so Web addresses quoted in this chapter may have changed by the time you read it. In all cases, we have tried to give the fullest detail of the body producing the site, so that if addresses have changed, it should be possible to trace any new locations taken up by the agencies producing the information.

In the case of the USA, for example, the Federal Interagency on Statistical Policy produces the Fedstats website (URL: http://www. fedstats.gov), which gives access to the full text of the *Statistical Abstract of the United States* (National Technical Information Service, annual). This performs a similar function to that of the *Annual Abstract of Statistics* in the UK, in that it gives a range of national statistics across a broad range of subject areas. However, it also has a very useful appendix which lists statistical sources under broad subject headings for example, 'recreation' – (i.e. a function very similar to that performed by the *Guide to Official Statistics* [Office for National Statistics, 1996] in the UK). Within these subject divisions, the resources listed are classified as to whether they are from official government sources, or from other bodies.

The Australian Bureau of Statistics has a comprehensive World Wide Web Information Service (URL: http://www.abs.gov.au), which includes some summary statistics which may be printed out from the site free of charge. As is the case with many of these government sites (including that of Statistics Canada [URL: http://www.statcan.ca/start.html] and the Statswebsite in New Zealand [URL: http://www.stats.govt.nz.STATSWEB.NSF]), searchable access to their publications catalogue is given, which can therefore be used as a bibliographic tool to trace availability of statistics in a given subject area. This catalogue is broken down into broad subject areas, including a section on 'Transport and tourism'. Under another chapter on secondary industries and distribution, a subsection on service industries gives information on tourism, theme parks, and other leisure and recreation pursuits. For each of the statistical sources listed, information is given on the content and scope of coverage.

Tracing industry and other sources of unofficial statistics can be more problematic, as no single body takes responsibility for collating and maintaining a database of the information available. There are some publications which aim to index unofficial statistics, including *Sources of United Kingdom Unofficial Statistics* (Mort and Siddall, 1997). This useful publication gives information on the source of the data, the year in which it was collected, and availability. There is also a comprehensive index. For international unofficial statistics, the *World Directory of Non-official Statistical Sources* (Euromonitor, 1997) covers more than fifty countries (including the USA, Canada, Australia and New Zealand), and gives references to statistics covering regions of the world (e.g. Eastern Europe), statistical sources by country, and then also a listing of publishers of unofficial statistics by country. The comprehensive subject index has a section on 'Leisure and entertainment', and gives titles of statistical sources and country of origin.

Tourism statistics

International tourism information

The World Tourism Organization (WTO) produces an annual publication, the *Yearbook of Tourism Statistics*, (World Tourism Organization, annual) giving details, by country, of numbers of tourists arriving at frontiers, numbers of foreign visitors, nights spent in tourism accommodation etc., giving up to five years' retrospective data. Published in two volumes, the second groups countries by regions, and gives some indication of trends in the tourism industry in those regions. Care has to be taken in the use of this volume as the data available for each country may differ hugely, and so direct comparisons may not always be made. The WTO also publishes *World Tourism Highlights 1997* (World Tourism Organization, 1998), which covers global development in the tourism industry, and gives statistics on the top tourism destinations, top tourism earners, and tourism receipts and arrivals in selected countries. *The Compendium of Tourism Statistics* (World Tourism Organization, 1997) covers thirty-four key areas of tourism supply and demand, for example arrivals by mode of transport; arrivals by purpose of visit; international inbound and outbound tourism. The WTO has a website (URL http://www.world-tourism.org/) which lists all of its publications. It also has a statistical database but this can only be accessed by WTO members.

The national tourism organizations of many countries provide domestic tourism figures, although they are frequently quoted as being sourced from the WTO publications mentioned above. In many cases, these figures can be accessed from the World Wide Web sites of national tourism organizations. Amongst such useful sources are Australia's Office for National Tourism website at http://www.dist.gov.au/tourism/index.html. This has a facts and figures section which links to a fact sheet (updated monthly) which provides statistics on the economic impact of tourism, and visitor arrival trends. For the USA, the Tourism Policy Council page is at http://tpcnet.doc.gov/main/stats.html. This body co-ordinates tourism policy at federal government level, and their website has a statistical information section which gives statistics provided by other related US government bureaus. The Tourism Industries Network (URL: http://www.tinet.ita.doc.gov/) is provided by the International Trade Administration – Tourism Industries, and aims to generate jobs through tourism exports. It provides statistics in a range of areas, including tourism arrivals information at state and city level. The New Zealand Tourist Board's Passport to New Zealand (URL: http://www/nztb.govt.nz/) does not give statistics on its own site, but does provide links to other useful government statistics pages.

UK information

Some of the most up-to-date and detailed statistics for the UK tourism market are supplied by the British Tourist Authority/English Tourist Board's publication, *Tourism Intelligence Quarterly* (British Tourist Authority, quarterly). This analyses international tourism in relation to the effects that worldwide trends will have on the UK tourism industry. The contribution tourism makes to the British economy is also covered. Figures are also given on UK tourists travelling abroad, and modes of travel. Whilst some of these figures are available in other publications, two of the major values of the *Tourism Intelligence Quarterly* are the currency of its information and frequency of publication.

The British Tourist Authority and English Tourist Board also jointly publish the *Overseas Visitor Survey* (British Tourist Authority, annual a). This covers the major factors contributing to the tourist experience when travelling to the UK, for example use of the BTA's overseas offices/commercial travel agents, participation in the arts when visiting the UK, accommodation and eating out, rail travel, use of tourist information centres, facilities available on Sundays and value for money/price competitiveness.

Travel Trends (Office for National Statistics, annual f) is the published results of the *International Passenger Survey* (British Tourist Authority, annual e), which collects data on travel to and from the UK. Visits by overseas residents are reported by country of origin and purpose of visit, and by mode of transport, amongst other categories. Outbound travel by UK residents is covered, broken down by similar criteria.

The *UK Tourist* is produced by the British Tourist Authority (British Tourist Authority, annual f) and the English, Welsh and Scottish tourist boards. This contains the published results of the *United Kingdom Tourism Survey*, which itself is sponsored jointly by the English, Northern Ireland, Scottish and Wales tourist boards and gives figures for numbers of tourists by purpose of their visit (for example, whether business and work tourism, visiting friends and relatives or holiday tourism). Categories of tourist are further broken down as to whether they are UK residents or not. Information is given on numbers of trips made, activities participated in, total nights spent, and expenditure.

Sightseeing in the UK (British Tourist Authority, annual c) is another joint publication of the national tourist boards. This covers numbers of available attractions, numbers of visits to these, trends in visits, expenditure, admission charges etc. Specific visitor numbers are provided for named attractions which receive high numbers of visitors (currently gauged at 30 000 visits or more). *Visits to Tourist Attractions* (British Tourist Authority, annual d), again a joint publication of the BTA and national tourist boards, breaks down attractions by type (e.g. historic houses, museums and galleries, country parks) and gives simple listings of each type of attraction by country and by name of attraction, providing numbers of visitors for the last two available years. *English Heritage Monitor* (English Tourist Board, annual) gives visitor numbers to monuments and historic buildings, with additional information given on English Heritage grants and amenities available at attractions.

In addition, statistical information may also be found in the published annual reports of each of the national tourism boards, and from their websites (see Appendix 1 at the end of this chapter).

The regional tourist boards of England and Wales produce *Regional Tourism Factsheets* (British Tourist Authority, annual b). Published annually, these give information, region by region, on tourism spending, age and social profile of tourists, accommodation and transport, and activities for UK tourists. Details of spending, season of visit, and accommodation used by overseas visitors are also provided. Figures are also given for visits to tourism attractions in the specific region. The information provided is up to date to the year preceding publication.

Leisure and sport

Whilst there are a number of statistics publications specifically covering this subject area (more detail later in this section), it is also likely that you will need to gather data from a wide range of sources depending on the particular emphasis of your research. To pick out some of the major elements of the subject, you could be looking at expenditure on leisure, participation in leisure pursuits, available time for leisure, and so on. We will be identifying and describing some of the specific collections of statistics from which you can gather information relevant to this range of subject areas.

Expenditure on leisure

The Office for National Statistics/Government Statistical Service in the UK collect and publish various series of social statistics, amongst which are *Family Spending* (Office for National Statistics, annual c) (prior to 1995 this was called the *Family Expenditure Survey*) and *Social Trends* (Office for National Statistics, annual e). *Family Spending* is based on a survey conducted (annually since 1957) amongst a large sample of households. It includes a chapter detailing household expenditure by region, and in this gives spending on items classified under 'Leisure services' and 'Leisure goods'. Depending on the scope of the definition of 'Leisure' which you are using for the purposes of your research, you may also need to include items from other sections, e.g. 'Fares and other travel costs', 'Alcoholic drink'. *Social Trends* (Office for National Statistics, annual e) which has been published since 1970 has a chapter on 'Expenditure', including household expenditure broken down by major items – some of this information is drawn from the *Family Expenditure Survey*, but there is also some from additional sources. Analyses of costs related to the Retail Price Index (RPI) are also given. Within the 'Lifestyles' chapter details are given of household expenditure on the National Lottery.

In the *United Kingdom National Accounts* (also known as the *Blue Book*) (Office for National Statistics, annual g), within the accounts given for various sectors of the economy (e.g. Central Government, Public Corporations) is a chapter on the 'Personal sector'. Within this, there are tables of statistics giving consumer expenditure by function, including expenditure on recreational goods and recreational and entertainment services.

Consumer Trends (Office for National Statistics, quarterly) breaks down consumer spending into broad categories, including alcohol and tobacco, books and magazines, but in this case total spending is the only figure given (i.e. there is no breakdown by age group or gender).

To find out what public bodies/local authorities are spending on leisure amenities, the Chartered Institute of Public Finance and Accountancy (CIPFA) statistical information service produces *Leisure and Recreation Statistics Estimates* (CIPFA, annual b) and *Charges for Leisure Services Statistics* (CIPFA, annual a). The first of these titles gives figures for expenditure by local authorities on leisure facilities, and also income generated by these. *Charges for Leisure Services Statistics* reports prices charged by local authorities for various types of leisure amenity (leisure centres; swimming pools; saunas; outdoor sports facilities), showing price increases relative to inflation.

Participation in leisure pursuits

Living in Britain: Results from the General Household Survey (Office for National Statistics, annual d) is a continuous survey conducted since 1971, which covers some main topics on a constant basis, but also covers a wider range of topics on an occasional basis, one of which is 'Sport and leisure activities'. The last time this topic was covered was in the survey which was carried out between April 1993 and March 1994 (since 1988 the research has been based on the financial as opposed to calendar year), and published as the

General Household Survey 1993. (Since 1994, the survey has been published under the title *Living in Britain: Results from the General Household Survey.*) The special chapter on 'Sport and leisure activities' covers participation rates for sports, games and physical recreation in general and is broken down by specific activity, and the same for leisure activities. Trends in participation are also given by a variety of categories (e.g. socioeconomic groupings, age, gender etc.).

The *Social Trends* (Office for National Statistics, annual e) chapter on 'Lifestyles' covers participation in leisure pursuits both within and outside the home. Participation rates are given, variously, by age and/or gender, and there is useful accompanying text describing trends, and generally fleshing out the details given in the tables.

The *UK Day Visits Survey 1994* (Countryside Recreation Network, 1996) is a biennial survey (so far conducted in 1994 and 1996) of the leisure day visits made by the adult (defined in this publication as people of fifteen years of age plus) population of the UK. The detailed survey looks at the types of people making visits, as well as the type of activity followed. Considerable analysis of the data collected is included in the published results.

Time available for leisure

The 'Lifestyles' chapter in *Social Trends* gives breakdowns of time use (giving percentages of time spent on major categories of activity) and use of free time (giving an average numbers of hours per week spent on leisure activities). To discover trends in the amount of time spent in work, the *Annual Abstract of Statistics* (Office for National Statistics, annual b) gives figures on average hours of full-time employees on adult rates. For more detailed breakdowns of working hours, see the *New Earnings Survey.* (Office for National Statistics, six per annum.)

Sport

A great deal of the information given above for leisure statistics will, of course, be applicable to research into sport. In some cases the most detailed information given will be for leisure in general (e.g. leisure spending) without this being broken down further into more specific categories.

For statistical information on specific sports, the most detailed coverage will probably be given by commercially produced publications intended for the sports fan market – for example, *Wisden Cricketer's Almanac* (1998). Official bodies or trusts associated with a particular sport may produce statistics – the Football Trust, for example, publishes the *Digest of Football Statistics* (Football Trust, annual). The annual reports and accounts of sports bodies (e.g. the UK Sports Council) and clubs (e.g. those football clubs which have been floated on the stock market) will contain some statistical information. Again, World Wide Web sites in this area are proliferating, both those produced by official bodies and those produced by sports fans. One site particularly worthy of note is the Sports Information Resource Centre (SIRC) statistics site. Based in Canada, this website gives good international statistical coverage (URL http://www.sportquest.com/statistics.shtml).

Sources of market research

Tracing market research

Market research reports are usually expensive because they contain commercially valuable information and, consequently, they can be difficult to obtain from libraries. Historical (out-of-date) information may be of interest to students but it is of limited value to anyone taking business decisions. The most expensive reports tend to be syndicated and continuous research data services which are available on subscription – these mainly cover food and retail markets. Reports covering leisure, sports and tourism markets tend to be annual or occasional publications. Research commissioned by a company for their own use is unlikely to be available commercially.

Directories

Marketsearch: International Directory of Published Market Research (Arlington Management Publications, annual) indexes nearly 20 000 market research studies which have been produced worldwide over the past five years. Each year new editions are added of around one fifth of these titles, and new publications are added (in 1997, 3500 titles were new). The studies are indexed by product, by publisher and by author. Under each product code there is a list of reports (details include the report title, countries covered, date, source and price); there is a source index at the back.

Findex: The World Directory of Market Research Reports, Studies and Surveys is produced annually by Euromonitor (Euromonitor, annual). This indexes around 10 000 reports by subject, geographic location, company, and publisher.

There is also a section with publishers' details. The information is updated by a telephone service, and by a mid-year supplement. It is also available electronically (on-line) in some libraries and on CD-ROM, produced by Cambridge Scientific Abstracts, and contains more material than the print version. With worldwide coverage, it contains abstracts of over 21 000 market and industry studies, including consumer markets.

Market research reports

Corporate Intelligence on Retailing and Travel and Tourism Intelligence

The Economist Intelligence Unit's publication divisions covering the retail sector and travel and tourism were taken over by the Corporate Intelligence Group in 1996. The two resultant companies have taken on the publications of these divisions and have continued the tradition of producing specialist research reports.

Corporate Intelligence on Retailing sector report titles include *In-store Catering in the UK* (1997), *Fast food in Europe* (1997) and *Retail and Leisure: The Essential Partnership?* (1996). Details of their publications can be found on their web page http://www.cior.com/

Travel and Tourism Intelligence (TTI) publish the journals *Travel and Tourism Analyst* (six per annum), and *International Tourism Reports* (quarterly) as well as sector reports. Examples of the latter include *International Business Travel* (1994), *Prospects for Tourism in South America* (1996) and *Airports in Europe* (1997). TTI's web page is at http://www.t-ti.com/

Euromonitor

Euromonitor is an established publisher of market research information whose journal titles include *Market Research Great Britain*, *Market Research Europe* and *Market Research International.* These monthly journals include regular analyses of leisure markets. Many of the reports contain valuable statistical data.

Euromonitor also publish a series of directories which include statistical information and retail information, for example *World Retail Directory* (3rd edn, 1997–8); *Directory of Consumer Brands and their Owners: Europe* (3rd edn, 1998); *International Marketing Data and Statistics* (22nd edn, 1998). Some products are now available via the internet or on CD-ROM as well as print format. Details of Euromonitor publications and access to subscription services can be found at http://www.euromonitor.com

Key Note

Key Note reports cover a wide range of sectors and include industrial markets. They include a useful series of reports on sport, leisure and tourism; these tend to cover broader subjects than reports produced by Mintel. Examples of recent reports include: *Betting and Gaming* (June 1997); *Football Clubs and Finance* (August 1997); *Hotels* (August 1997); *Leisure and Recreation (UK)* (September 1997); *Travel and Tourism (UK)* (July 1997).

Reports are available in print, CD-ROM or electronic format. The CD-ROM is monthly and gives access to executive summaries, outline key findings, and contents pages, plus the full text of any titles which have been purchased by the library/information service you are using. Ordering details are available on their web page http://www.keynote.co.uk/ and free executive summaries of the reports can be accessed from here.

Leisure Forecasts

Leisure Forecasts (Leisure Industries Research Centre, annual) contains information on market sectors in leisure including commentary, statistical data and five-year projections. It consists of two volumes – *Leisure in the Home* and *Leisure away from Home*. There is consistency between issues so that comparisons can be made across the years. The 'Special features' section highlights current issues in leisure markets, and an international focus has been introduced to this section with a feature on European leisure industries in the 1998 edition.

Leisure Forecasts is now produced by the Leisure Industries Research Centre – previously it was produced by Leisure Consultants, and during 1995–8 by both organizations in partnership.

Leisure Futures

Leisure Futures (Henley Centre for Forecasting, quarterly) looks at how people spend their time and their money. Analyses of economic, demographic, social and technological factors are used to forecast the prospects for a wide range of leisure markets. Special reports focus on particular topics each quarter.

MAID (Market Analysis and Information Databases)

An on-line service which makes available market reports from a range of major producers, including Key Note and Euromonitor. The reports are full text and market coverage is worldwide. Maid Plc have merged with Knight-Ridder to form the Dialog Corporation.

MarkIntel

This is another on-line service which is regularly updated and hosts market research reports from a wide range of providers. Reports are indexed by industry, company, product, geographic region and business topic. One of the providers, CountryLine International, produces market information and statistics on up to 180 countries including coverage of leisure, recreation and tourism. Other contributors provide analysis of the North American leisure markets.

Mintel

Mintel claims uniqueness as the only market analyst to include original research in its reports. The company produce a wide range of reports covering consumer markets including a large collection of reports covering leisure markets and aspects of leisure. These cover topics as diverse as *Long Haul Holidays* (March 1997), *Garden Furniture* (May 1995), *Broadcast Sponsorship* (June 1997), *The Football Business* (November 1996) and *Aerobics and Exercise Classes* (March 1998).

Mintel reports are available by subscription in print format (as a serial), on CD-ROM (updated monthly), or on-line via the internet at http://www.mintel. co.uk.

New Leisure Markets

These reports include key trends, market analyses, and details of major companies in the sector. Major market reviews which are updated annually include *Tourism in the UK* (1998) *Top Leisure Companies* (1998), *Sport and Recreation* (1997) and *Entertainment and the Arts* (1997). In addition occasional market reports cover specific aspects of leisure markets in the UK.

Conclusion

In this chapter, we have illustrated the important role both statistics and market research can play in tourism and leisure research. The tourism and leisure industries both represent fast-changing markets, and the statistical and market research information that is available to support research in these areas will inevitably reflect that. Alongside this, the increasing use of rapidly developing technologies (a prime example of which is the Internet) to deliver this information means that the major sources are constantly changing – there are far more good quality, authoritative websites in these subject areas now than there were two years ago, for example, and there will no doubt be many more in the near future. The basic need to follow sound research methods will therefore become ever more important as the information available continues to proliferate. Ensuring that you are using the most up-to-date material available to you, from a reputable source, and drawing sensible conclusions across comparable data will remain of high priority when you are using statistical and market research information from whatever source.

Appendix 1: World Wide Web sites for statistics

Australian Bureau of Statistics Australian Bureau of Statistics World Wide Web Information Service
URL: http://www.abs.gov.au (accessed 26 May 1998).
British Tourist Authority, The British Tourism Authority Web Site
URL: http://www.visitbritain.com/frameset.htm (accessed 26 May 1998).
Canadian Tourism Commission Canadian Tourism Information Network
URL: http://206.191.33.50/tourism/stats (accessed 26 May 1998).
Federal Interagency on Statistical Policy Fedstats
URL: http://www.fedstats.gov (accessed 26 May 1998).
International Trade Administration – Tourism Industries Tourism Industries Network
URL: http://www.tinet.ita.doc.gov/ (accessed 28 May 1998).
New Zealand Tourist Board New Zealand Tourist Board Passport to New Zealand
URL: http://www.nzt.govt.nz/ (accessed 28 May 1998).
Office of National Tourism Office of National Tourism
URL: http://www.dist.gov.au/tourism/index.html (accessed 28 May 1998).
Statistics Canada Welcome to Statistics Canada!
URL: http://www.statcan.ca/start.html (accessed 26 May 1998).
Statistics New Zealand Statsweb
URL: http://www.stats.govt.nz.STATSWEB.NSF (accessed 26 May 1998).
Tourism Policy Council Tourism Policy Council
URL: http://www/tpcnet.doc.gov/main/stats.html (accessed 28 May 1998).

World Tourism Organization
http://www.world-tourism.org/ (accessed 2 June 1998).

Appendix 2: Company details

Corporate Intelligence on Retailing
51 Doughty Street, London WC1N 2LS
0171 696 9006
http://www.cior.com/
Euromonitor plc
60–61 Britton Street, London EC1M 5NA
0171 251 1105
http://www.euromonitor.com
Henley Centre for Forecasting
9 Bridewell Place, London EC4V 6AY
0171 353 9961
Key Note Ltd
Field House, 72 Oldfield Road, Hampton, Middx TW12 2HQ
0181 783 0755
http://www.keynote.co.uk/
Leisure Industries Research Centre
Unit 1, Sheffield Science Park, Howard Street, Sheffield S1 2LX
0114 225 3972
http://www.shu.ac.uk/schools/lfm/lfmcent/lirc/
MAID (The Dialog Corporation)
The Communications Building, 48 Leicester Square, London WC2H 7DB
0171 930 6900
Markintel
The Investext Group (Boston, MA)
http://www.investext.com
Mintel International Group Ltd
18–19 Long Lane, London EC1A 9HE
171 606 4533
http://www.mintel.co.uk/
New Leisure Markets
Marketscape Ltd, 5th Floor, 29–30 Warwick Street, London W1R 5RD
0171 727 3443
Travel and Tourism Intelligence
51 Doughty Street, London WC1N 2LS
0171 696 9006
http://www.t-ti.com/

References

Arlington Management Publication (annual). *Marketsearch: International Directory of Published Market Research.*

Australian Bureau of Statistics (annual a) *Australia at a Glance.*

Australian Bureau of Statistics (annual b) *Year Book Australia.*

British Tourist Authority (annual a) *Overseas Visitor Survey.*

British Tourist Authority (annual b) *Regional Tourism Factsheets.*

British Tourist Authority (annual c) *Sightseeing in the UK.*

British Tourist Authority (annual d) *Visits to Tourist Attractions.*

British Tourist Authority (annual e) *International Passenger Survey.*

British Tourist Authority (annual f) *UK Tourist.*

British Tourist Authority (quarterly) *Tourism Intelligence Quarterly.*

CIPFA Statistical Information Service (annual a) *Charges for Leisure Services Statistics.*

CIPFA Statistical Information Service (annual b) *Leisure and Recreation Statistics Estimates.*

Countryside Recreation Network (1996) *UK Day Visits Survey 1994.*

English Tourist Board (annual) *English Heritage Monitor.*

Euromonitor (1997) *World Directory of Non-official Statistical Sources.*

Euromonitor (annual) *Findex: The World Directory of Market Research Reports, Studies and Surveys.*

Euromonitor (monthly a) *Market Research Great Britain.*

Euromonitor (monthly b) *Market Research Europe.*

Euromonitor (monthly c) *Market Research international.*

Football Trust (annual) *Digest of Football Statistics.*

Henley Centre for Forecasting (quarterly) *Leisure Futures.*

Leisure Industries Research Centre (annual) *Leisure Forecasts.*

Mort, D. and Siddall, L. (1997) *Sources of United Kingdom Unofficial Statistics.* Gower.

National Technical Information Service (annual) *Statistical Abstract of the United States.* US Department of Commerce.

Office for National Statistics (1996) *Guide to Official Statistics.*

Office for National Statistics (annual a) *Key Data.*

Office for National Statistics (annual b) *Annual Abstract of Statistics.*

Office for National Statistics (quarterly) *Consumer Trends.*

Office for National Statistics (annual c) *Family Spending.*

Office for National Statistics (annual d) *Living in Britain: Results from the General Household Survey.*

Office for National Statistics (annual e) *Social Trends.*

Office for National Statistics (annual f) *Travel Trends.*

Office for National Statistics (annual g) *United Kingdom National Accounts.*

Office for National Statistics (six per annum) *New Earnings Survey.*

Statistics Canada (biennial) *Canada Year Book.*

Statistics New Zealand (monthly) *Key Statistics.*

Statistics New Zealand (annual) *New Zealand Official Yearbook.*

Travel and Tourism Intelligence (quarterly) *International Tourism Reports.*

Travel and Tourism Intelligence (six per annum) *Travel and Tourism Analyst.*

United States Census Bureau (annual) *US Statistics in Brief.*

Wisden Cricketer's Almanac (1998) Penguin.

World Tourism Organization (1997) *Compendium of Tourism Statistics.* (17th edn).

World Tourism Organization (1998) *World Tourism Highlights 1997.*

World Tourism Organization (annual) *Yearbook of Tourism Statistics.*

7

Finding and using official European Union information sources on sport, leisure and tourism

Bob Burns

Although the European Union (EU) has historically had little formal competence in the areas of tourism, sport and leisure, a number of EU policy sectors are of considerable relevance to the subjects of concern to this book, and the importance of official EU information to researchers in these areas must not be underestimated. In areas such as social policy, transport policy, regional policy and competition policy the EU has taken a long-standing active interest in topics which impinge directly upon tourism, leisure and sport. In more recent years the EU has taken a far more direct interest in tourism and sport in particular, and the signs are that official EU publishing in these areas is likely to increase significantly in the immediately forthcoming years.

The intention of this chapter is to concentrate on looking at methods researchers can use to track down particular kinds of official EU information, together with outlining the various kinds of information centres and libraries such researchers can visit to gain access to hard-copy or electronic versions of useful documents, and specialist information staff help in researching their particular topic of interest. In addition there will be some more detailed analysis of existing publications emanating from the EU, both in hard copy and electronic form, which actually examine issues related to tourism, sport and leisure.

The chapter will examine the ever-widening range of EU institutions which currently, or potentially could, publish actively in the areas under consideration, discussing the types of publication they produce and the methods by which these can be tracked, either via the Internet, CD-ROM databases, or hard-copy indexing services.

The hope is that this chapter will be of considerable practical use to those researching in the subject areas, particularly those who are novices in terms of finding and using EU information. In this context readers' attention is immediately drawn to the appendices at the end of this chapter which include lists of different kinds of libraries and information centres throughout the English-speaking world which specialize in providing access to official EU information, and have staff able to deal with EU-related enquiries. Also included amongst the appendices are website addresses (URLs) for a whole host of useful sites on the Internet.

The remainder of the chapter divides into six distinct sections:

- the institutions and agencies of the EU, and the documents they publish
- statistical information
- information on funding
- information available on the Internet
- information available on CD-ROM databases
- places to visit or contact for further help or information.

The institutions and agencies of the European Union

Having already stated that the EU has not yet published a huge amount of material relevant to tourism, leisure and sport, it is equally true to say that a huge number of the EU's institutions have a latent interest in the area and are potential sources of future information, if not yet current publishers in the fields. There is no intention here to make any detailed analysis of the organizational and administrative structure of the EU, but rather to cover each relevant institution and its pertinent paper and electronic publications.

European Commission

Of all the EU's institutions the European Commission is by far the most prolific in terms of publishing. To look at it in its simplest fashion the Commission can be viewed as the prime policy formulation body within the EU. Most EU laws have their bases in proposals from the European Commission, which are examined, commented upon, and in many cases substantially amended by other EU institutions before actually becoming a piece of EU legislation. However the initial role of the European Commission is vital.

The European Commission is a non-elected body, based in Brussels, which itself comprises some twenty-four Directorate Generals (or DGs as they are often known), each responsible for a different area of activity. Each DG is headed by a Commissioner, backed up by a substantial expert staff. Each DG is responsible for monitoring EU policy in its own area, producing not only proposals for new pieces of legislation, but also reports and studies which may investigate particular topics of interest or which may evaluate the impact of earlier EU programmes, policies or legislation in a specific field.

The two DGs with most specific responsibility for tourism, leisure and sport are:

- DG X – Information, Communication, Culture and Audiovisual Media
- DG XXIII – Enterprise Policy, Distributive Trades, Tourism and Co-operatives.

It is clear that both DGs have wide remits and only deal with the subjects of concern to this book as part of their work. In addition a large number of other DGs may deal with matters of concern to those interested in tourism, leisure and sport. Those worth highlighting are listed below:

- DG II – Economic and Financial Affairs
- DG III – Industry
- DG IV – Competition
- DG V – Employment, Industrial Relations and Social Affairs
- DG VIII – Transport
- DG XVI – Regional Policies
- DG XXIV – Consumer Policy.

Most publications emanating from the Commission are actually published by the Commission as a whole or by the EU's publishing arm the Office for Official Publications of the European Communities, often known simply as OOPEC, or more commonly now as EUR-OP. Although individual DGs do publish documents themselves these are often notoriously difficult to track down, even via a Brussels source, and many are really intended purely as internal European Commission working documents.

Legislation and proposals for legislation

All European Commission proposals for new legislation or amendments to existing legislation begin life as Commission Documents, normally referred to as 'COM docs'. The COM doc. will contain not only the Commission's proposal for the new piece of legislation, but also an accompanying explanatory memorandum, which details the background to the Commission's initiative. Each year's COM docs are issued in a chronological running sequence. For example, in 1988 the Commission put forward a proposal for a directive on package travel. This original proposal was published with the document number COM (88) 41. All COM doc. references should look like this.

The proposal was subsequently amended and reissued a year later as COM (89) 348, and in 1990 was resubmitted as a re-examined proposal COM (90) 232. In this form it eventually became a directive later in 1990, as Council Directive 90/314.

This illustration is actually a fairly simple example of how an initial proposal can be amended several times before becoming a piece of EU legislation. The situation is now considerably more complex with the European Parliament having far more influence in the areas of initiating and amending legislation. It is also worth noting that, although the Commission initially proposed the directive, it was known throughout as a proposal for a Council directive. The European Council will be discussed later in this chapter but this gives an indication of how confusing the EU legislative process can be to a novice user.

As well as being published in COM doc. format each stage of the legislative process is also published in the *Official Journal of the European Communities*, although publication is often several weeks, or possibly even months, behind the COM doc. stage. Another disadvantage with the *Official Journal* version is that it does not include the explanatory memorandum but just the text of the proposal or amended proposal. The *Official Journal of the European Communities* itself divides into two parts, the L series, which publishes all legislation such as directives and regulations once they have been finalized; and the C series, which publishes all proposals and amended proposals together with a whole raft of other official documents which come under the rather nebulous heading of 'information and notices'. Thus the initial proposal stage for the package travel directive (COM (88) 41) mentioned above was published in the C series at: OJC 96/1988/04/12/p.5, which translates as page 5 of issue 96 of the C series of the *Official Journal*, dated 12 April 1988.

It is important to note that eventual final pieces of legislation do not appear in the COM doc. series, but are only published in the L series of the *Official*

Journal, so there can often be a frustrating delay prior to the publication of the final version. Consequently the actual directive 90/314 on package travel was published at: OJL 158/1990/06/23/p.59, which translates as page 59 of issue 158 of the L series of the *Official Journal*, dated 23 June 1990.

It is evident that there are a huge number of COM docs and *Official Journal*s published per year, with normally something like one issue of each series of the *Official Journal* per day. The number of COM docs varies from year to year but, for example, in 1997 there were well over 600.

As far as access to the COM docs and *Official Journal*s is concerned, as a rule COM docs are more likely to be found at specialist centres for European information, such as European Documentation Centres in the UK, whereas a wider range of libraries may hold copies of the *Official Journal*. For example in the UK many university libraries servicing large Law faculties will hold the *Official Journal of the European Communities*.

First-time or infrequent users of the *Official Journal of the European Communities* are likely to find the index difficult to use and those looking for either a known piece of legislation, or attempting to find all the legislation on a particular topic will undoubtedly find *European Communities Legislation: Current Status*, a two-volume publication from UK legal publishers Butterworths, easier to use. This lists all Directives and Regulations in chronological sequences, giving *Official Journal* publication citations. It also has a detailed subject keyword index. The main work comprises two volumes, with a supplementary updating volume issued every six months. The whole work is kept up to date by means of a fortnightly newsletter.

Policy documents

This has very briefly covered the legislative output of the Commission, but the COM doc. series includes a far wider range of publications than proposals for legislation. A large proportion of COM docs will be policy documents, as opposed to proposals for legislation. These documents may be discussion papers on which future legislation may be based, or may take the form of a review of EU activity in a particular area. Some such reviews may appear on an annual basis.

Such documents can come in various forms, but are technically known as communications or reports. In many cases though they will be referred to both officially and popularly as either white papers or green papers. Two recent examples of this form of policy COM doc. are:

- COM (95) 97 – Commission green paper on the role of the European Union in the field of tourism
- COM (97) 332 – Report from the Commission on Community measures affecting tourism (1995/96).

In many instances such policy COM docs are later reprinted in a more professional book format with full ISBN details, but it appears this was not the case with either of these two publications.

Monographs and periodicals

Whilst legislation, proposals for legislation and policy COM docs represent a substantial part of the Commission's publishing output, they are supplemented by a huge range of one-off monograph-type reports and studies, together with a large number of periodical titles.

A quick search made during research for this chapter revealed forty-five 'books' published by the Commission containing some information on tourism between 1983 and 1997. There is no scope here for a full listing of these titles but a selection appear in the References at the end of the chapter.

One hybrid title published jointly by DG III of the Commission and the Commission's statistical Office Eurostat deserves highlighting however. *Panorama of EU Industry* (European Commission, DG III, 1997) is an annual publication giving commentary and some basic statistics on a wide range of industries and business sectors. Tourism has its own chapter.

Currently there are no Commission periodicals which concentrate their emphasis on tourism, sport or leisure, but there are some which touch on these subjects in a peripheral way. These periodicals vary enormously in style and content from basic newsletters to heavyweight titles looking in depth at issues such as European Monetary Union. The best way to search for articles in these titles is to use one of the CD-ROM databases mentioned later in this chapter, but it is perhaps worth mentioning one title at this stage, EURO-INFO, a newsletter aimed at small businesses, which appears ten times per year and often includes information on EU policies in relation to tourism.

Two general periodical titles which should be highlighted here are the *Bulletin of the European Union* and the *General Report on the Activities of the European Union*, both published by the Commission. The *Bulletin* is a monthly current awareness service covering all areas of EU activity. Each issue has an excellent subject keyword index, enabling the user to track down any recent developments relevant to sport or tourism. The *General Report* is an annual publication which takes a retrospective overview of the EU's activities again with a user-friendly index.

Council of the European Union

Unfortunately the structure and working methods of the Council of the European Union, often referred to as the Council of Ministers, are somewhat complex to explain. Basically the Council is the body which ultimately adopts the legislative proposals put forward by the Commission, hence the fact that the aforementioned Commission proposal on package travel eventually became a Council directive.

The Council is composed of one member from each member state, but the composition is not fixed and membership varies according to topics under discussion. The members are ministers of state from each member country, but meetings take place at sporadic intervals depending on the nature of the topics under discussion. The two Councils most relevant to the subject matter of this book are the Tourism Council and the Culture Council, each of which met once in 1997.

Twice a year the heads of each member state will meet together with the President of the European Commission at what is called a European Council, at which the really important matters concerning the development of the EU are discussed.

Each member state has the Presidency of the Council for a six-month period on a prearranged timescale. At the time of writing, in early 1998, the UK has the Presidency, to be followed in rotation by Austria, Germany and Finland up to the end of 1999. The administrative work of the Council is provided for by a well staffed General Secretariat.

Having outlined this complex structure, it has to be said that the Council's overall publishing output is infinitely smaller than that of the Commission, and in relation to tourism, leisure and sport is very limited indeed.

All Council legislation – directives, regulations and suchlike are published in the L Series of the *Official Journal of the European Communities*. The General Secretariat publishes an *Annual Review of the Council's Work*, but this can appear up to two years late. The 1995 edition makes absolutely no mention of sport or tourism, although both topics are referred to very briefly in earlier editions.

A good way of keeping track of recent Council meetings is by using the monthly *Bulletin of the European Union* published by the Commission. This includes a section listing all recent Council meetings with information on specific topics discussed. The best way of tracking more detailed information on the meetings is via the Commission's RAPID database, available to European Documentation Centres on the World Wide Web. This database will be explained in more detail later.

European Parliament

The powers of the European Parliament have increased considerably in recent years, most notably with the introduction of the co-decision procedure by the Maastricht Treaty, but it must still be looked upon largely as a consultative rather than a legislative body. It has no power to initiate legislation, but does have the opportunity to amend Commission proposals and block legislation.

The European Parliament meets in full session once a month over two or three days, and the topics for discussion are as wide-ranging as in any national Parliament. The minutes of the sittings are normally available in printed form within a month. They make up an entire single edition of the C series of the *Official Journal of the European Communities*. The verbatim texts of the debates take considerably longer to produce, normally about a year. These are published in a special Annex to the *Official Journal of the European Communities*, with each issue of the Annex containing the debates of a particular monthly sitting.

Written questions from individual MEPs addressed to either the Commission or the Council are also published, with answers, in the C Series of the *Official Journal* on a frequent, but irregular, basis.

The European Parliament also has a strong committee structure, with each committee examining issues in a particular field of EU activity and producing reports, formerly also known as session documents or working documents. Many of these reports are responses to suggested pieces of Commission legislation, but the committees are also able to produce own-initiative reports on subjects which they feel need highlighting. The committees of most relevance here are those dealing with transport and tourism; and culture, youth, education and media. Two recent examples of their respective publications are the resolution on the Commission's green paper on the role of the EU in the field of tourism; and the report on the role of the EU in the field of sport.

European Parliament documents have historically been notoriously difficult to track down without knowing the individual document number, but now the European Parliament's excellent website and various commercially produced CD-ROMs have vastly improved both the methods of access and the availability of full text copies. The website and the CD-ROMs will be discussed at further length later.

European Court of Justice

It will probably be of little surprise to discover that the European Court of Justice has published little material relevant to our concerns here. This is primarily because the vast bulk of the Court's publishing output consists of reports of decisions in cases heard before it. Most cases which go before the Court concern interpretation of Community laws, such as the provisions of the founding and subsequent treaties (Rome, Maastricht etc.), and articles within directives and regulations. As we have seen, sport and tourism are not areas on which the EU has passed any significant amount of legislation, hence it is no great surprise to find a very small amount of case law relevant to our interests.

However, it is worth highlighting a couple of cases, if only again to point out the potential publications in which researchers may find useful information in the future. One of the Court's most famous recent decisions was in the case of Jean Marc Bosman (C-415/93), which effectively put an end to the existing transfer regime for footballers moving between clubs based in different EU member states. This case shows how EU freedom of movement for workers legislation can influence the sporting world. In another case (C-375/92) Spain was found to have not properly implemented EU legislation on the mutual recognition of educational qualifications by insisting that all people working as tour guides in Spain had to possess a recognized Spanish qualification, rather than simply an equivalent qualification from another member state.

All case reports are published in the series Reports of Cases before the Court of Justice and the Court of First Instance. The series should be available at all European Documentation Centres, and at many other university law libraries.

The manner in which the European Court Reports series is indexed is not especially helpful, particularly to novice or infrequent users. A better way of tracking down specific cases or cases on a particular topic is to use *Butterworths EC Case Citator and Service* (Isaacs, 1994–) republished in a cumulative form every six months by Butterworths, one of the UK's leading legal publishers. The publication is continually updated by a fortnightly newsletter service.

Economic and Social Committee

The Economic and Social Committee (ECOSOC) is an often overlooked body, perhaps because its powers are considerably more limited than those of the institutions mentioned above, but because of its composition its publications may be of some interest to those looking for information on tourism, leisure and sport.

In short it comprises government-nominated members from each member state drawn from groups such as employers' organizations, workers' organizations, small firms, consumers, the professions etc. It produces opinions on pieces of proposed EU legislation in a limited number of areas, primarily those with some socioeconomic relevance. It has no power to amend legislation, but its members represent important interest groups throughout the Union and as such the opinions may carry some weight. The opinions are published as individual documents, but are also reprinted in the C series of the *Official Journal of the European Communities* at a, sometimes considerably, later date. To give an example, in 1996 ECOSOC published an opinion on the PHILOXENIA (1997–2000) programme, the first multinational programme to assist European tourism. In addition to its individual opinions ECOSOC publishes a brief annual report summarizing its work.

Committee of the Regions

The Committee of the Regions (COR) is the most recently established of the EU's main institutions, and has a similar role to that of ECOSOC. Its 222 members are drawn from the local, district and regional authorities throughout the EU, and they are consulted on matters which have a regional policy dimension. Like ECOSOC the body has no power to amend legislation, but the COR also produces opinions of either a consultative, or more recently, an own-initiative nature. Two recent opinions focused on the interaction between education and sport, and the development of rural tourism. In addition the COR has held forums targeting particular issues at some of its plenary sessions, and on 17–18 September 1997, a forum looked at sport as a vehicle for the identity of cities and regions. Opinions are published individually, and from 1994 are available via the C series of the *Official Journal of the European Communities*.

Court of Auditors

The task of the Court of Auditors is to audit the accounts of EU institutions, checking on whether money has been correctly spent and whether necessary standards of financial management have been upheld. It reports back to the relevant institutions. The body has produced two special reports of direct relevance to tourism:

- Special report 4/92 on expenditure relating to the European Year of Tourism
- Special report 3/96 on tourist policy and the promotion of tourism (reprinted together with the Commission's replies in OJC 17/1996/01/16/p.1).

European Investment Bank

The EU's only other major institution is the European Investment Bank, but as yet it has, predictably, not published any documents with a direct relevance to tourism or sport.

Agencies

In addition to its main institutions the EU encompasses a number of additional quasi-autonomous agencies, based in different parts of the Union. As yet these agencies have taken little active interest in the subjects we are concerned with, and some by their very nature never will. However, it is worth briefly mentioning four of the agencies. For further information see their websites listed in the appendices at the end of the chapter.

The European Centre for the Development of Vocational Training, based in Greece, is the first of these agancies and has a brief which covers vocational education and training. It has published a few documents relevant to the tourism industry, including a huge 1994 report on occupations in the tourist sector, which includes a country-by-country analysis of job profiles. It has also published individual studies of a similar nature on the UK, Portugal, Greece, Italy, France and Germany, although these are somewhat older and all, with the exception of the UK volume, are in French. A full list of relevant CEDEFOP publications is included in the References at the end of this chapter.

The other three agencies are:

- the European Environment Agency
- the European Foundation for the Improvement of Living and Working Conditions
- the European University Institute.

Statistical information

The European Commission's statistical office Eurostat published its first volume of *Tourism: Annual Statistics* in 1990, covering the year 1987. The latest edition appeared in 1997 covering the year 1994. It is a highly detailed publication running to around 300 pages each year. It covers such items as tourist accommodation, resident and non-resident guest flows in accommodation establishments, travel agencies, tourist expenditure, employment in the tourist industry and tourist consumer prices. For more up-to-date but much less detailed statistics there is the monthly short-term statistics publication, *Distributive Trade, Services and Transport* (Eurostat, monthly), which includes tourism statistics in each issue. Since 1996 Eurostat have also been publishing a series *Statistics in Focus: Distributive Trade, Services and Transport* (Eurostat, four times per year). Published quarterly each issue, normally about ten pages in length examines a specific topic. As yet there have been none relating to tourism, but there are likely to be in the future. In 1995 Eurostat and DG XXIII of the European Commission jointly published a study entitled *Tourism in Europe*, which includes a wealth of statistical data and commentary on recent trends in the tourist industry together with individual chapters on each of the EU and European Free Trade Association (EFTA) member states. To date there appear to be no Eurostat publications which cover sport.

Information on funding

The best official publication covering EU funding is *Grants and Loans from the European Union: A Guide to Community funding* (European Commission, DG X, 1997). It provides a broad overview of European Union funded projects together with practical details on how to apply for funding. There are individual sections devoted to tourism and sport. The guide is also available on the Europa website, presumably updated in an ongoing fashion. The tourism section can be found at http://europa.eu.int/comm/sg/aides/en/p3ch3.htm, with the sport section at http://europa.eu.int/comm/sg/aides/en/p3ch8.htm.

Information available on the World Wide Web

Having spent some time outlining directly and potentially useful publications from the most relevant EU institutions, it is important to stress the increasing importance of the Web as a tool for accessing information on EU policy and documentation. Not only has the Union developed its own excellent website, Europa, but many other independent sites have evolved covering EU matters with links provided to relevant information on the official pages. In the following section the key websites will be highlighted, and specific documents relevant to sport and tourism available in full text will also be indicated. Inevitably the website addresses will be scattered throughout the text and readers wishing to examine the sites immediately may prefer to use the list of relevant website addresses (URLs) provided at the end of the chapter.

Official EU websites

Europa: http://europa.eu.int/index-en.htm

Europa is the EU's official website and during 1998 it is likely to develop into one of the largest websites in the world. From this homepage you can access a wide variety of information from the various institutions covered in the previous section of this chapter. The site is reliant on a very graphical interface, and can be somewhat slow to use. Also navigating around the site is not an entirely self-evident process, and many useful documents and information sources can easily remain hidden from the user. However, the sheer quantity of information available makes the website invaluable, and the Union should also be praised on the speed with which new documents are added and information is updated.

From the homepage you can move around the site in a variety of ways, either going to a news section for current information; an institutions section which leads into information from the different bodies; or via a policies link, which adopts a thematic approach to the content of the site. There is also a fairly basic keyword search facility available from the homepage. A useful, but not very self-evident link from the homepage is via the information icon in the bottom right of the screen. From here you can access, amongst other items, some useful databases. An example is IDEA, effectively a Who's Who of the EU institutions (http://158.169.50.70/idea/ideaen.html). This is an on-line equivalent of the annual printed volume *Who's Who in the EU*. It allows you to carry out a hierarchical search on the EU staff structure so, for example, you can discover the names, addresses, telephone/fax numbers and in some cases even e-mail addresses of all staff working on tourism within DG XXIII of the Commission.

In a very recent development the EU's bibliographical database SCAD has been made generally available over the Web (http://europa.eu.int/comm/ sg/scadplus/scad_en.htm). Going under the name of SCADplus, this website offers access to recent developments in EU policy as well as full access to the SCAD database, which for many years has only been available to information professionals via a complicated searching procedure. The SCAD database is enormously useful to anyone researching any aspect of EU policy, covering various categories of material from the early 1980s up to very recent weeks. The categories, or sectors as they are referred to by the database, are:

A – European Union legislation, proposals for legislation, and opinions on proposals for legislation.
B – Other official non-legislative EU publications (policy documents, monographs, articles in EU-published periodicals).
C – Articles on EU-related matters from over 2000 commercially published periodicals from all over the world.
D – Opinions on EU matters from employers' and trade union organizations.

SCAD is not a full-text database, but simply gives references as to where the full text of documents can be found, along with short abstracts of their contents. The availability of information in sector C is a real bonus for students and other academic researchers in particular, since documents in this sector offer analysis and criticism of EU policies and legislation, rather than the more factual or descriptive approaches which the official documents from sectors A and B obviously adopt.

The database is genuinely multilingual, but as yet the keyword search option is only available in French, with other languages to be added in the future. An alternative is to search for a word in the title or abstract of a document. Subject searches can be further limited by language, publication year or sector (A, B, C or D above). One drawback is that the database can only take a limited number of concurrent user sessions, so at times it is difficult to access, but its provision on the Web certainly marks a major breakthrough in the provision of EU information to a wider audience. SCAD could easily be used to find references on topics such as fire safety in hotels or broadcasting rights in relation to European football matches.

The database has been commercially available in CD-ROM format from two commercial suppliers in the UK for some time, and the CD versions certainly offer greater flexibility in searching, together with an English keyword structure already in place. For information on the CD-ROM versions see the CD-ROM section later in this chapter.

Another highly useful database available from the Europa site is RAPID (http://europa.eu.int/rapid/start/welcome.htm), a full-text database of press releases from the various EU institutions. The database is updated on a daily basis and covers material dating from the mid-1980s. It is searchable by free text words or phrases.

Early in 1998 a new on-line Web-based service called EU-LAW should also become available via the Europa site. This will give general access to a huge quantity of EU legislation in full text, together with the full text of the most recent twenty issues of both the C and L series of the *Official Journal of the European Communities.*

Such information is currently only available via the CELEX database, which itself only became available on the Web in the latter part of 1997. The EU-LAW service will effectively be a subset of the CELEX database, which is currently a charged-for subscription service. Those users wishing to make use of the CELEX database without taking out a subscription could try contacting their local European Documentation Centre, who will have access to the Web version of CELEX free of charge and, given available staff time, will be able to carry out searches on behalf of researchers. CELEX is particularly useful if you need to track down a particular piece of EU legislation but do not know its precise reference, or if you want to find out if a piece of EU legislation has been subsequently amended by a later piece of legislation. The database contains the full text of the following categories of material:

1 All the founding and amending treaties of the EU (Treaty of Rome, Single European Act, Maastricht Treaty etc.).
2 All EU secondary legislation (directives, regulations etc.).
3 Recent proposals for legislation, and any subsequent opinions on them (proposals from the Commission, amendments from the European Parliament, and opinions from the Economic and Social Committee and the Committee of the Regions).
4 European Court of Justice case law.
5 Agreements between the EU as a whole and other countries.

It also contains bibliographic references to, but not full text of:

- written questions from the European Parliament (but not the answers)
- older proposals for legislation, as in item (3) above.

The CELEX database has been available in CD-ROM format for some time from the same two commercial publishers who produce the CD-ROM versions of SCAD. The CD-ROM versions offer a greater flexibility in terms of searching, and will be covered in the CD-ROM section later in this chapter.

Another exceptionally up-to-date database available from the Europa site is EUDOR (http://www.eudor.com:8444/EUDOR/PROC/orientation?LANGUAGE =english). This has no full text, but indexes the titles of all COM docs and all documents published in either the C or the L series of the *Official Journal of the European Communities* from January 1996 onwards. It is searchable by title keyword or by various other criteria based on document numbers, dates etc. Those users with a budget and a credit card available can make use of EUDOR's other main function which is as a document delivery service. Specific documents can be ordered on-line at variable costs, with delivery available by fax or e-mail. This option may suit those with finances available and little opportunity to access materials via a local European information centre, such as a European Documentation Centre.

Having dealt with the general structure of the Europa website, and covered some of the comprehensive databases available from it, it is now worth looking at the websites of some of the individual institutions of the European Union.

European Commission: http://europa.eu.int/en/comm.html

As may be expected the Commission's website reflects its prime importance in terms of printed publications, and there is a wealth of information available from the links on this page. For example selected green papers (http:// europa.eu.int/comm/off/green/index.htm) and white papers (http://europa.eu. int/comm/off/white/index.htm) are available in full text, as are recent issues of the *Bulletin of the European Union* (http://europa.eu.int/abc/doc/off/bull/en/ welcome.htm).

By using the link to the Directory of the European Commission, it is possible to access the homepages of individual Directorates General. DG X's homepage (http://europa.eu.int/en/comm/dg10/dg10.html) has a recently established link to information on sport and the EU (http://europa.eu.int/ en/comm/dg10/sport/en/index.html). The information on these Web pages marks a substantial step forward in the provision of documentation on the EU's role in relation to sport. Included is information on the EURATHLON programme, designed to provide a framework for EU subsidies for sport, with details given on the criteria and procedure for 1998 applications, and a full list of the projects supported in 1997. There is also a section on EU financial support for sport for the disabled. The agenda, minutes and journal of the 1996 European Sports Forum are also available in full text. Perhaps most useful of all is the Sport Info Europe service, which gives information on the administrative structure of sport in all the member states, with lists of useful addresses and links to related external websites. The Sport Info Europe service also offers an e-mail enquiry service via these web pages.

The DG XXIII also has its own website (http://europa.eu.int/en/comm/dg23/index.htm) with a specific subsection dedicated to information on tourism (http://europa.eu.int/en/comm/dg23/tourisme/tourisme.htm). Here you will find information on the PHILOXENIA programme, aimed at promoting European tourism, together with an evaluation of the first Community Action Plan to Assist Tourism (1993–5). Also included are a series of comprehensive travel guides for tourists with disabilities, covering all fifteen member states, and a short section entitled 'Main facts on European tourism'.

Another document relating specifically to tourism available from the Commission website is the tourism section from the European Commission's Progress report on the implementation of the EC's Fifth Environmental Action Programme (http://europa.eu.int/en/comm/dg11/env-act5/prog-rep/chapt1-5.htm 130). This dates from January 1996 and provides a substantial evaluation of the impact of tourism on the environment.

From the Commission's website links can also be made to many of the Commission's offices around the world. Connections to the websites of the offices in ten of the fifteen member states are available, together with a selection of others. Amongst those that readers may find most useful are:

- UK (http://www.cec.org.uk/)
- Ireland (http://www.cec.ie/)
- USA (http://www.eurunion.org/)
- Hong Kong (http://www.ust.hk/~webeu/).

Council of the European Union: http://ue.eu.int/angl/summ2.htm

The Council's website currently has virtually no information pertinent to tourism or sport, but it does have a downloadable full-text version of the new Amsterdam Treaty for those who are interested. There is also a link to the website of the UK Presidency of the EU (January–June 1998) (http://presid.fco.gov.uk/). A related site is the retrospective database of documents relating to the rolling 1996 Inter-Governmental Conference (IGC) (http://europa.eu.int/en/agenda/igc-home/index.html) which undertook much of the work leading up to the drafting of the Amsterdam Treaty. One particularly useful document which can be found amongst the links here is 'Community tourism policy: the integration of tourism into the Treaty: a proposal by the AIT & FIA to the Intergovernmental Conference' (http://europa.eu.int/ en/agenda/igc-home/instdoc/industry/ait-en.htm). This paper dates from March 1996 and is a submission from the Alliance Internationale de Tourisme and the Fédération Internationale de Automobile to the Intergovernmental Conference.

European Parliament:
http://www.europarl.eu.int/sg/tree/en/default.htm

Far more useful is the European Parliament's website, which contains an increasing variety of documents in full text. Included amongst these are a developmental database of written questions from June 1996 onwards, information on the Committee on Transport and Tourism, and keyword searchable databases of reports tabled and texts adopted at plenary sessions from respectively 1997 and 1996 onwards. For example the Committee on Culture, Youth, Education and the Media's 1997 report on sport and the European Union is available in full text (http://wwwdb.europarl.eu.int/dg7-bin/seid.pl).

European Foundation for the Improvement of Living and Working Conditions: http://www.europa.eu.int/agencies/efilwc/index.htm

This agency has until very recently produced little of use to those researching into tourism or sports-related industries, but has just made available an excellent database of full-text articles on industrial relations. The database goes by the name of EIRO (http://www.eiro.eurofound.ie/index.main.html), and allows users to search by keyword for articles on an EU-wide or individual member state basis.

Other institutions and agencies

The websites of other institutions are currently less useful, but may become so in the future. Some of the potentially useful sites are listed below:

- European Court of Justice (http://europa.eu.int/cj/en/index.htm)

- Economic and Social Committee (http://europa.eu.int/ces/ces.html)
- Committee of the Regions (http://www.europa.eu.int/comreg/comreg.html)
- CEDEFOP, European Centre for the Development of Vocational Training (http://www.cedefop.gr/)
- European Environment Agency (http://www.eea.dk/)
- European University Institute (http://www.iue.it/).

Eurostat: http://europa.eu.int/en/comm/eurostat/serven/home.htm

Eurostat's website is largely a publicity tool for its hard-copy publications, but it does have a useful press release section searchable by keyword, which at the time of writing contains two press releases on tourism from 1996 and 1997. Press releases can also be viewed chronologically, and it is worth noting that the appearance of a press release on the website usually heralds the imminent arrival of a more detailed paper publication on the subject.

Non-official websites providing access to EU information

In addition to the Europa website and the related sites of the various EU institutions, there are a number of other sites which provide alternative methods of accessing EU resources. Two of the best are covered below.

European Information Association (EIA): http://www.hull.ac.uk/php/lbsebd/eia_html/

To quote from its website:

> the European Information Association (EIA) is an international body of information specialists concerned with developing, co-ordinating and improving information about the European Union. Regular EIA events and training courses give members the opportunity to develop ideas and skills, exchange experience and make new contacts at local, national and European level. Members include public, academic and government libraries, information units of professional, voluntary and pressure groups, European Documentation Centres, Euro Info Centres, local authorities, publishers, companies and law firms.

The EIA's website, set up and maintained by Eric Davies at the University of Hull, is an excellent alternative way of tapping into official EU information on the Web. In fact many users may find its text only interface a considerably simpler, and certainly faster, way of directly accessing information on the official websites mentioned above as opposed to using the Europa homepage's somewhat obtuse layout. It has clearly evident links to all the institutional websites mentioned above and an excellent 'recent additions' section.

Eurotext: http://eurotext.ulst.ac.uk/index.html

Another site well worth visiting is the Eurotext site at the University of Ulster. Eurotext is a joint project between the Universities of Ulster and Hull, designed to provide a resource bank of learning materials on Europe, through the provision of full-text EU documents on the Web. As such it is primarily aimed at students, although others looking for information on tourism in particular may find it useful. As yet there appear to be no documents on Eurotext which relate to sport or the leisure industry, but the coverage of tourism, whilst still developing, is already excellent.

Commercially published CD-ROM databases

Two UK companies have established themselves as market leaders in the commercial provision of official EU information via CD-ROM. The companies concerned are ILI and Context. Their addresses and website URLs are included in the appendices at the end of this chapter. The author is much more familiar with the ILI products, but in practice both companies' products offer flexible searching of databases mentioned earlier in the chapter. Commercial researchers may wish to consider taking out subscriptions to one or more of the CD-ROMs. Individuals are more likely to want to consult them in relation to specific questions, and are more likely to want to visit an institution which has a subscription to the relevant CD-ROM and makes the product available to visitors. It is likely that many UK European Documentation Centres, or their equivalents in other parts of the world, will allow access to one or more of the CD-ROM products mentioned below, but it is always worth telephoning first to make sure of availability and access.

Eurolaw (ILI) and CELEX (Context)

These are CD-ROM equivalents of the primarily full-text CELEX database of EU legislation and case law. Benefits of the CD-ROM versions include easier and more flexible search options, superior links between related documents, and the additional availability of related information from the UK Government's Department of Trade and Industry. The CD-ROMs can be updated on either quarterly or monthly subscriptions, so those looking for really up-to-date information will have to make use of the Web version of CELEX.

EU Infodisk (ILI) and European References (Context)

These are CD-ROM equivalents of the EU bibliographic database SCAD, available via the Web. Again the CD-ROM versions offer more flexible search options amongst other benefits. The Web version of SCAD has a limit on the number of users able to search it concurrently and can therefore sometimes be difficult to access. The CD-ROM versions also have added English keyword descriptors for all documents, whereas currently the Web version only offers French, with English to be added in the near future. The CD-ROMs are updated quarterly, so again those looking for very recent references will find the Web version more useful.

Official Journal C series (Context only)

This highly useful CD-ROM contains the full text of all documents published in the C series of the *Official Journal of the European Communities* from January 1990 onwards. The main benefit here is that it contains the full text of all legislative proposals and subsequent amendments (legislative COM docs), to which other databases only give references as opposed to full text. One word of warning here is that this CD-ROM is likely to be held by a far smaller number of European Documentation Centres than the four mentioned above.

Places to visit or contact when looking for official EU information

The European Commission has set up a series of information relays throughout the European Union member states to provide access to official documentation and specialist information staff help for a variety of different user groups. In addition a more limited network of information centres has been established in non-member states. Consequently researchers in the UK and Ireland are more likely to find a genuinely local centre which they can actually visit, as opposed to those in other parts of the English-speaking world who, particularly outside major urban centres, may be more reliant on the telephone enquiry services offered at the resource centres which provide access to official EU documentation.

European Documentation Centres (EDCs)

The network of EDCs is genuinely worldwide although, as mentioned above, the concentration of centres is greater in the EU member states. Also in some countries outside the EU, centres which are equivalent to EDCs may go by slightly different names, such as EU Depository Libraries in the USA.

European Documentation Centres receive free of charge the vast majority of the EU's official publications. Certainly all EDCs should have copies of all the publications mentioned earlier in this chapter. The main area in which EDCs do not receive all publications by right is that of statistical publications, where in recent years the number of publications distributed freely has been reduced. Also it is important to remember that many publications at Commission Directorate General level will not necessarily be made available to EDCs. In addition to receiving the printed publications free of charge, EDCs also have free access to the otherwise charged-for Web version of the CELEX database, and should be able to carry out searches on the database for personal visitors and telephone enquirers.

Many will also provide access to the CD-ROM databases mentioned in the immediately preceding section, although it is important to highlight that in most cases if you wish to make use of the CD-ROMs it will be worth telephoning your appropriate EDC first to ensure that you are able to access them and that a qualified member of staff will be present at the time of your visit to help you use them.

All EDCs are staffed by at least one information professional with responsibility for the management of the official EU collection. This person will also be available to help visitors with specific enquiries, although if you are undertaking genuine research rather than just looking for a specific document to read or photocopy it will again be worth telephoning in advance to make an appointment with the EDC librarian.

Virtually all EDCs are housed within university libraries and are primarily aimed at the academic community, both staff and students. However, they are also available to visitors from private companies, local authorities, non-governmental organizations and the general public. In the UK some EDCs do not allow access to students of school age, or those from further education colleges or those studying for GNVQs. The information held at EDCs tends to be very detailed and/or technical and is not really appropriate for the needs of these users, who should instead contact one of the European Resource Centres for Schools and Colleges mentioned below.

A full listing of all EDCs in the UK, Ireland, USA, Canada, Australia, New Zealand, South Africa and Hong Kong appears in the appendices to this chapter.

In addition to the network of EDCs there are also a small number of European Depository Libraries (DEPs) both in EU member states and other countries. These depositories tend to be located in major national libraries or large public libraries in major cities. Those in the UK are listed in the appendices.

European Information Centres (EICs) (EU member states only)

European Information Centres were set up about ten years ago specifically to cater for the needs of small and medium-sized business enterprises. The information on EICs provided by the European Commission's London Office website describes the functions of EICs as follows:

- to provide up-to-date information on the European Union to small and medium-sized enterprises (SMEs)
- to give EU-related advice on matters such as public contracts, taxation, company law and EU funding
- to provide access to EU databases, including Tender Electronic Daily
- to assist companies looking for business partners in the EU, through BC-Net.

European Information Centres should be the first port of call for those working in small and medium-sized business enterprises in the UK or Ireland, although EICs may well pass enquiries on to EDCs if their resources appear more suitable in relation to specific enquiries. A full list of UK and Irish EICs appears in the appendices at the end of this chapter.

Carrefours (EU Rural Information Centres) (EU member states only)

Some researchers either working in tourism or the leisure sector in rural areas, or interested in the impact of tourism or the leisure industry upon rural communities, may find it most appropriate to contact their local Carrefours. These centres have been set up to with three aims in mind:

- to provide information on Community policies and measures affecting rural society
- to promote awareness of rural development
- to encourage dialogue, partnership and co-operation between members of rural society and regions on common problems.

A full list of UK and Irish Carrefours appears in the appendices to this chapter.

European Resource Centres for Schools and Colleges (UK only)

These have recently been set up to act as a first port of call for schoolchildren, further education college students, GNVQ students, and their teachers. The resource centres have collections encompassing books, journals, directories and brochures. In addition they have access to the databases mentioned earlier in the chapter. They have a brief to provide information on European issues in a broad context and not just matters that relate specifically to the EU. Further information is available on the European Commission's London Office website (http://www.cec.org.uk/relays/relhome.htm). A list of the resource centres appears in the appendices.

Public Information Relays (EU member states only)

Recently the EU has set up a network of public information relays based in public libraries and aimed at providing basic EU information to the general public. The relays have a basic stock of reference materials and also some brochure-type literature available for people to take away. The relays have not been set up to deal with detailed or technical EU enquiries and it is unlikely that they will have much material to help the serious researcher. However, they may have certain publications which can act as a starting point for research on tourism or sport in the EU. The sheer number of relays makes listing them in the appendices impossible, but regionalized lists of the UK relays can be found on the European Commission's London Office website (http://www.cec. org.uk/relays/relhome.htm).

All information in this chapter was current at 1 February 1998. Any specific queries can be sent to the author by e-mail at r.d.burns@qmw.ac.uk. Anyone who would like a copy of the website appendix e-mailed to them to enable 'copying and pasting' of addresses into a browser can e-mail the author at the same address.

Appendix 1: Useful website addresses (URLs)

General websites

Bulletin of the European Union, http://europa.eu.int/abc/doc/off/bull/en/ welcome.htm
CEDEFOP, European Centre for the Development of Vocational Training, http://www.cedefop.gr/

Committee of the Regions, http://www.europa.eu.int/comreg/comreg.html

Council of The European Union, http://ue.eu.int/angl/summ2.htm

DG X of the European Commission, http://europa.eu.int/en/comm/dg10/dg10.html

DG XXIII of the European Commission, http://europa.eu.int/en/comm/dg23/index.htm

Economic and Social Committee, http://europa.eu.int/ces/ces.html

EIRO – full text article database on industrial relations in Europe from the above agency, http://www.eiro.eurofound.ie/index.main.html

EUDOR – indexing database and document delivery service covering recent years of the *Official Journal of the European Communities* and COM docs, http://www.eudor.com:8444/EUDOR/PROC/orientation?LANGUAGE=english

EUROPA – European Union's web server, http://europa.eu.int/index-en.htm

European Commission green papers, http://europa.eu.int/comm/off/green/index.htm

European Commission, http://europa.eu.int/en/comm.html

European Commission white papers, http://europa.eu.int/comm/off/white/index.htm

European Court of Justice, http://europa.eu.int/cj/en/index.htm

European Environment Agency, http://www.eea.dk/

European Foundation for the Improvement of Living and Working Conditions, http://www.europa.eu.int/agencies/efilwc/index.htm

European Information Association, http://www.hull.ac.uk/php/lbsebd/eia_html/

European Parliament, http://www.europarl.eu.int/sg/tree/en/default.htm

European University Institute, http://www.iue.it/

Eurostat – EU's statistical office, http://europa.eu.int/en/comm/eurostat/serven/home.htm

Eurotext – full text of EU legislative and policy documents, including several on tourism, http://eurotext.ulst.ac.uk/index.html

Hong Kong Office of the European Commission, http://www.ust.hk/~webeu/

IDEA – database of *Who's Who in the European Union*, http://158.169.50.70/idea/ideaen.html

Intergovernmental Conference retrospective database, http://europa.eu.int/en/agenda/igc-home/index.html

Ireland Office of the European Commission, http://www.cec.ie/

RAPID – full-text database of EU press releases, http://europa.eu.int/rapid/start/welcome.htm

SCAD database – indexes EU legislation, stages in the legislative process, other official EU non-legislative publications, articles from over 2000 periodicals on EU-related matters, and publications from European employers' and employ-

ees' organizations, http://europa.eu.int/comm/sg/scadplus/scad_en.htm
UK Office of the European Commission, http://www.cec.org.uk/
UK Presidency of the Council of the European Union, http://presid.fco.gov.uk/
US Office of the European Commission, http://www.eurunion.org/

Websites dealing specifically with tourism

Funding information for tourism-based projects, http://europa.eu.int/comm/sg/
aides/en/p3ch3.htm
Paper on the impact of tourism on the environment, http://europa.eu.int/en/
comm/dg11/env-act5/prog-rep/chapt1-5.htm 130
Paper presented to the IGC on incorporation of tourism into Amsterdam
Treaty, http://europa.eu.int/en/agenda/igc-home/instdoc/industry/ait-en.htm
Tourism information from DG XXIII of the Commission, http://europa.eu.int/
en/comm/dg23/tourisme/tourisme.htm

Websites dealing specifically with sport

European Parliament Committee Report on sport and the EU,
http://wwwdb.europarl.eu.int/dg7-bin/seid.pl
Funding information for sports-related projects, http://europa.eu.int/comm/sg/
aides/en/p3ch8.htm
Sport and the EU – information from DG X, http://europa.eu.int/en/comm/
dg10/sport/en/index.html

Appendix 2: European Documentation Centres in the UK

England

North West

University of Lancaster, Tel: 01524 65201/592539
University of Manchester, Tel: 0161 275 3770
University of Salford, Tel: 0161 745 5846

North East

University of Durham, Tel: 0191 374 3041/3044
University of Northumbria, Tel: 0191 227 4136

Yorkshire and Humberside

Leeds Metropolitan University, Tel: 0113 283 3126
Sheffield Hallam University, Tel: 0114 253 2126
University of Bradford, Tel: 01274 383 402
University of Hull, Tel: 01482 465 941
University of Leeds, Tel: 0113 233 5040

West Midlands

Coventry University, Tel: 01203 838 295
Keele University, Tel: 01782 583 238
University of Birmingham, Tel: 0121 414 7574/6570
University of Central England, Tel: 0121 331 5298
University of Warwick, Tel: 01203 523 523, ext 2041
University of Wolverhampton, Tel: 01902 322 300

East Midlands

Loughborough University, Tel: 01509 222 351/343
University of Leicester, Tel: 0116 252 2044
University of Nottingham, Tel: 0115 951 4579

Greater London

British Library of Political and Economic Science, LSE,
Tel: 0171 955 7273/7229
Queen Mary and Westfield College, Tel: 0171 775 3321
University of North London, Tel: 0171 753 5142

East Anglia

University of Cambridge, Tel: 01223 333 138
University of East Anglia (Norwich), Tel: 01603 592 431
University of Essex (Colchester), Tel: 01206 873 181

South West

University of Bath, Tel: 01225 826 826 x 5594
University of Bristol, Tel: 0117 928 7944
University of Exeter, Tel: 01392 262 072

South East

University of Kent (Canterbury), Tel: 01227 764 000, ext 3111
University of Oxford, Tel: 01865 271 463
University of Portsmouth, Tel: 01705 843 239
University of Reading, Tel: 0118 931 8782
University of Southampton, Tel: 01703 593 451
University of Surrey (Guildford), Tel: 01483 259 233
University of Sussex (Brighton), Tel: 01273 678 159
Wye College (Ashford), Tel: 01233 812 401, ext 512

Scotland

University of Aberdeen, Tel: 01224 273 819
University of Dundee, Tel: 01382 344 102
University of Edinburgh, Tel: 0131 650 2041
University of Glasgow, Tel: 0141 330 6722

Wales

University of Wales (Aberystwyth), Tel: 01970 622 401
University of Wales (Cardiff), Tel: 01222 874 262

Northern Ireland

Queens University (Belfast), Tel: 01232 245 133, ext 3605
University of Ulster (Coleraine), Tel: 01265 324 029

Appendix 3: European Information Centres in the UK

England

North West

Euro Info Centre North West (Liverpool), Tel: 0151 298 1928
Manchester Business Link, Tel: 0161 237 4000

North East

Newcastle Euro Info Centre, Tel: 0191 261 0026/5131(direct)

Yorkshire and Humberside

Leeds Metropolitan University Library, Tel: 0113 283 3126
Sheffield Hallam University, Tel: 0114 253 2126
University of Hull, Tel: 01482 465 940
WYEBIC, Economic Initiatives Division (Bradford), Tel: 01274 754 262

West Midlands

Birmingham European Business Centre, Tel: 0121 455 0268
Shropshire and Staffordshire Business Link (Telford), Tel: 01952 208 213
Staffordshire European Business Centre (Stoke), Tel: 01782 202 222

East Midlands

Leicester Euro Info Centre, Tel: 0116 255 9944
Notts Chamber of Commerce and Industry (Nottingham), Tel: 0115 962 4324

Greater London

Euro Info Centre, London Chamber of Commerce, Tel: 0171 489 1992
Euro Info Centre – Westminster (Regent Street), Tel: 0171 734 6406

East Anglia

Euro Info Centre East Anglia (Norwich), Tel: 01603 625 977

South East

Euro Info Centre Sussex (Burgess Hill), Tel: 01444 259 259
Kent Euro Info Centre (Maidstone), Tel: 01444 259 259
Southern Area Euro Info Centre (Southampton), Tel: 01703 832 866
Thames Valley Euro Info Center (Slough), Tel: 01753 577 877

South West

Bristol Chamber of Commerce and Industry, Tel: 0117 973 7373
Euro Info Centre South West (Exeter), Tel: 01392 214 085

Scotland

Glasgow Euro Info Centre, Tel: 0141 221 0999
Inverness Euro Info Centre, Tel: 01463 702 560

Wales

Cardiff Euro Info Centre, Tel: 01222 229 525
Mold Wales Euro Info Centre, Tel: 01352 704 748

Northern Ireland

Belfast Euro Info Centre, Tel: 01232 491 031

Appendix 4: European Depository Libraries in the UK

Business and Information Library
William Brown Street
LIVERPOOL L3 8EW
Tel: 0151 225 5434
Fax: 0151 207 1342

City of Westminster Central Reference Library
35 St Martin's Street
Westminster,
LONDON WC2 7HP
Tel: 0171 798 2034
Fax: 0171 798 2040

Appendix 5: Carrefours (EU Rural Information Centres) UK

England

Cirencester, Gloucestershire, Tel: 01285 653 477
Garstang, Lancashire, Tel: 01995 601 207

Scotland

Highlands and Islands Rural Carrefour, Inverness, Tel: 01463 715 400

Wales

Canolfan Ewropeaidd – Carrefour, Ynys Mon, Llangefni (Anglesey), Tel: 01248 752 491
West Wales European Centre, Carmarthen, Tel: 01267 233 3333

Northern Ireland

Carrefour Ulster, Clogher, Co. Tyrone, Tel: 016625 49438

6: UK European Resource Centres for Schools and Colleges

England

North West

Liverpool, Tel: 0151 225 8110
Manchester, Tel: 0161 234 1992

North East

Jarrow, Tel: 0191 420 1711
Morpeth, Tel: 01670 533559
Stockton on Tees, Tel: 01642 335392

Yorkshire and Humberside

Hull, Tel: 01482 466 834
Leeds, Tel: 0113 214 4068

West Midlands

Birmingham, Tel: 0121 446 4203

East Midlands

Loughborough, Tel: 01509 416 950

Greater London

Central Bureau
10 Spring Gardens
LONDON SW1A 2BN
Tel: 0171 389 4697/4723

Centre for Information on Language Teaching and Research
20 Bedfordbury
LONDON WC2N 4LB
Tel: 0171 379 5110

East Anglia

Cambridge, Tel: 01223 424 022
Colchester, Tel: 01206 863 839

South West

Gloucester, Tel: 01452 427 204

South East

Chichester, Tel: 01243 777 578
Maidstone, Tel: 01622 605 704
St Albans, Tel: 01582 830 318

Wales

Bangor, Tel: 01248 383 874
Cardiff, Tel: 01222 265 104

Scotland and Northern Ireland

The EC Commission's London Office website does not list any Resource Centres for Scotland or Northern Ireland, so presumably they have yet to be set up.

Appendix 7: European Documentation Centres in Ireland

The Library, St Patrick's College Maynooth. Co Kildare, Tel: 01 6285222
The Library, Trinity College Dublin, Tel: 01 6772941
The Library, University College Cork, Tel: 021 276871
The Library, University College Dublin, Tel: 01 7067777
The Library, University College, Galway, Tel: 091 24411
The Library, University of Limerick, Tel: 061 333644

Appendix 8: European Information Centres in Ireland

Bord Trachtala, Dublin 4
European Information Centre, 67 South Mall, Cork
Galway Chamber of Commerce, Merchants Road, Galway, Tel: 091 62624
Shannon Development, Limerick
Sligo Chamber of Commerce, 16 Quay Street, Sligo, Tel: 071 61274
Waterford Chamber of Commerce

Appendix 9: Carrefours (EU Rural Information Centres) in Ireland

Cahirciveen, Co Kerry, Tel: 066 72724
Galway, Tel: 091 24411
Waterford, Tel: 058 54646

Appendix 10: European Documentation Centres in the USA

American University
Council on Foreign Relations (New York)
Duke University
Emory University
George Mason University
Harvard University
Illinois Institute of Technology
Indiana University
Library of Congress
Miami University of Ohio
Michigan State University
New York Public Library
New York University
Northwestern University
Ohio State University
Pennsylvania State University
Princeton University
Stanford University
State University of New York
Texas Christian University
University of Arizona
University of Arkansas
University of California
University of Chicago
University of Colorado
University of Florida
University of Georgia
University of Illinois
University of Iowa
University of Kansas
University of Kentucky
University of Maine

University of Michigan
University of Minnesota
University of Nebraska
University of New Mexico
University of New Orleans
University of Notre Dame
University of Oklahoma
University of Oregon
University of Pennsylvania
University of Pittsburgh
University of Puerto Rico
University of South Carolina
University of Southern California
University of Texas
University of Utah
University of Virginia
University of Washington
University of Wisconsin
Washington University
Yale University

Appendix 11: European Documentation Centres in Canada

Halifax – Dalhousie University
Kingston – Queen's University
Montreal – McGill University and Universite de Montreal
Ottawa – Carleton University
Toronto – University of Toronto
Winnipeg – University of Manitoba

Appendix 12: European Documentation Centres in Australia

Bundoora – La Trobe University
Canberra – National Library of Australia
Hobart – University of Tasmania
Melbourne – State Library of Victoria
Sydney – State Library of New South Wales and University of Sydney

Appendix 13: European Documentation Centres in New Zealand

Auckland – Auckland Public Library and University of Auckland
Christchurch – University of Canterbury
Wellington – Parliamentary Library

Appendix 14: European Documentation Centres in South Africa

Cape Town – South African Library
Johannesburg – City of Johannesburg Public Library

Appendix 15: European Documentation Centres in Hong Kong

Hong Kong Baptist University

Appendix 16: European Commission offices around the world

UK

London

European Commission Representation in the United Kingdom
Jean Monnet House
8 Storey's Gate
LONDON SW1 P3 AT
Tel: 0171 973 1992
Fax: 0171 973 1900/1910

Belfast

European Commission Representation in Northern Ireland
9/15 Bedford Street (Windsor House)
BELFAST BT2 7AG
Tel: 01232 240 708
Fax: 01232 248 241

Cardiff

European Commission Representation in Wales
4 Cathedral Road
CARDIFF CF1 9SG
Tel: 01222 371 631
Fax: 01222 395 489

Edinburgh

European Commission Representation in Scotland
9 Alva Street
EDINBURGH EH2 4PH
Tel: 0131 225 2058
Fax: 0131 226 4105

Ireland

Dublin

European Commission Representation in Ireland
Dawson Street 18
DUBLIN 2
Tel: 353 1 662 5113
Fax: 353 1 662 5118

USA

2300 M Street, 3rd floor, NW
DC 20037 Washington
Tel: 1-202 862 9500/1/2
Fax: 1-202 429 1766

Canada

111 Albert Street
Suite 330
K1P 1A5 Ottawa (Ontario)
Tel: 1 613 238 6464
Fax: 1 613 238 5191

Australia

18 Arkana Street, Yarralumla ACT
2600 Canberra
Tel: 61 6 271 2721/2777
Fax: 61 6 273 4445/4944
Postal address:
PO Box 609
2600 Canberra

New Zealand

No office.

South Africa

2 Green Park Estate
27 George Storrer Drive
Groenkloof 0181 Pretoria
Tel: 27 12 464 319
Fax: 27 12 469 923
Postal address:
PO Box 945
Groenkloof 0026 Pretoria

Hong Kong

Office of the European Commission in Hong Kong
19/F St John's Building
33 Garden Road, Central
Tel: 852 2537 6083
Fax: 852 2522-1302

Appendix 17: Commercial suppliers of CD-ROM databases

Context Limited
Grand Union House
20 Kentish Town Road
LONDON NW1 9NR
Tel: 0171 267 8989
Fax: 0171 267 1133

DX 121900 Kentish Town 3
E-mail: sales@context.co.uk
Website: http://www.justis.com/homepage.html

ILI
Index House
ASCOT
Berkshire SL5 7EU
Tel: 01344 636400
Fax: 01344 291194
E-mail: databases@ili.co.uk
http://www.ili.co.uk/
or
ILI
610 Winters Avenue
Paramus
NJ 07652
USA
Tel: 1 201 986 1131
Fax: 1 201 986 7886
E-mail: sales@ili-info.com

References

Bates, and Wacker, S. C. (eds) (1996) *Tourism and the European Union: A Practical Guide: EU Funding, Other Support, EU Policy and Tourism.* OOPEC.

Committee of the Regions (1995) *Opinion on a Policy for the Development of Rural Tourism in the Regions of the European Union.* (OJ C210, 14/08/1995, p.99), OOPEC.

Committee of the Regions. (1996) *Opinion on 'Interaction between Education of Young People and Sport: A Proposal for Union-level Actions to Promote Positive Effects of Sport in Europe'.* (OJ C337, 11/11/1996, p.60), OOPEC.

Cooper, C. P. and Messenger, S. (1991) *The Structure of Professional Profiles for Tourism in the United Kingdom.* OOPEC (CEDEFOP).

Council of the European Communities (1990) *Council Directive 90/314 of 13 June 1990 on Package Travel, Package Holidays and Package Tours.* (OJ L158, 23/06/1990, p.59), OOPEC.

Court of Auditors (1996) *Special Report No. 3/96 on Tourist Policy and the Promotion of Tourism, Together with the Commission's Replies.* (OJ C17, 16/01/1997, p.1), OOPEC.

Economic and Social Committee of the European Communities (1996) *Opinion on the First Multinational Programme to Assist Tourism (1997–2000) PHILOXENIA.* (CES 1094/96, reprinted in OJ C30, 30/01/1997, p.1), OOPEC.

European Commission (1995) *The Role of the Union in the Field of Tourism: Commission Green Paper.* COM(95)97, OOPEC.

European Commission (1996) *Amended Proposal for a Council Decision on a First Multinational Programme to Assist European Tourism 'PHILOXENIA' (1997–2000)*. COM(96)635, OOPEC.

European Commission (1996) *Historic Gardens: Safeguarding a European Heritage*. OOPEC.

European Commission (1996) *Proposal for a Council Decision on a First Multinational Programme to Assist European Tourism 'PHILOXENIA' (1997–2000)*. COM(96)168, OOPEC.

European Commission (1996) *Report on the Evaluation of the Community Action Plan to Assist Tourism 1993–95*. COM(96)166, OOPEC.

European Commission (1996) *The European Union and Sport*. OOPEC.

European Commission (1997) *Report from the Commission to the Council, the European Parliament, The Economic and Social Committee and the Committee of the Regions on Community Measures Affecting Tourism (1995/96)*. COM(97)332, OOPEC.

European Commission (1997) *Who's Who in the European Union? Interinstitutional Directory*. OOPEC.

European Commission, DG III (1997) *Panorama of EU Industry: An Extensive Review of the Situation and Outlook of the Manufacturing and Service Industries in the European Union*. (Annual volumes since 1989), OOPEC.

European Commission, DG X (1997) *Grants and Loans from the European Union: A Guide to Community Funding*. OOPEC.

European Commission, DG XXIII (1995) *Tourism in Europe*. OOPEC.

European Commission, DG XXIII Tourism Unit (1993) *All-Season Tourism: Analysis of Experience, Suitable Products and Clientele*. OOPEC.

European Commission DG XXIII, Tourism Unit (1993) *Impact of Completion of the Internal Market on the Tourism Sector*. OOPEC.

European Commission, DG XXIII Tourism Unit (1993) *Pour une Signaletique Europeenne Harmonisee dans le Domaine du Tourisme Rural et Analyse des Circuits d'Information de Distribution et de Vente*. OOPEC.

European Commission, DG XXIII Tourism Unit (1993) *Tourism Customers in Central and Eastern Europe: Perspectives of Development*. OOPEC.

European Commission, DG XXIII Tourism Unit (1993) *Tourism Resources in Eastern Europe: Problems and Prospects for Cooperation*. (Two volumes), OOPEC.

European Commission, DG XXIII Tourism Unit (1994) *Eurotourism: Culture and Countryside: 48 Projects Co-financed by the European Commission in 1992*. (Forty-eight project cards in ring binder), OOPEC.

European Commission, DG XXIII Tourism Unit (1994) *Le Tourisme Culturel en Europe*. OOPEC.

European Commission, DG XXIII Tourism Unit (1994) *Les Differentes Notions du Tourisme Social: L'evolution de L'offre et de la Demande*. OOPEC.

European Commission, DG XXIII Tourism Unit (1994) *Taking Account of Environment in Tourism Development*. OOPEC.

European Commission, DG XXIII Tourism Unit (1994) *The Evolution in Holiday Travel Facilities and in the Flow of Tourism Inside and Outside the European Community*. (Two volumes), OOPEC.

European Commission, DG XXIII Tourism Unit (1996) *Making Europe Accessible for Tourists with Disabilities: Handbook for the Tourism Industry*. OOPEC.

European Commission, DG XXIII Tourism Unit (1997) *Yield Management in Small and Medium-Sized Enterprises in the Tourist Industry*. (Two volumes), OOPEC.

European Court of Justice (1994) Case C-375/92, Commission of the European Communities v. Kingdom of Spain. (Reported in *European Court Reports*, 1994, Vol. 1, p. 923), OOPEC.

Eurostat (1987–) *Tourism: Annual Statistics*. (Published annually).

Eurostat (monthly) *Distributive Trade, Services and Transport: Short Term Statistics*. (ISSN 1019-0619).

Eurostat (published four times per year) *Statistics in Focus: Distributive Trades, Services and Transport*. (ISSN 1017-589X).

Ferreira Duarte, A. (1991) *Analyse de la structure des profils professionnels dans le secteur touristique au Portugal*. OOPEC.

Fissamber, W. (1991) *Analyse de la Structure des Profils Professionnels dans le Secteur Touristique en Grece*. OOPEC (CEDEFOP).

Geary, M. and Snell, C. (eds). (1994–) *European Communities Legislation: Current Status, 1952–*. (Two main volumes with additional supplements), Butterworths.

Guerra, D. and Peroni, G. (1994) *Occupations in the Tourist Sector: A Comparative Analysis in Nine Community States*. CEDEFOP.

Isaacs, S. (consultant ed.) (1994–) *Butterworths EC Case Citator and Service*. (Two issues per year, kept up to date by fortnightly looseleafs), Butterworths.

Lasok, D. (1994) *Law and Institutions of the European Union*. 6th edn, Butterworths.

Lohmann, M. (1991) *Analyse de la Structure des Profils Professionnels dans le Secteur Touristique en Republique Federale d'Allemagne*. OOPEC (CEDEFOP).

Muller-Warson, L. (1992) *Vocational Training in the Tourist Industry: A Documentary Study*. OOPEC (CEDEFOP).

Passat, J. (1991). *Analyse de la Structure des Profils Professionnels dans le Secteur Touristique en France*. OOPEC (CEDEFOP).

Seary, B. (1992) *Brussels in Focus: EC Access for Sport*. Sports Council.

Thomson, I. (1989) *The Documentation of the European Communities: A Guide*. Mansell.

European Court of Justice (1995) Case C-415/93, Union Royale Belge des Societes de Football Association ASBL and Others v. Jean-Marc Bosman and Others. (Reported in *European Court Reports*, 1995, Vol. 1, p. 4921), OOPEC.

8

Leisure and tourism organizations

C. Michael Hall

Organizations are an essential part of public life. However, despite the central-ity of organizations in the formulation of public and private policy, and their importance to economy and society, organizations have only been subject to significant analysis in the leisure and tourism fields over the past decade. Research on leisure and tourism organizations has tended to focus on public sector organizations at the national and regional level and their contribution to policy and development (Hall, 1994; Hall and Jenkins, 1995; Heeley, 1989; Pearce, 1992), with only minor attention being given to the private sector (Dunning and McQueen 1982a, 1982b; Heeley 1986). More recently, interor-ganizational relationships have been given greater scrutiny (Long, 1997; Selin and Beason, 1991), while the role of interest groups in influencing leisure and tourism policy is also a growing area of interest (Craik, 1991; Hall and Jenkins, 1995).

This chapter aims to provide an overview of the complexity of studying leisure and tourism organizations, their roles as information sources, their inter-relationships with each other and their overall leisure and tourism functions. The chapter is divided into several sections. The first section provides an overview of organizations in tourism and leisure and explains the difficulties inherent in conducting research in this area. A framework is provided to help give an overview of the field and also to provide a basis for the following sections. Those sections then discuss information sources available at various levels of analysis for different sectors; at each level examples are provided of the type of information that may be available and how this might be utilized. The conclusion notes the importance of research on leisure and tourism organizations and highlights that the significance of the research cannot be seen in isolation but must be related to both the availability of information and the methods and approach of the student of leisure and tourism organizations.

Leisure and tourism organizations

There are almost as many different definitions of 'organization' as there are definitions of 'leisure and tourism'! However, for the purposes of this chapter, the term 'organization' is defined as a collective entity which has been established in order to achieve a goal (or set of goals) or purpose. Organizations can be categorized in several ways, for example we describe them in terms such as private or public, voluntary or non-voluntary, profit or non-profit driven. They may also be conceived as 'machines', 'organisms', 'cultures', 'political systems', 'instruments of domination' or other metaphors, such as a 'prison' (Morgan, 1986). We are all involved in organizations, whether it be in work (e.g., our company employer) or leisure (e.g., a sports club). Suffice it to say that organizations occupy all aspects of life outside the private internal realm of the individual, and they substantially affect it, e.g., think of the way in which people talk of 'fitting into an organizational culture'. Given the almost all-encompassing field of organizations, how can we fit them neatly into categories of leisure and tourism?

The answer is we cannot. But we can at least come up with some suggestions as to how tourism and leisure organizations may be conceptualized and, therefore, understood. Probably the central issue in trying to define the field of leisure and tourism organizations is whether we are discussing organizations which have been established specifically to further leisure- and tourism-related goals or whether we also include organizations which are affected by leisure and tourism activities, issues and policies, and which therefore seek to influence leisure and tourism. The former approach may be conceptually neat but it is extremely narrow and fails to convey the richness of the leisure and tourism field. For example, such an approach would exclude many environmental organizations which are clearly a component of the leisure and tourism field and which, therefore, function as information sources for this very important subfield of tourism and leisure, especially in the provision of information from environmental interest groups. Furthermore, the former approach might also exclude organizations which have leisure and tourism as only a minor concern in terms of their overall direction but which, for leisure and tourism interests, is a major concern. For example, the World Trade Organization, Association of South East Asian Nations (ASEAN) or even a corporation like Coca-Cola which influences sport and leisure through its sponsorship relationships, are all a part of the leisure and tourism system and of the provision of information within that system. Therefore, in an effort to provide a more complete picture of leisure and tourism information sources, this chapter will take a broad perspective of leisure and tourism organizations.

This broad approach is an organizational studies equivalent to Leiper's (1989, 1990) concept of partial industrialization. According to Leiper (1989: 25) partial industrialization refers to the condition in which only certain organizations providing goods and services directly to tourists are in the tourism industry. The proportion of (a) goods and services stemming from that industry to (b) total goods and services used by tourists can be termed the index of industrialization, theoretically ranging from 100 per cent (wholly industrialized) to zero (tourists present and spending money, but no tourism industry).

This situation offers one explanation for the difficulties in gaining co-ordination within the tourism and leisure industry, because different organizations have different degrees of tourism industrialization and therefore different goals with respect to the industry overall. For example, although we can recognize that many segments of the economy benefit from tourism, it is only those organizations with a direct relationship to tourists that become actively involved in fostering tourism development or in marketing. Nevertheless, there are many other organizations, such as food suppliers, petrol stations, and retailers, sometimes described as 'allied industries', which also benefit from tourists but are not readily identified as part of the tourism industry (Hall, 1995).

Leiper's perspective is far more encompassing of organizations than a narrow supply-side approach used by Smith (1988, 1991, 1993) which paid particular attention to the commodities which tourism produces. From a supply-side perspective, the tourism industry may be defined as 'the aggregate of all businesses that directly provide goods or services to facilitate business, pleasure, and leisure activities away from the home environment' (Smith, 1988: 183). However, a supply-side approach still means you have to draw an arbitrary line as to what constitutes direct provision. Some organizations will be included, but many would be left out. Such discussions are not just academic arguments, because the complexity of defining what we mean by leisure and tourism organizations can make it extremely difficult for researchers to not only track down individual organizations and their responsibilities, but also the interrelationships that exist between them.

Table 8.1 Number of international organizations listed by the Union of International Associations 1909–95

Year	Number
1909	213
1956	1 117
1960	1 422
1968	3 547
1977	6 474
1981	14 273
1984	22 456
1986	25 124
1988	28 942
1990	26 656
1991	28 200
1992	32 068
1993	34 004
1994	36 486
1995	41 722

Source: Adapted from Union of International Associations

Another complicating factor in studying leisure and tourism related organizations is their sheer growth in recent years. Table 8.1 illustrates the overall growth in international organizations (government and non-government) listed by the Union of International Associations 1909–95. Since the Second World War there has also been a tremendous expansion in the number and scope of interest groups (also described as pressure groups) (Cigler, 1991; Cigler and Loomis, 1986). Up until the 1960s, interest groups were primarily business association based. However, since the early 1960s, there has been rapid growth in Western nations of the number of citizen and public interest groups, particularly in the area of consumer and environmental concerns (Schlozman and Tierney, 1986).

Leisure and tourism has not been immune from the growth in interest groups. Until the mid-1960s, tourism-related interest groups were generally confined to industry and professional associations. However, the growth of consumer and environmental organizations extended the number of groups who had an interest in tourism issues, particularly as it related to aspects of tourism develop-

Table 8.2 Leisure and tourism organizations

Government and intragovernmental organizations	Producer organizations	Non-producer organizations	Single interest organizations
International World Tourism Organization; World Heritage Committee (UNESCO); Committee for the Development of Sport; OECD (Organization for Economic Co-operation and Development)	World Travel and Tourism Council; International Air Transport Association; Tourism Sport International Council; International Olympic Committee	Tourism Concern; World Wildlife Fund; World Leisure and Recreation Association; Greenpeace Friends of the Earth	World Congress Against the Commercial Sexual Exploitation of Children
Supranational APEC tourism working group; Tourism Council of the South Pacific; ASEAN Promotion Centre on Trade and Investment; European Commission	Pacific Asia Travel Association (PATA); Baltic Sea Tourism Commission; Play Fair Europe; European Surfing Federation; National Olympic Committees	Sierra Club; International Downtown Association; Travel and Tourism Research Association	End Child Prostitution in Asian Tourism (ECPAT)
National Indonesian Directorate General of Tourism; English Sports Council; Countryside Commission; Australian Tourist Commission; Irish Tourist Board	British Sports and Allied Industries Federation; Tourism Council Australia; Institute of Leisure and Amenity Management (ILAM)	National Trust; Australian Conservation Foundation; Australian Consumers Association	The Wilderness Society; Hispanic Association for Corporate Responsibility; ECPAT (Australia)
Regional (including provincial and state) Tourism Alberta; Natal Parks Board; Western Australian Tourism Commission (WATC); Scottish Tourist Board; Tourism British Columbia	Tourism Council Australia (WA Division); Scottish Confederation of Tourism; Shannon Development; Coalition of Minnesota Business	Western Australian Conservation Council	Tasmanian Wilderness Society
Local Local government involvement in leisure and tourism provision, e.g. Tourism Dunedin; Calgary Economic and Development Authority; Tourism Vancouver	Local chambers of commerce and industry associations; local sporting clubs and private sport and leisure centres	Ratepayers and resident associations, e.g. Waikiki Improvement Association	Single issue organizations such as 'friends of a park' or a group which has been formed in order to prevent particular developments such as a hotel or airport

ment at the local level. In the 1980s and the early 1990s, the range of groups was extended still further as social issues, such as sex tourism, and international trade became significant. Therefore, it is important to realize that tourism interest groups go well beyond those that are part of the tourism industry and include a vast array of community, public and special interest groups (Hall and Jenkins, 1995).

Table 8.2 represents a framework by which leisure and tourism organizations may be categorized. On one axis leisure and tourism organizations can be classified according to the scale in which they operate. Five levels are identified local, regional (including state and provincial organizations), national, supranational and international. The supranational category has become increasingly important given the emergence of regional economic associations, such as the European Union or the Association for South East Asian Nations, which may have substantial impacts on leisure and tourism policy and development. The other axis classifies leisure and tourism organizations along a continuum, according to their degree of institutionalization, as government and intragovernmental organizations, producer organizations/groups, non-producer organizations/groups and single interest organizations/groups (after Hall and Jenkins, 1995; Matthews, 1976).

Government, as the dominant actor in the set of institutional arrangements which surround leisure and tourism, produces organizations which tend to have a high level of continuity in terms of their activities, goals and policies. Producer groups, such as business and professional organizations and labour organizations, tend to have a high level of resources, a stable membership maintained by the ability of the group to provide benefits to members, and substantial ability to gain access to government. In non-producer groups, institutionalization has occurred on the basis of a common interest of continuing relevance to members, e.g., organizations such as consumer and environmental groups. Single-interest groups are at the other end of the continuum from producer groups and are characterized by their limited degree of organizational permanence, as they will likely disappear altogether once their goals have been achieved or have been rendered unattainable (Hall and Jenkins, 1995). Clearly the nature of an organization will influence the information it provides. Indeed, the activist function of interest groups in terms of trying to influence government policy and the development of leisure and tourism will often mean that these organizations will be information rich for students of tourism and leisure issues.

Nevertheless, it is important to note that organizations are not static and that they may progress through various categories. For example, local and regional conservation organizations may become nationally or even internationally based (e.g., the Sierra Club of United States and Canada started from a small California-based organization). Similarly, changes in perceptions of the role of government in leisure and tourism may also lead to organizational change. For example, the Australian National Travel Association (an industry body which promoted Australia overseas in the 1950s and 1960s) was the forerunner to the Australian Tourist Commission, a government funded organization responsible to the federal minister for tourism, which promotes Australia overseas, and Tourism Council Australia which is the peak industry body (Hall, 1995). A further point to note is that increasingly the boundaries between government and producer organizations are becoming blurred as public–private partnerships, such as regional development corporations, are formed.

Now that a framework for understanding leisure and tourism organizations has been developed, it is appropriate to turn to the various information sources that are available. Obviously, much will depend on what level is being searched and the actual purpose of search. Although it is difficult to generalize on the availability of information we can note that activity-based information (e.g. holiday-taking, conference and business travel, places to go and see, things to do) is widely available from leisure and tourism producer organizations. Government and quasi-government organizations, e.g. national and regional tourist organizations or sports councils, will also generally have such information, some will also detail their policies and development plans. However, if students want information about development issues, especially social and environmental impact, then they will often have to refer to interest groups for such information. Tourism and leisure is often categorized as a 'good news' industry (Hall, 1995). Therefore, if students want the negative side of development they will have to start looking outside of the formal industry sectors.

Increasingly, leisure and tourism organizations will have websites. Indeed, in the author's search for relevant information sources on and by leisure and tourism organizations it was noted that CD-ROM, on-line searches and the availability of Internet and website access had led to many paper-based directories no longer being purchased by university and public libraries. However, printed broad-scale organizational directories are still extremely useful (e.g., Daniels and Schwartz, 1997; Maconie, 1992; Millard, 1988). Nevertheless, unless you know exactly which organization or issue you are looking for, the most useful starting point for a search will be at the international, supranational and national level, as organizations at this level will often have membership deriving from the level(s) underneath them. In addition, it cannot be emphasized enough that, in many cases, you will need to 'browse' around your subject because of the very diffuse structure of the leisure and tourism system. Therefore, much of the chapter will focus on these macrolevel organizations because of the key role they play as information sources for what is occurring at all levels of leisure and tourism. The next section will examine some of the key international and supranational leisure and tourism organizations information sources.

International and supranational organizations

When searching for information regarding leisure and tourism organizations at the international and supranational level, readers are blessed with some readily available and user-friendly information sources. The section will commence with a discussion of one of the major sources on international organizations, the Union of International Associations, and it will then examine a number of indexes and organizations including the Global Index of Chambers of Commerce and Industry, the General Association of International Sporting Federations, the World Travel and Tourism Council and the World Tourism Organization.

Union of International Associations

One of the key global sources to government and non-government tourism and tourism-related organizations are the publications of the Union of International Associations (UIA). The UIA was founded in June 1907, in Brussels, Belgium, as the Central Office of International Associations, by Henri La Fontaine and Paul Otlet, Secretary-General of the then International Institute of Bibliography, now the International Federation for Documentation (FID). The UIA became a federation under the present name in 1910 at the 1st World Congress of International Associations. The UIA is an independent, non-governmental, non-profit body which is apolitical in character and is almost completely self-financed. The balance in funding is made up from donations and sponsorships from several governments (most notably Belgium, France and Switzerland) and a number of official and private bodies. Registered under Belgian law as an international association with scientific aims its primary aim is to facilitate the evolution of the activities of the worldwide network of non-profit organizations, especially non-governmental or voluntary associations.

One of the most significant aspects of the quality and comprehensiveness of the way the UIA works is the extent of its external relations with other international bodies. The UIA has close relations with United Nations bodies, such as UNESCO and the International Labour Office (ILO), and with other organi-

Table 8.3 Union of International Associations International organizations and non-governmental organizations website overview (http://www.uia.org/homeorg.htm uia)

Descriptive information

Profiles of international organizations (over 44 000 bodies, 104 000 links)
Intergovernmental organizations and networks (5900)
International associations – NGOs (38 000)
Universal membership organizations (529)
Intercontinental organizations (1050)
Regional (subcontinental) organizations and networks (4100)
Informal, transnational associations and networks
Transnational religious orders (850)
International funds, foundations and banks
Semi-autonomous international bodies (2700)
Internationally oriented national organizations (4500)

Alphabetical checklist (15 000 organizations and NGOs)
Demonstration (141 hyperlinked organizations and NGOs)

Websites of other international organizations and NGOs
Links to over 1000 international organizations (alphabetical order/subject order)
Links to over 70 sites related to international organization and organizations (resources, information etc.)

Statistics on international organizations (and NGOs)

By type, By year
By country of secretariat, By country of membership
Conferences of international organizations
Organization strategies and world problems

Publications (and CD-Roms) describing international organizations

Yearbook of International Organizations (4 volumes each year); (CD-Rom)
Whos Who in International Organizations
Directory of International Organization Abbreviations and Logotypes
World Guide to Religious and Spiritual Organizations
International Association Statutes Series
Transnational Associations/AssociationsTransnationales (6 a year)

Bibliographical information on international organizations

Publications and periodicals of international organizations
Publications on concerns of international organizations
Bibliography of research on transnational organizations

UIA studies of international organization and NGOs
Selected reports (downloadable documents)
Documents for the study of international NGO relations
Research papers

Frequently asked questions (FAQs)

Relating to international organizations
Relating to international NGOs

Feedback

Report new international organizations and networks
Indicate corrections to descriptive information (changes of address, etc.)
Indicate new website and e-mail addresses

zations such as the Council of Europe, and the Commonwealth Science Council. The *Yearbook of International Organizations* is prepared co-operatively by the United Nations and the UIA. The UIA maintains contact with over 25 000 international non-governmental organizations (NGOs) eligible for inclusion in the *Yearbook of International Organizations*, while the website overview proclaims that it is the 'Clearing house for information on over 40,000 international non-profit organizations and constituencies' (Union of International Associations, 1997, http://www.UIA.org/homeorg.htm uia). Table 8.3 provides an overview of the website. The UIA also has close links with the Federation of International Associations established in Belgium (FAIB), the Union of International Nongovernmental Organizations established in France (UOIF), Federation of Semi-Official and Private International Institutions established in Geneva (FIIG) and the Conferences of NGOs in consultative status with the Economic and Social Council of the United Nations (ECOSOC) and UNESCO. However, the comprehensiveness of the UIA's publications and sites means that their material can be used as a 'first-stop' secondary data source.

The main working languages of the UIA are English and French. Most publications are produced in English, with French versions where there is sufficient demand. The *Yearbook of International Organizations* is indexed in all languages used by international organizations. The periodical *Transnational Association* contains articles in both English and French. As well as being available in hard copy (printed) form and on CD-ROM much of the work of the UIA is available on their website.

Yearbook of International Organizations

One of the most important information sources produced by the UIA of interest to researchers on tourism and leisure organizations is the *Yearbook of International Organizations* which is the most comprehensive and authoritative account of organizations in the world today. The 1997 publication in four volumes was the 34th edition of the *Yearbook*. The four volumes are:

- Volume 1: *Organization Descriptions and Cross-references*
- Volume 2: *International Organization Participation (Country Directory of Membership)*
- Volume 3: *Global Action Networks (Subject Guide and Index)*
- Volume 4: *International Organizations Bibliography and Resources.*

The four volumes of the *Yearbook* are each published annually and are also available on CD-Rom. Each can be used as an independent working tool, or as a complement to the other volumes. Government and non-government organizations are distinguished within the *Yearbook*, although they are not grouped into separate sections of the volumes. Organizations appear in order of their English title (or other major language if they have no English title). Included in the alphabetical sequence are the other language titles and the abbreviations by which the organizations are known, cross-referenced to the full descriptions. Descriptions vary in length from several lines to several pages. The descriptions, based almost entirely on data supplied by the organizations themselves, include:

- organization names in all relevant languages
- principal and secondary addresses including e-mail and World Wide Web
- executive officer or other contacts
- main activities and programmes
- events and conferences
- personnel and finances
- technical and regional commissions
- history, goals, structure
- interorganizational links
- languages used
- membership by country.

Volume 2 provides a country directory of secretariats and membership with addresses provided. Volume 3 is one of the most valuable if the researcher is unsure of the exact organization he or she is seeking information on. International organizations are listed by subject with travel and tourism organizations being classified under 'Transportation and telecommunications' and sport, leisure, recreation and some environmental organizations classified under the heading of 'Recreation'. Subjects are grouped into both general and detailed categories. The classification scheme highlights functional relationships between various categories. Classified by region, international organizations are also listed by subject according to the region with which they are particularly concerned. The index includes:

- keywords from organization names
- former names in various languages
- alternative names/initials in various languages
- organization subject categories in English, French, German, Russian and Spanish
- the names of principal executive officers
- the names of the organization's founders.

Volume 4 is a useful information source if the researcher is seeking information on organizational outputs. It is divided into three main sections and has a full index to enable cross-referencing between the various sections. Part I contains the bibliographical information also contained in Volume 1 of the *Yearbook*, including periodical and other publications of international organizations. Part II provides bibliographical information under the headings of 'World problems', 'Action strategies' and 'Human values', and is of most value if the researcher is interested in NGOs and the activities of the United Nations family of organizations. Part III is a collection of bibliographic materials (just over 9000 citations) relevant to the study of international NGOs and refers to recent studies, documents and information on a variety of international associations.

Other UIA publications

As well as the *Yearbook*, the UIA produces several other publications which are of value in leisure and tourism organizational research. Established in 1948 *Transnational Associations* is an interdisciplinary bilingual journal (articles in English or French) which focuses on the actions, achievements and interests of the international NGOs profiled in the *Yearbook of International Organizations*. Topics covered in the journal include social organization, humanitarian law, scientific co-operation, language and culture, and economic development. The journal also has regular update sections which profile new listings of the UIA. In a similar format to the *Yearbook* the UIA publishes a *World Guide to Religious and Spiritual Organizations* (1996) which lists almost 3500 associations, orders, fraternities, institutes, networks and programmes. Given the impact of religious organizations on leisure activities and, in some cases, travel and tourism, e.g. the Muslim pilgrimage to Mecca, the *World Guide* is a potentially extremely useful information source for the study of the interrelationships between religion, leisure and travel. Finally, the UIA also produces a *Who's Who in International Organizations* (1995) which is a biographical reference work to 13 000 individuals associated with over 7000 international organizations ranging from international non-government and non-profit bodies, international committees, centres and institutes, to national non-profit groups concerned with international issues. The volume is useful for the researcher because as well as providing information on heads of the larger international organizations it also profiles divisional heads, senior staff of medium-sized organizations, and heads of smaller NGOs. Indexes provide ease of access to the entries and are filed by nationality, main field of work and international organization.

One cannot leave discussion of the UIA without also noting the potential information source which their website provides. The UIA provides an integrative matrix which reflects the contents of Volume 3 of the *Yearbook of International Organizations*. Two addresses will be of most interest to readers, the website listings on the subject of transportation and telecommunications (http://www.UIA.org/webints/websw25.htm) and the recreation listings (http://www.UIA.org/webints/websw34.htm). Both of these sites represent excellent opportunities to obtain substantial amounts of information with relatively little effort from a database that is very comprehensive.

Other general international and supranational listings

Although the UIA provides a comprehensive listing of United Nations system of organizations, students of tourism and leisure might also wish to consider referring to the UN official website locator (http://www.unsystem.org/index.html) which provides an alphabetical index of UN organizations, the official classification system for such organizations, a frequently requested information section and other relevant links including cross-agency and thematic links. It is worth noting that many of the United Nations organization's websites are amongst the most information rich in the environment, culture and heritage area. Several other valuable organizational listings are also available on the Web. The 'Philanthropy Journal Online' provides a wide range of information about non-profit organizations throughout the world, but especially in the USA, with a major research tool being the 'Meta-Index for Nonprofit Organizations' (http://www.philanthropy-journal.org/plhome/plmeta.htm). The Index refers to other links, organizations and information sources and also has specific reference points for human rights, civil liberties and politics, health and environmental issues. Two other useful organizational directories in the environmental area are the 'Environmental Organization Web Directory' (http://www.webdirectory.com/) and the Envirolink Library entries on environmental organizations (http://www.iccwbo.org).

One of the most important sources of information on business organizations is the International Chamber of Commerce (ICC) which is an international association of Chambers of Commerce and Industry. As with many business organizations the activities of the ICC are increasingly becoming electronically based. Indeed, the ICC is specifically trying to encourage electronic commerce and is developing special projects, such as the 'Electronic Silk Road' and an electronic World Network of Chambers of Commerce, which are receiving considerable support from private corporations and from government authorities. The ICC site provides numerous pages which detail the operations of the organization, national committees and affiliates, and global business (http://www.iccwbo.org/). Perhaps of most interest to students of leisure and tourism is the 'Global Index of Chambers of Commerce and Industry' operated by the Consortium for Global Commerce which provides not only listings and links to various Chambers but also links to several business networking projects which include leisure and tourism activities (http://www.worldchambers.com/chambers.html). Those students searching for information about Chambers of Commerce and regional business development organizations should also consider directly contacting their own local chamber as they will usually be extremely helpful in providing linkages with other national and international chambers

Yahoo, a tool for searching for information on the Web, offers numerous points of information on organizations with the most valuable being an organizations category in its business and economy listing (http://www.yahoo.com/yahoo/economy/organizations). The category contains many sites of public and private sector organizations which are involved in tourism and leisure development from the international to the local scale. Several subcategories are also provided including economic development, professional, small business and trade associations. A search by the author through these pages revealed a wealth of references to tourism- and leisure-related organizations. Although not containing a separate tourism category (it does contain an entertainment and leisure section) Internet Public Library Associations on the Internet has a collection of over 700 Internet sites providing information on a wide range of associations and organizations (http://www.ipl.org/ref/AON/).

Tourism

The World Tourism Organization (WTO) based in Madrid, Spain, produces a wealth of tourism-related information. However, although the statistical and other research publications of the WTO are useful for the tourism student the greatest amount of organizational information, such as details of other tourism organizations around the world including countries which are not members of the WTO, are to be found on their website (http://www.world-tourism.org). The WTO website contains information on the statistics service (although for access to the actual statistics database payment is required), publications, newsletter and press releases, much of which is downloadable for free. Of particular value for those interested in national and supranational tourism organizations is the 'Information from Official Tourism Organizations' page (http://www.world-tourism.org/tourworl.htm) which details information received from official tourism organizations from around the world, each of which is converted into a separate site. Where organizations use e-mail or have a website that link has also been made. In order to make access easier, readers should note that the WTO have further categorized tourism organizations by region: Africa, Americas, Asia, Europe and the Middle East.

There are several useful sources of producer information also available on the Web. One of the best access points is the World Travel and Tourism Council (WTTC), an international coalition of major travel and tourism corporations, based in London. WTTC shares its site (http://www.wttc.org/) with ECONETT, the European Community Network for Environmental Travel and Tourism which also has an on-line database of information about developments in sustainable tourism. Some of the information on ECONETT is also available in Spanish, German, French and Italian. The Pacific Asia Travel Association (PATA) also produces a significant number of statistical, industry and research publications on tourism in the Asia Pacific region. However, as with many other tourism organizations, the best sources of information about organizational roles, resources and activities are to be found on the website rather than in hard copy. In the case of PATA website (http://www.pata.org), categories of information include material about PATA itself, travellers' links, news, events, divisional information (Asia, Pacific, Europe and Americas) and resources.

Sport

Researchers are fortunate that there are a number of excellent on-line sources of information on sport and related subjects such as recreation, sports medicine, events and sports tourism. The General Association of International Sports Federations (GAISF) based in Monaco has an extremely comprehensive website (http://www.worldsport.com/worldsport/gaisf/home.html) which, apart from information on the GAISF, contains links to sites which detail member congresses, federations, multisport games, news and results, press releases and several lists of relevant addresses. The site is one of the best available in terms of identifying the responsible international organizations for individual sports and sports-related activities, i.e. sports journalism, events and sports medicine. The list of GAISF members (67 full members, 16 associate members and five provisional members) and relevant links are to be found at http://www.worldsport.com/worldsport/gaisf/members.html. In addition to the GAISF, students should also look at the publications and listings of the International Olympic Committee. The Olympic Movement website contains a wealth of information on the Olympics, including the relevant Summer and Winter Games sports federations, a list of national Olympic Committees (e.g. the British Olympic

Association, http://www.olympics.org.uk/), and links to forthcoming Olympic Games (http://www.olympic.org/).

A producer association which has useful country resources is The World Federation of the Sporting Goods Industry (WFSGI) website (http://www. sportlink.com/international) which contains market research by country, environmental information, legal information and organizational information. One of the greatest single sources of information on sporting organizations at the international, national and regional levels is the Sport Information Resource Center (SIRC) based in Gloucester, Canada. Information on SIRC and its activities is available on-line and through CD-ROM as well as some information also being available in hard copy. The SIRC homepage and index (http://www. sirc.ca/index.html) provides a good outline of the areas that they cover, which includes all aspects of sport and recreation, as well as some related areas such as sports tourism. The SIRC website is called Spotquest. It also produces a database called Sportdiscus which is an index to sports publications and SIRC offers a document delivery service (see http://www. sportquest.com/sirc/sportexpress.html for details). In addition, the SIRC website also contains a directory of sporting organizations with separate pages for sport-related national and international associations, university and college World Wide Web sites with sport-related programs, and information centres which specialize in the sport and fitness areas (see http://www. sportquest.com/questassoc.cfm).

National, regional and local organizations

National organizations offer a range of information for the leisure and tourism student. However, students will often experience substantial difficulties in trying to identify organizations responsible for the area they are interested in. This is because different nations have different political systems and institutional arrangements for the co-ordination, development, management and promotion of heritage, culture, leisure, recreation, sport and tourism. In federal systems for example, much of the responsibility for an area may be at the state or provincial level rather than the national. Similarly, in certain countries, the private profit or non-profit sector may provide the co-ordination for an area rather than central government. For example, in the USA, SIRC lists over 200 sporting organizations which have a national or multistate focus (http://www.sportquest.com/questassoc.cfm). Similarly, in Australia, there is a federal government body as well as a ministry responsible for sport, while each state and territory will also have a ministry and, often, a separate state sports commission or similar.

Despite the substantial variation between different countries and different sectors several good examples of information rich national organizations can be identified. One of the most significant is the Australian Sports Commission (ASC) which provides both an excellent website (http://www.ausport.gov.au/home.html) and a series of paper-based directories:

- the *Australian Sports Directory* which contains a listing of Australian sporting organizations
- the *Australian Sports Science Directory* which offers a listing of sport scientists operating in Australia by sport and discipline
- the *Australian Sports Industry Directory* which offers contacts for Australian sporting organizations as well as those involved in the sporting industry, including manufacturers, sports and fitness centres, media, marketing management, public relations, hospitality, event management, education and training, venues, and professional and trade associations.

The ASC website is extremely valuable as it contains links to various international sports organizations, outlines the organization of sport in Australia (including government policies), and also contains a series of topics in sport. The depth of information on the ASC site can be favourably contrasted with some of the sites of other countries, e.g., New Zealand (Hillary Commission, http://www.hillarysport.org.nz/).

One very important source of information on national and regional organizations is the directory of government departments and agencies that nearly every country produces. Indeed, many countries will have a central government information centre that can then pass you on to the relevant authority. In addition, government printers or publishing agencies will also be able to pass on information such as annual reports and other relevant material on government and departmental activity. Examining government directories can also be a useful way to see the vast range of government and semi-government organizations that impinge on the leisure and tourism field. For example, the Department for Culture, Media and Sport in the United Kingdom, the central UK Government Department responsible for arts, sport, recreation, museums, galleries, heritage and tourism, sponsors forty-five executive and advisory non-departmental public bodies nearly all of which have an input into the leisure and tourism field, e.g. Arts Council of England, British Tourist Authority, English Heritage, English Tourist Board, Millennium Commission, National Heritage Memorial Fund, National Maritime Museum, Sports Council, and the Victoria and Albert Museum (http://www.culture.gov.uk/ABOUT.HTM).

At the local and regional level the information resources of tourism organizations tend to be quite poor, especially with respect to tourism statistics as these tend to be gathered more at the national level. However, marketing and policy information will often be available. In contrast, sports, leisure and recreation information tends to be more readily available at the local and regional level, most likely because this is the level from which most of the organizational clients will be drawn. While websites are proliferating at this level, the most common source of information will be a community directory which is produced by the local government authority. These directories will typically source sports clubs and associations, recreation and leisure groups, as well as providing information on community services groups (e.g. Wellington City Council, 1997).

Conclusions

As this chapter has demonstrated, leisure and tourism organizations can provide an extremely rich source of information for students of the area. However, the broad nature of leisure and tourism means that identifying relevant organizations can be very difficult if the information that is being searched for is issue rather than organizational driven. In particular, this chapter emphasizes the importance of looking beyond the boundaries of government and producer organization to also consider the information of interest groups, especially in relation to environmental and social issues.

This chapter only provides a brief taste of some of the information and resources that are available. As in other areas of the information revolution, material is increasingly becoming available on the Internet to the exclusion of some of the traditional print forms. For example, many directories are becoming so CD-ROM and website driven that some libraries will now only buy the electronic and not the printed form. Finally, we should note the influence that new technology is having on our search patterns for information. Nowhere is this becoming more significant than in the leisure and tourism system with its inherent characteristic of partial industrialization. In this ever interconnected world we are increasingly looking to the global to understand the local.

Acknowledgements

The author would like to acknowledge the assistance of Maria Aptakar, Dave Crag, Penny Forrest and Gary Johnson in examining the use and availability of information on leisure and tourism organizations.

Appendix 1: Key international leisure and tourism organization information sources

Asia-Pacific Economic Co-operation (APEC) Secretariat
438 Alexandra Road
14-00, Alexandra Point
Singapore 119958
Tel: 65 276 1880
Fax: 65 276-1775
E-mail: info@mail.apecsec.org.sg
Website: http://www.apecsec.org.sg/apecnet.html

General Association of International Sports Federations (GAISF)
Villa Le Mas 4
bd du Jardin Exotique
MC 98000
Monaco
Website: http://www.worldsport.com/gaist/home.html

Pacific Asia Travel Association (PATA) Headquarters
1 Montgomery Street
Telesis Tower, Suite 1000
San Francisco
CA 94194-4539
USA
Tel: 1 415 986 4646
Fax: 1 415 986 3458
E-mail: patahq@pata.org
Website: http://www.pata.org/patanet/index.html

Sport Information Resource Center (SIRC)
1600 James Naismith Dr
Gloucester, Ontario
Canada KIB 5N4
Fax: 1 613 748 5701
E-mail: moreinfo@sirc.ca
Website: http://www.sirc.ca

Tourism Council of the South Pacific
PO Box 13119
Suva
Fiji Islands
Tel: 679 304 177
Fax: 679 301995

Union of International Associations (UIA)
Rue Washington 40
B-1050 Brussels
Belgium
Tel: 32 2 640 18 08
Fax: 32 2 646 05 25
E-mail: uia@uia.be
Website: http://www.uia.org/

World Federation of the Sporting Goods Industry (WFSGI)
BP 480, Le Hameau CH
1936 Verbier
Switzerland
Tel: 41 26 35 35 70
Fax: 41 26 35 35 79
E-mail: 100736.1547@compuserve.com
Website: http://www.sportlink.com/international

World Tourism Organization (WTO)
Capitán Haya, 42
28020 Madrid
Spain
Tel: 34 1 567 8100
Fax: 34 1 571 0757
E-mail: omt@world-tourism.org
Website: http://www.world-tourism.org

Appendix 2: A selection of sport leisure and tourism organizations

International and regional organizations

Association of South-East Asian Nations (ASEAN) Secretariat
70A, Jalan Sisingamangaraja
Jakarta 11210
Indonesia
Tel: 62 21 7262991
Fax: 62 21 7398234
Website: http://www.asean.or.id/

Carribbean Tourism Organization
20 East 46th Street
New York
NY 100174258
USA
Tel: 212 682 0435
Fax: 212 697 4258

Indian Ocean Tourism Organization
IOTO Secretariat
6th Floor, 16 St Georges Terrace
Perth
Western Australia 6000
Tel: 61 08 9220 1896
Fax: 61 08 9220 1810
Website: http://www.cowan.edu.au/pa/ioto/

International Air Transport Association (IATA)
Viale di Val Fiorita 00144
Rome, Italy
Tel: 06 5912442
Fax: 06 5913517
Website: http://194.184.148.170/info/iata.htm

International Association for Sports Information
c/o Albert Remans 'L'ESPACE DU 27 SEPTEMBRE' 4e etage
Boulevard Leopold II
44 1080 – Brussels
Belgium
Tel: 02 413 28 93
Fax: 02-413 28 90
Website: http://www.sportquest.com/iasi/index.html

International Association of Amusement Parks and Attractions
1448 Duke Street
Alexandria
VA 22314-3464
USA
Tel: 703 836 4800
Fax: 703 836 4801
E-mail: iaapa@iaapa.org
Website: http://www.iaapa.org/

Organization for Economic Co-operation and Development
2 Rue André-Pascal
75775 Paris CEDEX 16
France
Tel: 33 01 45 24 82 00
Fax: 33 01 45 24 85 .00
E-mail: webmaster@oecd.org
Website: http://www.oecd.org/

Organization of American States, Inter-Sectoral Unit for Tourism
1889 F Street, N W
Washington
DC 20006
USA
Website: http://www.oas.org/EN/PROG/TOURISM/home.htm

Pacific Asia Travel Association
PATA Headquarters
One Montgomery Street
Telesis Tower, Suite 1000
San Francisco
CA 94104-4539
USA
Tel: 415 986 4646
Fax: 415 986 3458
Conference fax: 415 834 0420
E-mail: patahq@pata.org
Website: http://www.dnai.com/~patanet/

Pacific Rim Institute of Tourism
Suite 930, 555 West Hasting
Vancouver
British Columbia
V6B 4N6
Canada
Tel: 604 682 8000

Sports Tourism International Council, International Headquarters
PO Box 5580-Station 'F'
Ottawa
Canada K2C 3M1

Tel and fax: 1 613 226 9447
E-mail: stic@winning.com
Website: http://www.sportquest.com/tourism/index.html

Tourism Concern
Stapleton House
277–281 Holloway Road
London N7 8HN
Tel: 0171 753 3330
Fax: 0171 753 3331
E-mail: tourconcern@gn.apc.org
Website: http://www.gn.apc.org/tourismconcern/

Tourism Council for the South Pacific
PO Box 13119
Suva
Fiji Islands
Tel: 679 315277
Fax: 679 301995

Travel and Tourism Research Association
546 East Main Street
Lexington
KY 40508
USA
Tel: 1 606 226 4344
Fax: 1 606 226 4355
E-mail: ttra@mgtserv.com
Website: http://www.ttra.com

World Federation of the Sporting Goods Industry
Le Hameau
PO Box 480
1936 Verbier
Switzerland
Tel: 41 27 775 35 70
Fax: 41 27 775 35 79
E-mail: wfsgi@verbier.ch
Website: http://www.sportlink.com/international/

World Heritage Centre, UNESCO
7, Place de Fontenoy
75352 Paris
France
E-mail: wh-info@unesco.org
Website: http://www.unesco.org/whc/

World Leisure and Recreation Association
WLRA Secretariat
3 Canyon Court West
Lethbridge
AB T1K 6V1
Canada
Tel: 403 381 6144
Fax: 403 381 6144
E-mail: wlra@hg.uleth.ca
Website: http://www.worldleisure.org/

World Tourism Organization
Capitán Haya
42 28020 Madrid
Spain
Tel: 34 1 567 81 00/20
Fax: 34 1 571 07 57
E-mail: omtweb@world-tourism.org
Website: http://www.world-tourism.org/

World Wildlife Fund International
Avenue du Mont-Blanc
CH-1196
Gland, Switzerland
Tel: 41 22 364 91 11
Website: http://www.worldwildlife.org/

Australia

Australian and New Zealand Association for Leisure Studies (ANZALS)
Department of Sport and Exercise Science (Tamaki Campus)
The University of Auckland
Private Bag 92019
New Zealand
Website: http://www.gu.edu.au/gwis/leis/services/lswp/index.htm

Australian Conservation Foundation
340 Gore Street
Fitzroy
Victoria 3065
Tel: 03 9416 1166
Fax: 03 9416 0767
Website http://www.peg.apc.org/~acfenv/

Australian Federation of Travel Agents
AFTA Headquarters
309 Pitt Street
Sydney
NSW 2000
Tel: 02 9264 3299
Fax: 02 9264 1085
E-mail: gina@afta.net.au
Website http://www.afta.com.au/

Australian Institute of Sport
PO Box 176
Belconnen
ACT 2616
Tel: 02 6214 1111
Fax: 02 6251 2680
Website: http://www.ausport.gov.au/aismenu.html

Australian Sports Commission
PO Box 176
Belconnen
ACT 2616
Tel: 61 06 252 1915
Fax: 61 06 252 1995
Website: http://www.ausport.gov.au/home.html

Department of the Environment, Sport and Territories
Moore Street
Canberra
ACT 2601
Tel: 61 2 6274 1111
Fax: 61 2 6274 1123
Website: http://www.dest.gov.au/index.html

Office of National Tourism
Department of Industry, Science and Tourism
GPO Box 1839
Canberra
ACT 2601
Tel: 61 6 279 7222
Fax: 61 6 279 7211
Website: http://www.dist.gov.au/tourism/

Queensland Office of Sport and Recreation
4th Floor Capital Hill Building
85 George Street
Brisbane
Queensland 4000
Tel: 61 7 3237 0098
Fax: 61 7 3237 0288
Website: http://www.sportrec.qld.gov.au/

South Australia Sports Institute
PO Box 219
Brooklyn Park
SA 5032
Tel: 08 416 6631

Canada

Canadian Business Travel Association
PO Box 6021
Station D
Calgary
AB T2P 2C7
Website: http://www.cndbus-travassoc.com/

Canadian Sport and Fitness Administration Centre, Inc.
1600 James Naismith Drive
Suite 307
Gloucester
Ontario
K1B 5N4
Tel: 613 748 5602
Fax: 613 748 5706

Canadian Olympic Association
Olympic House
2380 Pierre Dupuy Avenue
Montreal
PQ H3C 3R4
Tel: 514 861 3371
Fax: 514 861 2896

Canadian Tourism Commission
235 Queen Street
400D, Ottawa
Ontario
K1A 0H6
Tel: 613 954 3943
Website: http://206.191.33.50/tourism/tindu.html

Hotel Association of Canada
Suite 1016
130 Albert Street
Ottawa
ON K1P 5GE
Tel: 613 237 7149
Fax: 613 238 8928
E-mail: info@hotels.ca
Website: http://www.hotels.ca/

North American Sports Library Network
Gretchen Ghent, Chair
c/o The University of Calgary Libraries
2500 University Drive NW
Calgary
Alberta T2N 1N4
Tel: 403 220 6097
Fax: 403 282 6837
E-mail: gghent@acs.ucalgary.ca
Website: http://www.sportquest.com/naslin/index.html

Tourism Industry Resource Centre
PO Box 2703
Whitehorse
Yukon
Y1A 2C6
Tel: 867 667 5449
E-mail: tirc@yknet.yk.ca
Website: http://www.yukonweb.com/government/tourism/tirc

New Zealand

Australian and New Zealand Association for Leisure Studies (ANZALS)
Department of Sport and Exercise Science (Tamaki Campus)
The University of Auckland
Private Bag 92019
New Zealand
Website: http: www.gu.edu.au/gwis/leis/services/lswp/index.htm

Hillary Commission
PO Box 2251
Wellington
E-mail: sitemail@hillarysport.org.nz
Website: http://www.hillarysport.org.nz/

New Zealand Recreation Association
PO Box 27-161
Wellington
Tel: 04 384 2450
E-mail: nzrec@actrix.gen.nz

New Zealand Tourism Board, Head Office
Fletcher Challenge House
89 The Terrace
PO Box 95
Wellington
Tel: 04 472 8860
Fax: 04 478 1736
Website: http://www.nztb.govt.nz/

Sport, Recreation and Fitness Industry Training Organization (SFRITO)
PO Box 2183
Wellington
Tel: 04 385 9047
Fax: 04 385 7024
E-mail: smith@sfrito.org.nz

Tourism Policy Group
Ministry of Commerce
PO Box 1473
Wellington
Tel: 64 4 472 0030
Fax:64 4 499 3670
E-mail: tourism@moc.govt.nz
Website: http://www.moc.govt.nz/tpg/

Travel Agents' Association of New Zealand
PO Box 1888
DX SX10033
Wellington
Tel: 04 499 0104
Fax: 04 499 0827
E-mail: taanz@tiasnet.co.nz
Website: http://www.taanz.org.nz

UK

Arts Council of England
14 Great Peter Street
London SW1P 3NQ
Tel: 0171 333 0100
Fax: 0171 973 6590
Website: http://www.artscouncil.org.uk/

Association of British Travel Agents (ABTA)
55–57 Newman Street
London W1P 4AH
Tel: 0171 637 2444
Website http://www.abtanet.com/

British Tourist Authority
Thames Tower
Blacks Road
Hammersmith
London W6 9 EL
Tel: 0181 846 9000
Fax: 0181 563 0302

Countryside Commission
John Dower House
Crescent Place
Cheltenham GL50 3RA
Tel: 01242 521381
E-mail: info@countryside.gov.uk
Website: http://www.countryside.gov.uk/

English Heritage
23 Savile Row
London W1X 1AB
Tel: 0171 973 3000
Fax: 0171 973 3001
Website: http://www.english-heritage.org.uk/

English Sports Council
16 Upper Woburn Place
London WC1H 0QP
Tel: 0171 388 1277
Fax: 0171 383 5740

Hotel, Catering and Institutional Management Association (HCIMA)
191 Trinity Road
London SW17 7HN
Tel: 0181 672 4251
Fax: 0181 682 1707
Website: http://hcima.org.uk/general/

Institute of Leisure and Amenity Management
ILAM House
Lower Basildon
Reading RG8 9NE
Tel: 01491 874800
Fax: 01491 874801
Website: http://www.ilam.co.uk/

Leisure Studies Association
Chelsea School Research Centre
University of Brighton, Eastbourne
BN20 7SP
Tel: 01323 640357

Scottish Sports Council
Caledonia House
South Gyle
Edinburgh, EH12 9DQ
Tel: 0131 317 7200
Fax 0131 317 7202

Sport and Recreation Information Group (SPRIG)
The Sports Library
Central Library
Surrey Street
Sheffield S1 1XZ
Tel: 0114 273 5929
E-mail: sports.library@dial.pipex.com

Sports Council for Wales
Sophia Gardens
Cardiff, CF1 9SW
Tel: 01222 300 500

USA

American Association for Active Lifestyles and Fitness
1900 Association Drive
Reston, VA 20191
Tel: 1 800 213 7193
Website: http://www.aahperd.org/aaalf/aaalf.html

American Hotel and Motel Association
1201 New York Avenue, NW, 600
Washington
DC 20005-3931
Tel: 202 289 -3100
Fax: 202 289 3199
E-mail: info@ahma.com
Website: http://www.ahma.com/

The Sporting Goods Manufacturers Association
200 Castlewood Drive
North Palm Beach
Florida 33408-5696
Tel: 561 842-4100
Fax: 561 863-8984
Web http://www.sportlink.com/

Travel Industry Association of America
1100 New York Ave NW
Suite 450
Washington
DC 20005-3934
Tel: 202 408 1832
Fax: 202 408 1255

US Congressional Travel and Tourism Caucus
US House of Representatives
House Annex, 2
Room 246
Washington
DC 20515
Tel: 202 225 3935
Fax: 202 225 9293

US Department of Commerce, International Trade Administration, Tourism
Industries
1401 Constitution Avenue, NW
Room 1860
Washington
DC 20230
Fax: 1 202 482 2887
Website: http://tinet.ita.doc.gov

US Travel and Tourism Administration
8070 NW 53rd Street
107, Springfield Building
Miami
FL 33166
Tel: 305 526 2912
Fax: 305 526 2915

References

Australian Sports Commission (1997) Australian Sport. http://www.ausport.gov.au/ (accessed 24 April 1998).

British Olympic Association (1996) British Olympic Movement. http://www.olympics. org.uk/ (accessed 24 April 1998).

Cigler, A. J. (1991) Interest Groups: A Subfield in Search of an Identity. In *Political Science: Looking to the Future, Vol. 4, American Institutions* (W. Crotty, ed.) Northwestern University Press.

Cigler, A. J. and Loomis, B. A. (eds) (1986) *Interest Group Politics*, 2nd edn. CQ Press.

Consortium for Global Commerce (1997) Global Index of Chambers of Commerce and Industry. http://www.worldchambers.com/chambers.html (accessed 24 April 1998).

Craik, J. (1991) *Resorting to Tourism: Cultural Policies for Tourist Development*. Allen and Unwin.

Daniels, P. K. and Schwartz, C. A. (eds) (1997) *Encyclopedia of Associations*, 31st edn. Gale Research Inc.

Department for Culture, Media and Sport (1997) About the Department. http://www.culture.gov.uk/ABOUT.HTM (accessed 22 April 1998).

Dunning, J. H. and McQueen, M. (1982a) Multinationals in the international hotel industry. *Annals of Tourism Research*, **9**, 69–90.

Dunning, J. H. and McQueen, M. (1982b) *Transnational Corporations in International Tourism*. United Nations Centre for Transnational Studies.

Envirolink Library (1997) Envirolink Library: Organizations. http://envirolink.org/orgs/ index.html (accessed 22 April 1998).

Environment Web Directory (1997) Environmental Organization Web Directory: Earth's Biggest Environment Search Engine. http://www.webdirectory.com/ (accessed 22 April 1998).

General Association of International Sports Federations (GAISF) (1997) World Sport Center. http://www.worldsport.com/worldsport/gaisf/home.html (accessed 24 April 1998).

General Association of International Sports Federations (GAISF) (1997) List of GAISF Members. http://www.worldsport.com/worldsport/gaisf/members.html (accessed 24 April 1998).

Hillary Commission for Sport, Fitness and Leisure (1997) Hillary Commission Home Page. http://www.hillarysport.org.nz/ (accessed 24 April 1998).

International Chamber of Commerce (1997) International Chamber of Commerce: The World Business Organization. http://www.iccwbo.org/ (accessed 24 April 1998).

Hall, C. M. (1994) *Tourism and Politics: Place, Policy and Power*. John Wiley and Sons.

Hall, C. M. (1995) *Introduction to Tourism in Australia: Planning, Development and Impacts*, 2nd edn. Longman Australia.

Hall, C. M. and Jenkins, J. (1995) *Tourism and Public Policy*. Routledge.

Heeley, J. (1986) Big Company Involvement in Scottish Tourism. *Fraser of Allander Quarterly Economic Commentary*, **11** (2), 75–9.

Heeley, J. (1989) Role of National Tourist Organizations in the United Kingdom. In *Tourism Marketing and Management Handbook* (S. F. Witt and L. Moutinho, eds), Prentice Hall.

International Olympic Committee (1997) The Olympic Movement: The World-Wide Web Home Page of the International Olympic Committee. http://www.Olympic.org/ (accessed 24 April 1998).

IPL Associations on the Net (1997) Internet Public Library of Associations on the Net. http://www.ipl.org/ref/AON/ (accessed 22 April 1998).

Leiper, N. (1989) *Tourism and Tourism Systems*. Occasional Paper No.1, Department of Management Systems, Massey University.

Leiper, N. (1990) Partial Industrialization of Tourism Systems. *Annals of Tourism Research*, **17**, 600–05.

Long, P. E. (1997) Researching Tourism Partnership Organizations: From Practice to Theory to Methodology. In *Quality Management in Urban Tourism*, (P. Murphy, ed.) John Wiley and Sons.

Maconie, R. (ed.) (1992) *The Top 3000 Directories and Annuals*, 10th edn. Dawson UK Ltd.

Matthews, T. (1976) Interest group access to the Australian Government Bureaucracy. In *Royal Commission on Australian Government Administration: Appendixes to Report, Volume Two*. Australian Government Publishing Service.

Millard, P. (ed.) (1988) *Trade Associations and Professional Bodies of the United Kingdom*, 9th edn. Pergamon Press.

Morgan, G. (1986) *Images of Organization*. Sage.

Pacific Asia Travel Association (1997) PATAnet The Pacific Asia Travel Association. http://www.pata.org (accessed on 22 April 1998).

Pearce, D. G. (1992) *Tourist Organizations*. Longman Scientific and Technical.

Philanthropy Journal Online (1997) Meta-Index for Nonprofit Organizations. http://www.philanthropy-journal.org/plhome/plmeta.htm (accessed 22 April 1998).

Schlozman, K. L. and Tierney, J. T. (1986) *Organized Interests and American Democracy*. Harper and Row.

Selin, S. and Beason, K. (1991) Interorganizational Relations in Tourism. *Annals of Tourism Research*, **18**, 639–52.

Smith, S. L. J. (1988) Defining Tourism: A Supply-Side View. *Annals of Tourism Research*, **15**, 179–90.

Smith, S. L. J. (1991) The Supply-Side Definition of Tourism: Reply to Leiper. *Annals of Tourism Research*, **18**, 312–18.

Smith, S. L. J. (1993) Return to the Supply Side. *Annals of Tourism Research*, **20**, 226–9.

Sport Information Resource Center (1997) SIRC Index. http://www.sirc.ca/index.html (accessed 24 April 1998).

Sport Information Resource Center (1997) Sport Associations. http://www.sportquest.com/questassoc.cfm (accessed 24 April 1998).

Union of International Associations (ed.) (1995) *Who's Who in International Organizations*, 2nd edn. 3 vols, K G Saur Verlag.

Union of International Associations (ed.) (1996) *World Guide to Religious and Spiritual Organizations*. K G Saur Verlag.

Union of International Associations (ed.) (1997) *Yearbook of International Organizations 1997/98*, 34th edn. 4 vols, K G Saur Verlag.

United Nations Committee on Co-ordination (1997) Official Web Site Locator for the United Nations System of Organizations. http://www.unsystem.org/index.html (accessed 22 April 1998).

Wellington City Council (1997) *Community Directory: Community Commissioning 1997/98*. Wellington City Council.

World Federation of the Sporting Goods Industry (1997) Sporting Goods Manufacturers International. http://www.sportlink.com/international (accessed 22 April 1998).

World Tourism Organization (1997) World Tourism Organization Information Centre. http://www.world-tourism.org (accessed 22 April 1998).

World Tourism Organization (1997) Information from Official Tourism Organizations. http://www.world-tourism.org/tourworl.htm (accessed 22 April 1998).

World Travel and Tourism Council (1997) Site map. http://www.wttc.org/ (accessed 22 April 1998).

Yahoo (1997) Business and Economy: Organizations. http://www.yahoo.com/yahoo/economy/organizations (accessed 22 April 1998).

9

Finding out about sport, leisure and tourism on video

Lesley Gunter

Introduction

The aim of this chapter is to give an overview of some of the possible ways to find video sources in the areas of sport, leisure and tourism. Much of the information contained in the chapter is a guide to further contacts, useful libraries and information centres, key organizations and a selection of video distributors with a guide to their holdings. There is also an analysis of the subjects covered that are available through general distributors, and a section on copyright gives a guide to the current legislation.

Although video has been used as an information medium for a number of years, it is still relatively difficult to research compared to other resources such as books and journals. There are the added difficulties that video cannot be browsed on the shelf, so an immediate appraisal of the contents is not possible, and standards do seem to vary enormously. Whereas all books have an international standard book number which is unique to each publication, there is no equivalent method of control for videos. Furthermore, most of the abstracts, indexes in bibliographies that are listed in Chapter 5 do not include videos. There is also a huge amount of high-impact type film, much of which is made with the armchair viewer in mind. The educational content of many of the videos available is minimal. The nature of the medium offers opportunities for thrilling the viewer, and sport is particularly well adapted to this type of production.

Many public and University libraries contain large collections of material held on video. Sometimes video is treated differently to printed material in that it is shelved separately and there may even be a special collection of video material. Some libraries produce seperate catalogues of video material so that it is possible to search only for material in the form of video. It is possible to find out what videos are available in many university libraries by searching their catalogues on the Internet. (See Chapter 3 for further details.) However, it is often very difficult or impossible to obtain videos through an interlibrary loan or document delivery system, so this will only be useful as a way of establishing that there are titles available.

An analysis of videos in sport, leisure and tourism

The following analysis of videos indicates the range available in each subject area. The analysis was carried out using *Videolog*. This is a loose-leaf trade publication available from:

Lukins – Trade Services Publications Ltd., Cherryholt Road, Stamford, Lincolnshire PE9 2HT

Tel: 01780 764331 Fax: 01780 757679

It contains listings and cross-references on currently available video titles in the UK, and is updated fortnightly.

The sections on sport, leisure and tourism are listed as follows:

Section 600 – Special interest

Section 620 – General interest (health and leisure)

Section 640 – Sport

The following activities are listed in *Videolog*. The number in brackets represents the number of titles listed for that activity in the publication dated 16 June 1997.

American football	(9)
Angling	(310)
Archery	(1)
Arena sports	(11)
Athletics	(22)
Badminton	(2)
Baseball	(21)
Basketball	(25)
Bodybuilding	(39)
Bowls	(6)

Boxing	(57)
Carriage driving	(4)
Cricket	(45)
Cycling	(74)
Equestrian	(216)
Field sports/hunting	(55)
Football	(709)
Golf	(185)
Gymnastics	(2)
Hockey	(3)
Ice hockey	(2)
Kickboxing	(20)
Martial arts	(89)
Motor cycle sports	(490)
Motor sport	(796)
Other sports/compilations	(66)
Powerboat racing	(66)
Rugby league	(8)
Rugby union	(50)
Sailing	(45)
Shooting	(10)
Skating/skateboarding	(12)
Skiing/snowboarding	(126)
Snooker/pool/billiards	(10)
Squash	(8)
Surfing/windsurfing/water skiing	(67)
Swimming	(5)
Tennis	(42)
Wrestling	(169)
Exercise/fitness	(284)
Places of interest/travel	(566)
Self-defence	(8)

Videolog lists thirty-nine sports/activities plus fitness and exercise, places of interest/travel/self-defence. These categories together list over 4700 titles.

Video distributors

The following is a selected list of distributors mainly in the UK who responded to a request for information on their products. Rather than list each video that they supply, a brief description of the types of video they distribute has been included to give some idea of the material available.

Astrion PLC
142 Great North Way, Hendon, London NW4 1EG
Tel: 0181 202 0011 Fax: 0181 202 3300
Small selection of motor sport and football.

AVID – Audio Visual Independent Distribution Ltd
Unit 2 Boeing Way, International Trading Estate, Brent Road, Southall, Middlesex UB2 5LB
Tel: 0181 893 5767 Fax: 0181 893 5955
Titles in rugby league, football (Bolton Wanderers) and golf.

BBC Video
See Video Plus Direct.

Beckmann Home Video
PO Box 44, Leatherhead, Surrey KT22 7AE
Tel: 01372 457358
Large selection including: boxing, chess, cricket, cycling, equestrian, field sports, fishing, football, golf, martial arts, tai chi, motorcycling, motoring, sailing, snooker, skiing, tennis. Also selection of touring videos covering popular areas of Britain.

Beekay International
Withy Pool, Henlow Camp, Bedfordshire SG16 6EA
Tel: 01462 816960 Fax: 01462 817253
Wide selection of fishing videos covering coarse, carp, pike, game and sea fishing.

Bell Media Group Ltd
Lamb House, Church Street, Chiswick Mall, London
Tel: 0181 996 9960 Fax: 0181 996 9966
Four titles only on motor sport, skiing, snowboarding and mountain biking.

Black Diamond Films Ltd
13 New Row, Covent Garden, London WC2N 4LF
Tel: 0171 497 3320 Fax: 0171 497 3069
Specialize in dramatic films of surfing, windsurfing, rock climbing, mountain biking and in-line skating – titles such as: *Gravity Sucks and Total Insanity.*

British Tourist Authority (BTA)
Commercial Department, Thames Tower, Black's Road, London W6 9EL
Tel: 0181 563 3011/3/5 Fax: 0181 563 3289
They have seven videos which are available direct from them, aimed mainly at visitors to the UK e.g. *England: A Country for All Time*; *Scotland: World of a Difference*. See also International Video Network who distribute all BTA videos.

Capricorn Productions
Delta House, 11–13 Albion Place, Maidstone, Kent ME14 5DY
01622 691431 Fax: 01622 688249
One title only – *On Top of the Weald: Discovering the Weald of Kent and East Sussex*.

Claremont Video Productions
2 Claremont Road, Dewsbury WF13 4LF
Tel: 01924 466340
A small selection of Yorkshire visitor videos called *The Journey Series*.

Classic Pictures Entertainment Ltd
Shepperton International Film Studios, Studios Road, Shepperton, Middlesex TW17 0QD
Tel: 01932 572016 Fax: 01932 572046
Small selection including some historical documentary in cricket and motor racing.

Coachwise
Units 2/3 Chelsea Close, Off Amberley Road, Armley, Leeds LS12 4HW
Tel: 0113 231 1310 Fax: 0113 231 9606
Coachwise is the marketing arm of the National Coaching Foundation. They produce an annual catalogue which covers the following subjects: general interest, sports coaching, physical education, general sports, sports science and medicine, leisure, recreation and sport management, health and fitness and fitness products. They have twenty-seven videos available in a range of subjects. They also supply other multimedia, and some audio products.

Creative Media Marketing Ltd
84–86 Grays Inn Road, London WC1X 8BQ
Tel: 0171 405 6165 Fax: 0171 405 6168
Sports and fitness including *The Winning Formula – The Football Association Official Coaching* tapes. Titles include *Direct Play*, *Scoring*, *Winning the Advantage*, *Defending to Win*, *Goal Keeping*, *Soccer Star*.

Dalesman Publishing Company Ltd
Clapham, Lancaster LA2 8EB
Tel: 01524 251225 Fax: 01524 251708
A series of titles including *Dalesman*, featuring visitor attractions in Yorkshire and Derbyshire.

Ettinger Bros Productions Ltd
3 Church Road, Penny Lane, Liverpool L15 9EA
Tel: 0151 734 2240 Fax: 0151 733 2468
Football documentary only.

Fifth Avenue Films
PO Box 2001, Hockley, Southampton SS5 6HU
Tel: 01702 232396 Fax: 01702 230944
Small selection of fishing videos.

Green Umbrella
The Old Forge, Ockham Lane, Ockham, Surrey GU23 6PH
Tel: 01483 223022 Fax: 01483 223099
Large selection of titles in cricket, fishing, football including some coaching, golf, health and fitness, horses, motor racing, skiing, squash, tennis. Also supply Newcastle United videos and a selection of titles for prospective travellers.

Hisha Trading (UK)
Gordon House, Woodstock Road, Charlbury, Oxford OX7 3ET
Tel: 01608 811093 Fax: 01608 810352
Karate – various disciplines.

Human Kinetics Europe
Units C2/C3, Wira Business Park, West Park Ring Road, West Park, Leeds LS16 6EB
Tel: 0113 278 1708 Fax: 0113 278 1709
Skills and strategies of various sports as well as sports science and movement.

Hyperactive Films Ltd
2 High Street, Lydney, Gloucestershire GL15 5SL
Tel: 01594 844394
Wide selection of fishing and some sport shooting.

IMC VIdeo Ltd
Godalming Business Centre, Woolsack Way, Godalming, Surrey GU7 1XW

Tel: 01483 427366

Small selection of aerobics. Also A–Z Sport series, and Greatest Moments series. Lonely Planets travel guides series.

Institut National du Sport et de l'Education Physique
11, Avenue du Tremblay – 75012 Paris, France
Tel: 01 41 74 41 50 Fax: 01 41 74 44 02
A catalogue of videos available from this organization is available on request.

Institute of Sport and Recreation Management (ISRM)
Giffard house, 36/38 Sherrard Street, Melton Mowbray LE13 1JX
Tel: 01664 65531 Fax: 01664 501155
The ISRM produce a series of videos to supplement the written guides that they offer, all of which are aimed at people working in the sport and leisure industry. One series is called Effective Duty Management, a video training pack aimed at duty managers and supervisors working in the sport and leisure industry. Others include Health and Safety Management, Effective Pool Supervision and Quality Customer Service in Sport and Recreation. Full details are available from the ISRM.

International Licensing and Copyright Ltd
Broadley Studios, Broadley House, Broadley Terrace, London NW1 6LG
Tel: 0171 258 0324 Fax: 0171 723 9606
Small selection of football, rugby union and British tourism.

International Video Network
500 Chiswick High Road, London W4 5RG
Tel: 0181 956 2226 Fax: 0181 956 2339
Distribute British Tourist Authority videos. Also have a large selection of tourism titles listed in the following categories: Video Visits, Video Expeditions, Supercities, Lonely Planet, Rhapsody, Where in the World, New Zealand, Alpine Adventure, Wild Animals, Reader's Digest.

Mega Mail
PO Box 148, Enfield, Middlesex EN3 4NR
Tel: 0181 292 4875 Fax: 0181 805 9987
Baseball – skills and documentary. Selection of football (documentary) also snooker and golf. Wide range of exercise and fitness.

MIA
70 Baker Street, London W1M 1DJ

Tel: 0171 935 9225 Fax: 0171 935 9565
Small selection of football and golf. Also women's boxing and wrestling.

New World Company Ltd
Paradise Farm, Westhall, Halesworth, Suffolk IP19 8RH
Tel: 01986 781682 Fax: 01986 781645
Mostly self-help, hypnosis and relaxation with one title on sports improvement.

The Original Video Production Company (OVC)
PO Box 885, Milton Keynes MK7 8PQ
Tel and Fax: 01908 645115
Large selection of fishing, mostly instructional.

Our Video Company Ltd
88 Berkeley Court, Baker Street, London NW1 5ND
Tel: 0171 402 9111 Fax: 0171 723 3064
Small selection of yoga, fishing and tennis.

Porter Publishing Ltd
PP Video Ltd
The Storehouse, Little Hereford Street, Bromyard, Hereford HR7 4DE
Tel: 01885 488800 Fax: 01885 483012
Motor sport and some titles for touring caravanners at home and abroad.

Professional Magnetics Ltd
Cassette House, 329 Hunslet Road, Leeds LS10 1NJ
Tel: 0113 270 6066 Fax: 0113 271 8106
Very wide selection of sport including American football, athletics, baseball, basketball, cycling/mountain biking, boxing, cricket, fishing, golf, horse riding, keep fit, motor cycling, motor racing, rallying, rugby, sailing, self-defence, skating/skiing/snowboarding, snooker, soccer, squash, tennis, water sports, wrestling, and a selection of miscellaneous titles. Also wide selection of special interest travel videos covering places of interest at home and abroad.

Quadrant Video
37a High Street, Carshalton, Surrey SM5 3BB
Tel: 0181 669 1114 Fax: 0181 669 8831
Large selection: baseball, basketball, bodybuilding, boxing, cricket, football, golf, horse racing, keep fit, martial arts, motorsport, rugby, squash, tennis. Mostly documentary with a few instructional titles.

Qualification and Curriculum Authority (QCA)
Newcombe House, 45 Notting Hill Gate, London W11 3JB
Information Tel: 0171 229 1234 Orders Tel: 0181 867 3333
They produce videos relating to the PE National Curriculum: *Exemplification of Standards: PE – Key Stage 3* videotape and booklet £6.50, *Expectations in PE – Key Stages 1 & 2* videotape and booklet £9.00

Quantum Leap Group Ltd
Quantum House, 26 Darin Court, Crownhill, Milton Keynes, Buckinghamshire MK8 0AD
Tel: 01908 561133 Fax: 01908 564414
A large selection including football, martial arts, equestrian, skiing – mostly documentary. Also some tourism videos covering areas of Britain.

Sain Cyf
Canolfan Sain, Llandwrog, Caernarfon, Gwynedd LL54 5TG
Tel: 01286 831111 Fax: 01286 831497
Local interest, visitor and countryside as well as a small selection of Welsh rugby union.

Screen Multimedia Ltd
9 Station Road, Radlett, Hertfordshire WD7 8ED
Tel: 01923 469043 Fax: 01923 469044
Exercise, fitness and yoga.

Striding Edge Productions
Crag House Farm, Wasdale, Cumbria CA19 1UT
Tel: 01622 850064 Fax: 01622 850063
A selection of outdoor titles including a series of Great Walks videos and the Wainwright series.

TV Choice Ltd
22 Charing Cross Road, London WC2H OHR
Tel: 0171 379 0873 Fax: 0171 379 0263
Leisure and tourism videos looking particularly at business, economic and environmental aspects. They specialize in films for classroom and training use. Titles include *Systems for Leisure* explaining how information systems work in a busy leisure centre, and *Too Much Tourism?* explores the growing conflict over the future of one of Britain's most popular National Parks.

Tourism Concern

Stapleton House, 277–281 Holloway Road, London N7 8HN

Tel: 0171 753 3330. Fax: 0171 753 3331

Website: http://www.gn.apc.org/tourismconcern/

Tourism Concern has a range of tourism videos available for hire to its members only.

Travel Television PLC

PO Box 60, Hindhead, Surrey GU26 6XL

Tel: (free phone) 0800 525509 Fax: 01428 604673

International travel videos aimed at the prospective visitor.

Venta Television Ltd T/A Tadpole Lane, Unit 13, Winnall Valley Road, Winchester, Hampshire SO23 8LU

Tel: 01962 841100 Fax: 01962 840004

Visitor attractions including many stately homes and gardens. Official National Trust and Royal Horticultural Society videos.

Video House International

Ash Street, Fleetwood, Lancs FY7 6TH

Tel: 01253 770510 Fax: 01253 776729

Distributors of the Independent Travellers Guide series which cover numerous destinations worldwide.

Video Martial Arts (VMA International)

Chojin Martial Arts Centre, 10 Low Friar Street, Newcastle upon Tyne NE1 5UE

Tel: 0191 261 9859 Fax: 0169 734 4958

A wide range of martial arts videos including a range of disciplines. Instructional and documentary.

Video Plus Direct

19–24 Manasty Road, Orton Southgate, Peterborough PE2 6UP

Tel: 01733 232800 (order desk) 01733 233464 (switchboard) Fax: 01733 230618

A very big distributor with an extensive selection of documentary and instructional in the following sports American football, athletics, baseball, basketball, bmx, cycling, boxing, cricket, fishing, golf, horses, martial arts, motor cycling, motor racing, rally sports, rugby, sailing, self-defence, skating, skiing, snooker, soccer, tennis, trucks, water sports, wrestling, also a selection of miscellaneous titles. They also supply BBC Sports videos including football (Match of the Day series), cricket, motor sport, golf, rugby, snooker and classic sporting moments.

Videoactive Leisure
Freepost, Mill House Studios, Malpas, Cheshire SY14 7BR
Tel: 01948 780564 Fax: 01948 780566
Fishing and special interest leisure videos including some steam railway and narrowboat travel guides.

VSI Visionsport International
96 High Street, Marlow SL7 1AQ
Tel: 01628 477007 Fax: 01628 475252
A wide range of football titles including many season review compilations of popular and less popular teams. Also some rugby union and keep fit titles.

Other ways of finding out about video

There are a number of ways in which you can search for video titles other than looking at publishers' and distributors' catalogues. The following pages list some of the other sources that you may find useful.

Publications

American Archives of the Factual Film catalogue
The catalogue of the American Archives of the Factual Film (AAFF) is available on the Internet free of charge at http://www.lib.iastate.edu/scholar/db/ aaffxx.html The AAFF is both an archive and a research centre for the study and preservation of non-theatrical films. At present, the archive contains some 25 000 films, with over 13 000 individual titles. These include corporate films from such sponsors as International Harvester, AT&T, and the Union Pacific Railroad, US Government films from the Department of Agriculture and NASA, and educational films produced by Coronet, McGraw-Hill, and the Encyclopedia Britannica Educational Corporation.
Further details available from Special Collections Department, 403 Parks Library, Iowa State University, Ames, Iowa 50011-2140, USA
Tel: 515 294 6672 Fax: 515 294 5525
E-mail: aaff@iastate.edu
Website: http://www.lib.iastate.edu/spcl/aaff/aaff.html

Bowker's Complete Video Directory 1997
This publication, which is in four volumes, indexes over 93 000 'special interest videos'. These include documentaries, some popular travel titles and some sports videos. For each title a short description is included and the details of

the distributor and the price are given. There is also a subject index and relevant index headings include: anthropology, sport – history, sport – biography, sport – general, sociology, travel and travel guides. The distributor index gives the addresses of video distributors, most of which are in the USA.
Published by R. R. Bowker
ISBN: 0835238733

British National Film and Video Guide
A quarterly publication which is produced by the National Film and Television Archive of the British Film Institute and made available in printed form by the British Library. It lists films, videos and multimedia programmes with a substantial moving picture element offered within the UK for non-theatrical loan or purchase. Materials covered include educational and training films, independent productions, documentaries, television programmes and feature films. It is arranged by subject.
Available on subscription from the British Library NBS, Turpin Distribution Services Ltd, Blackhorse Road, Letchworth, Hertfordshire SG6 1HN
Tel: 01462 672555 Fax: 01462 480947.

Film and Television Collections in Europe: The MAP TV Guide
Edited by Daniela Kirchner
Blueprint inprint (Routledge), 1995
ISBN: 1 85713 015 4
£75.00

Film and Television Handbook
Edited by Eddie Dyja
British Film Institute
This annual publication is a very useful general handbook which provides information and contacts on the film, video and television industry. It also includes some statistics and market information.

Film Researchers' Handbook: A Guide to Sources in North America, Asia, Australasia and Africa
Edited by Jenny Morgan
Blueprint imprint (Routledge)
ISBN: 0415 151236
£50.00

Finding and Keeping: Researcher's Guide to Audiovisual Resources in Australia
Compiled by Marjorie Roe, Pam Dunlop and Bert Cornelius.

Canberra, Australia
Published for Australian Library and Information Association Press by AGPS,
1989
ISBN: 0644109130

Footage: World Moving Image Source Book
Second Line Search Publications
196 Broadway, 5th Floor, New York 10023
Tel: 212 787 2583 Fax: 212 787 3454
ISBN: 1 890979 24 4
Website: http:\\www.footage.net
Descriptions of moving image sources in the USA and Canada. The database
can be accessed from the website.

Online Sports
9070 Rotherham Avenue, San Diego, CA 92129-3125
Tel: 800 856 2638 or 760 749 6792 Fax: 800 856 2632 or 760 749 2966
Website: http://www.onlinesports.com
This is a business database of sports-related products which are available to
purchase on-line. It can be searched by sport, category, players, team etc. and
will then link to a list of products relating to the search, which gives price and
suppliers name. There are a large number of videos listed. Ordering can be on-
line or by using more traditional methods. All the information about how to
use the catalogue and order products is set out clearly in the introduction.

SportDiscus
This is an international database which is updated quarterly and is available on
CD-ROM in many university libraries. It includes over 400 000 citations on all
aspects of sports, physical fitness, physical education, sports medicine and
exercise physiology published since 1975. It is produced by the Sport Information Research Centre (SIRC), 1600 James Naismith Drive, Gloucester, Ontario,
K1B 5N4, Canada. Fax: 1 613 748 5701. They also have an Internet indexing
service called Sport Quest which is accessible free of charge on the Internet at
http://www.sportquest.com
A search of SportDiscus reveals that nearly 2000 videotapes are indexed. Many
of them include an abstract and some detail on the source. Over 500 of the
videos indexed are Australian. Obtaining them from outside Australia may be
a problem as only a small percentage will be distributed in the UK and North
America. For the Australian titles it may be possible to get help from the
National Sport Information Centre, Australian Sports Commission, PO Box 176,
Belconnen, ACT 2616, Australia. The website is http://www.ausport.gov.au

Tour CD

Leisure, Recreation and Tourism Abstracts on CD-ROM. This CD is produced by the Commonwealth Agricultural Bureau (CAB) International. It contains over 250 references to video, where video is used as a medium for analysing performance or as an educational tool, but this database does not index videos as a format. Most of the citations are articles and reports, many of which look at the uses and applications of video in the leisure industry.

Useful organizations

British Universities Film and Video Council
77 Wells Street, London W1P 3RE
Tel: 0171 393 1500 Fax: 0171 393 1555
Website: http://www.bufvc.ac.uk/
The British Universities Film and Video Council (BUFVC) exists to promote the use, production and study of film and related audiovisual media (television, video, computer-based multimedia) for higher education and research. Membership of the council is open to organizations with an interest in higher education and research; this includes UK universities, other further and higher educational establishments including overseas universities, commercial companies and broadcasters, schools with sixth forms and individual researchers.

The council has a library and specialist information service, which holds current catalogues from over 700 British distributors of audiovisual materials. They maintain the Slade Film History Register which holds the written records of the leading British cinema newsreel companies which operated between 1910 and 1979. Also a research index is maintained which catalogues non-fiction television broadcasts (since 1987) by subject. Although the council is not a major distributor of film and video it does assist in making available material in the UK which is suitable for higher education and research, and might not otherwise be obtainable. It maintains a film and video hire collection – the Higher Education Film and Video Library – which is handled by Concord Video and Film Council in Ipswich. A hire catalogue can be obtained from the BUFVC.

The council publishes a magazine called *Viewfinder* three times per year. This magazine is free of charge to members or £10.00 for three issues. ISSN: 0952 444.

A CD-ROM – *Audio Visual Materials for Higher Education* has recently been produced. Updated twice yearly it contains the AVANCE database with over 15 000 records of audiovisual programmes and related print materials. Entries include films, videos, tape-slide sets, sound recordings, computer courseware and interactive multimedia. It is available at all educational establishments who are members of BUFVC – which is virtually all British universities and many colleges.

They produce a number of useful publications, but the most useful one for those seeking information or carrying out research is the *Researchers Guide to British Film and Television Collections*, ISBN 0 901299 68 5, £35.00. A copy should be available in most good reference libraries. The *Researchers Guide* describes over 300 film and television collections in the UK and Ireland. National and regional film archives, television companies and stock shot libraries as well as smaller collections held by local authorities, museums, industrial companies and private individuals. The subject index includes a listing under 'Sport', with cross-references to a number of individual sports. It also includes a heading 'Travel and Transport'.

British Film Institute (BFI)
21 Stephen Street, London W1P 2LN
Tel: 0171 255 1444
Website: http://www.bfi.org.uk/

The BFI is a publicly funded body, which receives a substantial part of its funding direct from central government. It is also supported – statutorily and voluntarily – by the film and television industry in the UK. It was first set up in 1933, and is now established by Royal Charter. BFI Library and information services holds the world's largest collection of documentation on film and television. It includes both published and unpublished material ranging from books and periodicals to news cuttings, press releases, scripts, theses and files of festival material.

FOCAL (Federation of Commercial Audio-Visual Libraries)
Room 203, Pentax House, South Hill Avenue, Northolt Road, South Harrow, Middlesex HA2 Tel and Fax: 0181 423 5853
Website: http://www.focalltd.demon.co.uk/

An international, non-profit making professional trade association representing commercial film/audiovisual libraries and interested individuals. They offer a free information service and can direct enquirers to libraries where specific footage is available. They have international contacts and detailed information about their members is available on their free website.

Sportspages

Caxton Walk, 94–96 Charing Cross Road, London WC2H 0JG

Tel: 0171 240 9604

Barton Square, St Anne's Square, Manchester, M2 7HAA

Tel: 0161 832 8530

Sportspages is a bookshop. They have two shops listed above which each maintain a large selection of videos covering a wide selection of sports. They will send out lists of titles available and they offer a postal ordering service.

Libraries

Adventure and Wildlife Stock Shot Library

Church House, 18 Parkmount, Leeds LS5 3HE

Tel: 0113 230 7150 Fax: 0113 274 5387

A wide range of adventure sports and wildlife footage, most shot on 16 mm or Super 16 mm and available on Beta SP or film.

American Archives of the Factual Film

Special Collections Department, 403 Parks Library, Iowa State University, Ames, Iowa 50011-2140, USA

Tel: 515 294 6672 Fax: 515 294-5525

E-mail: aaff@iastate.edu.

Website: http://www.lib.iastate.edu/spcl/aaff/aaff.html

Australian Institute of Sport

National Sport Information Centre (NSIC), Australian Sports Commission, PO Box 176, Belconnen, ACT 2616, Australia

Website: http://www.ausport.gov.au

The information centre indexes all commercially available videotapes purchased by the NSIC for the Sport Database (SportDiscus – see section on CD-ROMs). Information contained in the database includes where the NSIC purchased its copy and video system requirements.

BBC Pebble Mill

Information Research Library, Pebble Mill Road, Birmingham, B5 7QQ

Tel: 0121 414 8888

BBC TV Sports Library

Kensington House, Richmond Way, Shepherds Bush, London W14 0AX

Tel: 0181 743 1272

All requests for research and access facilities must go through: Sport, News and Current Affairs Sales, BBC Enterprises Ltd. Woodlands, Wood Lane, London, W12 0TT
Tel: 0181 576 2185

British Film Institute Library
21 Stephen Street, London W1P 2LN
Tel: 0171 255 1444, ext. 2120
Fax: 0171 436 2338
E-mail: library@bfi.org.uk
Website: http://www.bfi.org.uk/framesets/library.htm

British Universities Film and Video (BUFV) Council Library
77 Wells Street, London W1P 3RE
Tel: 0171 393 1500 Fax: 0171 393 1555
Website: http://www.bufvc.ac.uk/
Provides a service for BUFV members (which includes most UK universities) only.

Channel Four Clip Library
124 Horseferry Road, London SW1P 2TX
Tel: 0171 306 8490 Fax: 0171 306 8363

Library of Congress
Motion Picture, Broadcasting and Recorded Sound Reading Room, Room 336, Madison Building, Library of Congress, Washington, DC 20540-4690, USA
Tel: 202 707-8572 Fax: 202 707-2371
Website: http://lcweb.loc.gov/rr/mopic/

New Zealand Television Archive
100 Victoria Street West, PO Box 3819, Auckland, New Zealand
Tel: 64 9 375 0941 Fax: 64 9 375 0872
E-mail: Vhills@tvnz.co.nz
Website: http://www.tvnz.co.nz/archive

Northern Ireland Film Council
21 Ormeau Avenue, Belfast BT2 8HD
Tel: 01232 232 444 Fax: 01232 312886

The Olympic Television Archive Bureau
TWI House, 23 Eyot Gardens, London W6 9TR
Tel: 0181 233 5353 Fax: 0181 233 5354

The International Olympic Committee owns a unique collection of film and television material covering the entire history of the Olympic Games from 1896 to 1994. Now it can be accessed via the Olympic Television Archive Bureau, which is administered by Transworld International.

Scottish Film Council
Downahill, 74 Victoria Crescent Road, Glasgow, G12 9JN
Tel: 0141 334 4445 Fax: 0141 334 8132

Sports Video Library
Transworld International, The Axis Centre, Level 5, Hogarth Business Centre, Chiswick, London W4 2TH
Tel: 0181 233 5500/5300 Fax: 0181 233 5301
Wide spectrum of sports collected including mainstream and unusual. Access by appointment.

Trans Video Productions Non-League Football Library
16 Old Road, Linslade, Leighton Buzzard, Bedfordshire LU7 7RD
Tel: 01525 383752
A collection of non-league football matches and other football-related footage dating from 1986. Access by appointment only.

Video Travel Stock Footage Library
International Video Network Ltd, 107 Power Road, Chiswick, London W4 5PL
Tel: 0181 742 2002
Telephone for access information.

Copyright

Copyright laws exist to protect the rights of both authors (which includes artists and performers) and publishers. Copyright law is extremely complex. Generally, an exclusive right is given to authors, artists, dramatists, composers, performers and producers of sound and video recordings, producers and principal directors of films, to authorize or prohibit rental and lending of their productions. In the UK at least, this right could be used to prevent libraries from lending audiovisual materials, without the consent of the owner of the lending rights. It can also be a breach of the copyright law to make a recording of a live performance. Consequently, if you are making recordings of television broadcasts, planning to make a video programme, playing a video to an audience or engaging in any similar activity you should check how your country's copyright law applies to your activities.

Australia

In Australia the law relating to copyright is contained in the Copyright Act 1968 and the decisions of courts. In addition to protecting written material it also protects works recorded on film and video. The Australian Copyright Council disseminates information about copyright in Australia. It is an independent non-profit organization and it has a website at http://www.copyright. org.au/ It produces a number of information sheets which are available on its website including a factsheet about copying videos (Australian Copyright Council, 1997). It also publishes a range of books about Australian copyright (e.g. Australian Copyright Council, 1996). Under normal circumstances it is not legal to make a copy of a video recording without the permission of the copyright owner. However, it is possible to copy a video for research or private study if the use is 'fair'. Use may not be considered to be fair if it is possible to purchase a copy instead of copying it. A scheme exists whereby educational establishments can pay copyright fees to an organization called Screenrights in order to make multiple copies of television programmes.

UK

Copyright legislation changes quite frequently, but the current regulations are laid down by the Copyright Designs and Patents Act 1988 which was amended by the Copyright and Related Rights Regulations 1996. (Statutory Instrument 1996 no. 2967.) Both the Act and the Statutory Instrument can be consulted in major reference libraries. Educational establishments may make copies of terrestrial television broadcasts for educational use only if they have purchased a licence from the Educational Recording Agency. They have a website at http://www.era.org.uk/index.html. There are a number of other agencies which issue licences permitting the copying and use of performances. The Copyright Licensing Agency issues licences to higher education institutions and its website has a list of similar agencies at http://www.cla.co.uk/www/copcon.htm There are numerous guides to copyright available such as Norman (1997) and Flint (1997).

USA

The copyright law of the USA is contained in Title 17 of the United States Code. This can be accessed on the Web at http://lcweb.loc.gov/copyright/

title17/ It gives the copyright owner the exclusive right to reproduce (copy) the work and in relation to motion pictures and videos copyright owners have the exclusive right to display and perform the work. Public performance of video programmes is an infringement of copyright. Videos may be performed publicly for educational purposes if all of the following conditions are met (American Library Association, 1998):

- The performance must be by instructors or by pupils.
- The performance is in connection with face-to-face teaching activities.
- The entire audience is involved in the teaching activity.
- The entire audience is in the same room or same general area.
- The teaching activities are conducted by a non-profit education institution.
- The performance takes place in a classroom or similar place devoted to instruction.
- The person responsible for the performance has no reason to believe that the videotape was unlawfully made.

There are numerous books available in both libraries and bookstores about copyright.

References and further resources

American Library Association (1998) *Video and Copyright*. Library and Research Center Fact Sheet No. 7. ALA. http://www.ala.org/library/fact07.html (accessed 15 May 1998).

Australian Copyright Council (1996) *A User's Guide to Copyright*. ACC.

Australian Copyright Council (1997) *Copying Video*. Information sheet 26. ACC. http://www.copyright.org.au/page3.htm (accessed 15 May 1998).

Batt, C. (1997) A licence to lend's all is required. *Library Association Record*, 99 (3) March, 131.

Bowker's Complete Video Directory 1997. Bowker.

British Film Institute (annual) *Film and Television Handbook*. BFI.

Bruwelheide, J. (1995) *The Copyright Primer for Librarians and Educators*, 2nd edn. American Library Association.

Flint, M. (1997) *A User's Guide to Copyright*. Butterworth.

Kirchner, D. (ed.) (1995) *Film and Television Collections in Europe: The MAP TV Guide*. Routledge.

Luckins Trade Services Publications Ltd (1997) *Videolog*. Luckins.

Morgan, J. (ed.) (1996) *Film Researcher's Handbook: A Guide to Sources in North America, Asia, Australia and Africa*. Routledge.

Norman, S. (1997) *The Copyright and Related Rights Regulations 1996: Summary of the Main Provision Affecting Libraries*. Library Association.

Roe, M., Dunlop, P. and Cornelius, B. (1989) *Finding and Keeping: A Researchers Guide to Audiovisual Resources in Australia*. Australian Library and Information Association Press.

Shoebridge, M. (1992) *Information Sources in Sport and Leisure.* Bowker Saur.
Sport and Recreation Information Group (SPRIG) (1989) *Finding Out about Video.* SPRIG Seminar No. 2, SPRIG.

Appendix: A selection of books on sport, leisure and tourism

Sport

Beck, P. (1998) *Scoring for Britain: International Football and International Politics, 1900–1939.* Cass.

Booth, D. (1998) *The Race Game: Sport and Politics in South Africa.* Cass.

Butler, R. (ed.) (1997) *Sports Psychology in Performance.* Butterworth-Heinemann.

Clark, G. and Humberstone, B. (eds) (1997) *Researching Women and Sport.* Macmillan.

Coakley, J. (1997) *Sports in Society.* 6th edn, Wm. C. Brown.

Cox, R. (1998) *Sport Psychology.* 4th edn, McGraw-Hill.

Dauncey, H. and Hare, G. (eds). (1998) *France and the 1998 World Cup.* Cass.

DeSensi, J. and Rosenberg, G. (1996) *Ethics in Sport Management.* Fitness Information Technology.

Digel, H. (1995) *Sport in a Changing Society: Sociological Essays.* Verlag Karl Hoffman.

Farmer, P. and Mulrooney, A. (1996) *Sport Facility Planning and Management.* Fitness Information Technology.

Figler, S. (1995) *Sport and Play in American Life: A Textbook in the Sociology of Sport.* 3rd edn, Brown & Benchmark

Hall, M. (1996) *Feminism and Sporting Bodies.* Human Kinetics.

Hill, C. (1996) *Olympic Politics.* 2nd edn, Manchester University Press.

Houlihan, B. (1997) *Sport, Policy, and Politics.* Routledge

Kew, F. (1997) *Sport: Social Problems and Issues.* Butterworth-Heinemann.

Kremer, J., Trew, K. and Ogle, S. (eds) (1997) *Young People's Involvement in Sport.* Routledge.

Male, M. (ed.) (1995) *The Social Roles of Sport in Caribbean Societies.* Gordon & Breach.

Mangan, J. (1996) *Tribal Identities: Nationalism, Europe, Sport.* Cass.

Mangan, J. (1998) *The Games Ethic and Imperialism: Aspects of the Diffusion of an Ideal.* Cass.

Mayall, D. and Cronin, M. (1998) *Sporting Nationalisms: Identity, Ethnicity, Immigration and Assimilation.* Cass.

Meinander, H. and Mangan, J. (eds) (1998) *The Nordic World: Sport in Society.* Cass.

Nauright, J. (1997) *Sport, Cultures, and Identities in South Africa.* Leicester University Press.

Parkhouse, B. (1996) *The Management of Sport.* 2nd edn, Mosby.

Pitts, B. and Stotlar, D. (1996) *Fundamentals of Sport Marketing*. Fitness Information Technology.

Polley, M. (1998) *Moving the Goalposts: A History of Sport and Society Since 1945*. Routledge.

Raitz, K. (ed.) (1995) *The Theater of Sport*. Johns Hopkins University Press.

Riordan, J. and Arnmaud, P. (eds) (1997) *Sport and International Politics*. Spon.

Thoma, J. and Chali, L. (1996) *Sport Governance in the Global Community*. Fitness Information Technology.

Tomlinson, A. (ed.) (1995a) *Ethics, Sport and Leisure*. Chelsea School Research Centre, University of Brighton.

Tomlinson, A. (ed.) (1995b) *Gender, Sport and Leisure: Continuities and Challenges*. Chelsea School Research Centre, University of Brighton.

Tranter, N. (1998) *Sport, Economy, and Society in Britain, 1750–1914*. Cambridge University Press.

Wagg, S. (ed.) (1995) *Giving the Game Away: Football, Politics and Culture on Five Continents*. Leicester University Press.

Leisure

Argyle, M. (1996) *The Social Psychology of Leisure*. Penguin.

Böröcz, J. (1996) *Leisure Migration: A Sociological Study on Tourism*. Elsevier Science.

Colclough, J. (1996) *Investigating the Leisure and Tourism Industries*. Hodder & Stoughton.

Collier, T. (1995) *Business Planning in the Leisure Industry*. Pitman.

Cushman, G., Veal, A. and Zuzanek, J. (eds) (1996) *World Leisure Participation: Free Time in the Global Village*. CAB International.

Eaton, B. (1996) *European Leisure Businesses*. ELM.

Edmonds, J. (1996) *Human Resources in Leisure and Tourism*. Hodder & Stoughton.

Evans, G. and White, J. (1997) *The Economic and Social Impact of the National Lottery: A Literature Review*. University of North London Press.

Flemming, S., Talbot, M. and Tomlinson, A. (eds) (1995) *Policy and Politics in Sport, Physical Education and Leisure*. Leisure Studies Association.

Haworth, J. and Iso-Ahola, S. (1997) *Work, Leisure and Well-being*. Routledge.

Henderson, K. (1996) *Both Gains and Gaps: Feminist Perspectives on Women's Leisure*. Venture.

Howell, S. (1996) *Performance, Monitoring and Evaluation in Leisure Management*. Pitman.

Johson, D. and Goodhead, T. (1996) *Coastal Recreation Management: The Sustainable Development of Maritime Leisure*. Spon.

Jordan, D. (1996) *Leadership in Leisure Services: Making a Difference*. Venture.

Kelly, J. (1996) *Leisure*. 3rd edn, Allyn & Bacon.

Merkel, U. and Tokarski, W. (eds) (1996) *Racism and Xenophobia in European Football*. Meyer.

Mommaas, H. (ed.) (1996) *Leisure Research in Europe*. CAB International.

Morgan, M. (1996) *Marketing for Leisure and Tourism*. Prentice Hall.

Naylor, D. (1997) *Case Studies in Financial Control and Performance Measurement in Leisure and Recreation Management*. Ravenswood.

Nicole, S. (ed.) (1996) *Women, Leisure and the Family in Contemporary Society.* CAB International.

Williams, S. (1995) *Outdoor Recreation and the Urban Environment.* Routledge.

Wiseman, E. (1996) *Finance in Leisure and Tourism.* Hodder & Stoughton.

Wynne, D.(1998) *Leisure, Lifestyle and the New Middle Class: A Case Study.* Routledge.

Youell, R. (1996) *The Complete A–Z Leisure, Travel & Tourism Handbook.* Hodder & Stoughton.

Tourism

Betteridge, D. (1997) *Event Management in Leisure and Tourism.* Hodder & Stoughton.

Boer, A., Thomas, R. and Webster, M. (1997) *Small Business Management: A Resource-based Approach for the Hospitality and Tourism Industries.* Cassell.

Boissevain, J. (1996) *Coping With Tourists.* Berghahn.

Brunt, P. (1997) *Market Research in Travel and Tourism.* Butterworth-Heinemann.

Burns, P. and Holden, A. (1995) *Tourism: A New Perspective.* Prentice Hall.

Butler, R. and Hinch, T. (eds) *Tourism and Indigenous Peoples.* Thomson.

Clark, M. (ed.) (1998) *Researching and Writing Dissertations in Hospitality and Tourism.* Thomson.

Cooper, C. and Wanhill, S. (eds) (1997) *Tourism Development.* Wiley.

Deegan, J. and Dineen, D. (1997) *Tourism Policy and Performance: The Irish Experience.* Thomson.

Elliott, J. (1997). *Tourism: Politics and Public Sector Management.* Routledge.

Field, D. (1997) *Marketing for Leisure and Tourism.* Hodder & Stoughton.

Gee, C., Makens, J. and Choy, D. (eds) (1997) *The Travel Industry.* 3rd edn, Van Nostrand Reinhold.

Getz, D. (1997) *Event Management and Event Tourism.* Cognizant Communication Corp.

Go, F. and Jenkins, C. (eds) (1997) *Tourism and Economic Development in Asia and Australasia.* Pinter.

Hall, M. (ed.) (1998) *Sustainable Tourism.* Longman.

Holloway, C. (1998) *The Business of Tourism.* 5th edn, Longman.

Inkpen, G. (1998) *Information Technology for Travel and Tourism.* 2nd edn, Longman.

Ioanides, D. (1998). *The Economic Geography of the Tourist Industry.* Routledge.

Johns, N. (ed.) (1996) *Productivity Management in Hospitality and Tourism.* Cassell.

Knowles, T. (1998) *Hospitality Management: An Introduction.* 2nd edn, Longman.

Laws, E., Moscardo, G. and Faulkner, B. (eds) (1998) *Embracing and Managing Change in Tourism.* Routledge.

Laws, E. (1997) *Managing Packaged Tourism.* International Thomson Business Press.

Lockhart, D. and Drakakis-Smith, D. (eds) (1997) *Island Tourism: Trends and Prospects.* Pinter.

Lumsdon, L. (1997) *Tourism Marketing.* Thomson.

Medlik, S. (1997) *Understanding Tourism.* Butterworth-Heinemann.

Middleton, V. and Hawkins, R. (1998) *Sustainable Tourism: A Marketing Perspective.* Butterworth-Heinemann.

Mullins, L. (1998) *Managing People in the Hospitality Industry.* 3rd edn, Longman.

Murphy, P. (ed.) (1997) *Quality Management in Urban Tourism.* Wiley.

Oppermann, M. and Chon, K. (1997) *Tourism in Developing Countries*. International Thomson Business Press.

Pattullo, P. (1996) *Last Resorts: the Cost of Tourism in the Caribbean*. Cassell.

Priestley, G., Edwards, A. and Coccossis, H. (eds) (1996) *Sustainable Tourism? European Experiences*. CAB International.

Richards, G. (ed.) (1996) *Cultural Tourism in Europe*. CAB International.

Ringer, G. (ed.) (1998) *Destinations: Cultural Landscapes of Tourism*. Routledge.

Rogers, T. (1998) *Conferences: A Twenty-first Century Industry*. Longman.

Ryan, C. (1997) *The Tourist Experience*. Cassell.

Selwyn, T. (ed.) (1996) *The Tourist Image: Myths and Mythmaking in Tourism*. Wiley.

Shaw, G. and Williams, A. (eds) (1997) *The Rise and Fall of British Coastal Resorts*. Pinter.

Teare, R. and Bowen, J. (1997) *New Directions in Hospitality and Tourism*. Cassell.

Thea Sinclair, M. (ed.) (1997) *Gender, Work and Tourism*. Routledge.

Tribe, J. (1997) *Corporate Strategy for Tourism*. International Thomson Business Press.

Veal, A. (1997) *Research Methods for Leisure and Tourism*. 2nd edn, Pitman.

Watt, D. (1998) *Event Management in Leisure and Tourism*. Longman.

Glossary of terms

Application   A computer software program designed for a particular purpose, such as word processing or sending e-mail.

Bandwidth   In very simple terms this refers to the capacity of a telecommunications link.

BIDS   A gateway to certain databases on the Web providing access to journal literature and conference papers in the arts, humanities, sciences and social sciences. (Housed at the University of Bath – **B**ath **I**nformation and **D**ata **S**ervices.)

BLDSC   (**B**ritish **L**ibrary **D**ocument **S**upply **C**entre) The lending division of the British Library, located at Boston Spa, Yorkshire. It provides inter-library loan and document delivery services both within the UK and internationally.

Browser   Software which is used to view documents on the World Wide Web. Two of the most popular browsers are Netscape, produced by Netscape Inc and Microsoft's Internet Explorer.

Call number   The number given to a book by a library which usually indicates where you will find it on the shelf in the library.

CD-ROM   (**C**ompact **D**isc-**R**ead-**O**nly-**M**emory) A medium for storing large quantities of data e.g. indexes and abstracts which can be read by a computer.

Citation   A detailed reference to another published work.

Citation index   An index of previously published articles and books which have been cited in later publications.

Classmark   The number given to a book by a library which usually indicates where you will find it on the shelf in the library.

Client A computer program which uses the services provided by another computer over a network. A Web browser is a specific kind of client program.

Cookie A piece of information sent by a Web server to a Web browser that the browser software is expected to save and to send back to the server whenever the browser makes additional requests from the server.

Cyberspace The word 'Cyberspace' is used to describe the whole range of information resources available through computer networks. Hence if it's on the Internet it's in Cyberspace.

Database A searchable collection of data. Although often associated with computers the term database can be used to refer to any searchable collection of data, such as information held on cards systematically filed in a filing cabinet.

Dissertation A substantial piece of written work produced for a degree at an institution of higher education. In North America dissertation refers to a piece of work completed for the award of a doctoral degree (PhD). In the UK it refers to a piece of work completed for the award of a degree below doctoral level, e.g. BA or MSc.

Domain name The unique name that identifies an Internet site. Domain names always have two or more parts, separated by dots. The part on the left is the most specific and the part on the right is the most general.

E-mail discussion group/list See Mail list below.

ERIC (**E**ducational **R**esources **I**nformation **C**enter) A US network of sixteen clearing houses, each responsible for collecting, analysing, abstracting and making available information resources.

File Transfer Protocol (FTP) A standard protocol (and an application) which allows files to be transferred between computers over the Internet.

Home Page The main Web page for a business, organization, person or simply the main page of a collection of Web pages or Website.

Hyper media Documents which contain text, images, video and audio.

Hypertext Markup Language (HTML) A computer code used to create documents which are on the World Wide Web.

Hypertext Transfer Protocol (HTTP)   The protocol used to exchange HTML documents on the World Wide Web.

Index   An alphabetical list of authors, titles and/or subjects.

Inter-library loans   A service which enables users of one library to borrow material not held in their own library from a library elsewhere, usually BLDSC.

Internet   An international network connecting millions of computers.

Internet Service Provider (ISP)   An organization that provides access to the Internet, usually on a commercial basis.

Internet Protocol (IP) address   A unique numeric address of a computer which is directly connected to the Internet.

Intranet   A private network inside a company or organization that uses the same kinds of software as the Internet, but that is for internal use only.

Java   A computer programing language which can be used to create animation and multimedia for the Web.

Journal   Sometimes called a periodical or serial. Published at regular intervals, journals contain articles written by different authors.

Literature search   A systematic and exhaustive search for published material in a specific subject.

Mail list (or mailing list)   A system that allows people to send an e-mail to one e-mail address and have it forwarded to people who have subscribed to that particular mailing list.

Monograph   Another word for a book, but more usually a book on a specific topic at an advanced level.

On-line database   A database containing bibliographic data which can be interrogated from a remote computer terminal.

On-line public access catalogue (OPAC)   A computerized library catalogue which is often accessible on the Internet.

Periodical   Sometimes called a journal or serial and published at regular intervals. Periodicals contain articles written by different authors.

Report literature   Reports of all kinds, which give results of research or development work. May include technical notes and memoranda, conference papers and proceedings, research and development reports and formal reports.

Serial   A periodical or journal.

Server   A computer which provides services to other computer programs over a network.

Spamming   An inappropriate attempt to send the same message to a large number of people who didn't ask for it through a networked communications facility, such as a mailing list.

Telnet   A protocol (and an application) that allows users to log on to remote computers over the Internet.

Thesaurus   Index of subject headings used in indexing and abstracting sources. Refers to related subject headings.

Thesis   A thesis is a statement of the findings of research and the conclusions drawn from it which is presented for the award of a degree at a university or other institution of higher education. In the UK the term thesis is used in relation to work completed at PhD level only while in North America it is used to describe work below that level only.

Uniform resource locator (URL)   The unique address of a document on the Web.

Web page   A document which is in HTML format and is accessible on the World Wide Web.

Website   A collection of Web pages, usually belonging to one individual or organization, held on a particular server.

White pages   A directory containing the e-mail addresses of individual people.

World Wide Web (WWW)   The part of the Internet that uses the http protocol to make available documents which contain hypertext and hyper media and can be viewed using a Web browser.

Yellow Pages   A directory containing the e-mail addresses of companies.

Index

Abstracting journals, 119, 120, 122–31
Abstracts, 57–8
  journal articles, 84–5
Academic journals, 77–8, 79–83
  attractions and heritage, 82
  hospitality management, 81
  leisure, recreation and sport, 80
  tourism, 80–1
  travel and transport, 81–2
  see also Journals
Academic libraries, 53–4
Academy of Leisure Services website, 44
American Archives of the Factural Film
  (AAFF), 242
Anbar, 122–3
Annual Abstract of Statistics, 142
Argus Clearing House, 35
Articles in Hospitality and Tourism, 123
Arts and Humanities Citation Index, 123
ASSIA (Applied Social Sciences Index
  and Abstracts), 123
Association of British Travel Agents
  (ABTA) website, 49
Association of National Tourist Offices
  website, 49
Australian Books in Print, 135
Australian Bureau of Statistics, 144
Australian Council for Health, Physical
  Education and Recreation
  (ACHPER) website, 44
Australian Education Index, 123–4
Australian Government Index of
  Publications, 124

Australian Sports Commission (ASC),
  213
  National Sport Information Centre
    (NSIC), 247
  website, 45, 213
Australian Tourism Index, 124

Bath Information and Data Services
  (BIDS), 120
Beckmann Home Video, 235
Bibliographic references:
  citation of, 61–3, 87–90
    Harvard method, 60–1, 62, 88–9
    Numeric (Vancouver) method, 60,
      61–2, 89, 90
  compilation of, 60–1
  journal articles, 85–6, 87–90
Bibliographie Touristique, 124
Bibliographies, 57–8, 119–20, 134–5
Bibliography of Education Theses in
  Australia, 133
Biz/ed, 35
Books in Print (USA), 135
Bookseller (UK), 135
Bowker's Complete Video Directory,
  242–3
Britannica Internet Guide, 35
British Education Index, 124–5
British Film Institute (BFI), 246
  library, 248
British Humanities Index, 125
British Library Catalogue, 134

British Library Document Supply Centre
(BLDSC), 59
British National Bibliography, 134
British National Film and Video Guide,
243
British reports, translations and theses,
132
British Tourist Authority (BTA), 145–7
BTA/ETB library, 54
videos, 236
website, 48
British Universities Film and Video
Council, 245–6
library, 248
BULB Information Service, 36

Canadian Education Index, 125
Canadian Tourism Commission (CTC),
Tourism, Reference and
Documentation Centre (TRDC)
library, 54–5
Canadian Tourism Information Network
website, 47
Carrefours (EU Rural Information
Centres), 179
Ireland, 189
United Kingdom, 186–7
CD-ROM databases, 127, 176–7
suppliers of, 193–4
CELEX database, 171–2, 176, 178
Centre for Leisure and Tourism Studies
(CELTS), 12–13, 14
Coachwise, 236
Committee of the Regions (COR), 166–7
Community Travel Research Database
(Texas) website, 49
Company information websites, 42–3
Conference proceedings, 132
Consumer market research, 140
Contents lists, 140–2
Copyright, 249–51
Corporate Intelligence on Retailing and
Travel and Tourism Intelligence, 151
Council of the European Union, 163–4
website, 173–4
Countryside Commission library, 54
Countryside Recreation Network website,
44

Court of Auditors, 167
Cumulative Book Index, 135–6
Current Contents (Social and Behavioural
Sciences), 125
Current Research in Britain: Social
Sciences, 133

Databases:
electronic database techniques, 120–2
European Union, 169–72
CD-ROM databases, 176–7
see also Abstracting journals;
Bibliographies; Indexes
Descriptive research, 12
Discussion lists, 39–41
Dissertations, 58–9, 133–4
Dissertations Abstracts, 133
Document delivery services, 59–60

ECoNETT website, 49, 211
Economic and Social Committee
(ECOSOC), 166
Education Index, 125–6
Electronic database techniques, 120–2
Electronic journals, 87
Electronic mail, 37–41
e-mail addresses, 38
e-mail discussion lists, 39–41
searching for e-mail addresses, 38–9
English Sports Council:
library, 55
website, 46
English Tourist Board (ETB), 145–6
BTA/ETB library, 54
Enlightenment, 2–3
EU Infodisk database, 177
EURATHLON programme, 173
Eurolaw database, 176
Euromonitor, 151–2
Europa website, 169–72
European Business ASAP, 126
European Commission, 158–63
legislation and proposals for legislation,
160–1
monographs and periodicals, 162–3
offices, 191–3
policy documents, 161–2
website, 172–3

European Court of Justice, 165–6
European Depository Libraries, 186
European Documentation Centres
    (EDCs), 177–9
  Australia, 190
  Canada, 190
  Hong Kong, 191
  Ireland, 188
  New Zealand, 191
  South Africa, 191
  United Kingdom, 182–4
  United States, 189–90
European Foundation for the
    Improvement of Living and Working
    Conditions website, 174
European Information Association (EIA)
    website, 175–6
European Information Centres (EICs),
    179
  Ireland, 188–9
  United Kingdom, 184–6
European Investment Bank, 167
European Parliament, 164–5
  website, 174
European References database, 177
European Resource Centres for Schools
    and Colleges, 180, 187–8
European Union, 157–94
  agencies, 167–8
  CD-ROM databases, 176–7
    suppliers of, 193–4
  information on funding, 168
  institutions, 158–67
  sites for access to EU information,
    177–80
  statistical information, 168
  websites, 169–76, 180–2
Eurostat website, 175
Eurotext website, 176
Evaluative research, 12
Explanatory research, 12

Film and Television Handbook, 243
Findex: the World Directory of Market
    Research Reports, Studies and
    Surveys, 150–1
FOCAL (Federation of Commercial
    Audio-Visual Libraries), 246

Gender Equity in Sports website, 46
General Association of International Sports
    Federations (GAISF) website, 211
General Household Survey (GHS), 11–12,
    148–9
Geographical Abstracts: Human
    Geography, 126
Global Index of Chambers of Commerce
    and Industry, 210
Government involvement in leisure and
    tourism research, 6–7
Government Reports Announcements
    and Index, 132
Government tourism organization
    websites, 46–9
Green Umbrella, 237
Green-Travel, 39
Guide to Official Statistics, 143

Harvard citation method, 60–1, 62, 88–9
Hawaii Tourism Office website, 48
Hillary Commission for Sport Fitness and
    Leisure website, 45
Hospitality, academic journals, 81
Hospitality-industries, 39–40
HOTEL-L, 40
House journals, 78
Hypertext markup language (HTML), 29

IDEA database, 169–70
Index New Zealand, 126
Index of Conference Proceedings, 132
Index to Theses Accepted for Higher
    Degrees in the Universities of Great
    Britain and Ireland, 133–4
Indexes, 57–8, 119, 120
  journal articles, 84–5
  list of, 122–31
  use of for statistics and market
    research, 140–1, 142
Infodisk database, 177
Information, 9, 52
Informational society, 9
Infotec-Travel, 40
Inside Information, 126–7
Institute of Sport and Recreation
    Management (ISRM), 238
Interdisciplinary research, 21–3

International Association for Sports
    Information website, 45
International Bibliography of the Social
    Sciences, 127
International Chamber of Commerce
    (ICC), 209–10
International ERIC, 127
International Hospitality and Tourism
    Database CD-ROM, 127
International Institute for Sport and
    Human Performance website, 46
International Olympic Committee, 211
    film and television library, 248–9
International organizations, 7, 204–12,
    216–20
International Video Network, 238
Internet, 27–9
    connecting to, 28–9
    literature searches, 57
    see also Internet search engines;
        Relevant websites; World Wide
        Web
Internet Hospitality Index, 36
Internet search engines, 32–7
    geographic search engines, 34–5
    leisure and tourism gateways, 36–7
    limiting searches, 34
    linking different concepts, 33
    searching for parts of words, 33
    searching for phrases, 33
    subject trees, 35–6
Internet service providers (ISPs), 29

Journals, 76–117
    bibliographic citation of, 87–90
    identifying relevant articles, 83–6
        abstracts and indexes, 84–5
        bibliographic references, 85–6
    list of, 90–117
    new developments, 83
    obtaining articles, 86–7
        electronic journals, 87
        interlibrary loan and document
            supply, 87
    see also Academic journals

Key Data, 141–2
Key Note, 152
Knowledge, 8–9

Leisure:
    academic journals, 80
    definitions of, 17
    economic importance of, 24
    expenditure on, 147–8
    participation in leisure pursuits, 148–9
    relevant websites, 44–5
    time available for, 149
Leisure and tourism research, 6–8, 17–24
    cross-disciplinarity, 21–3
    newness of, 19–21
Leisure centres, satisfaction with, case
    study, 16–17
Leisure Forecasts, 152
Leisure Futures, 152
Leisure Information Network website, 44
Leisure Recreation and Tourism
    Abstracts, 127–8
Leisure Studies Web Pages, 36
Leisurenet, 40
Libraries, 51–60
    abstracts, indexes and bibliographies,
        57–8
    academic libraries, 53–4
    Australia, 63–5
    Canada, 66–7
    document delivery services, 59–60, 87
    interlibrary loan, 87
    library catalogues, 56–7
    New Zealand, 67
    obtaining journal articles, 86–7
    public libraries, 53
    special libraries, 45–55
    statistics, 58
    theses and dissertations, 58–9
    United Kingdom, 68–71
    United States, 71–4
    use of the Internet, 57
    video libraries, 247–9
    see also Literature searches
Literature searches, 55–6
    electronic databases, 120–2
    journals, 83–6
    library catalogues, 56–7
    see also Abstracting journals;
        Bibliographies; Indexes; Internet
        search engines
Local organizations, 214

MAID (Market Analysis and Information Databases), 153
Market research, 140
  company details, 155
  sources of, 150–3
  using indexes and contents lists, 140–2
Marketsearch: International Directory of Published Market Research, 150
MarkIntel, 153
Meta-Index for Nonprofit Organizations, 209
Metatourism, 22
Mintel, 153
Modems, 28–9
Monthly Catalog of United States Government Publications, 128
Museum Abstracts, 128
Museums, academic journals, 82

National Library of Australia, 135
National Lottery case study, UK, 9, 13–14
National organizations, 212–14, *see also* Organizations
National Union Catalogue, 134
Natural sciences, 10–11
Netscape, 29–30
New Leisure Markets, 153
New Zealand Bibliographic Network (NZBN), 136
New Zealand Books in Print, 136
New Zealand Tourism Board website, 47
Numeric (Vancouver) citation method, 60, 61–2, 89, 90

Office of National Tourism (Australia) website, 47, 145
Official Journal C series, 177
Olympic Movement website, 211–12
Online Public Access Catalogues (OPACs), 56, 86
Online Sports website, 244
Organizations, 197–228
  Australia, 220–2
  Canada, 222–4
  definition of, 198
  government tourism organization websites, 46–9
  information sources, 215–16

international organizations, 7, 204–12, 216–20
leisure and tourism research, 6
national, regional and local organizations, 212–14
New Zealand, 224–5
United Kingdom, 225–7
United States, 227–8
video information, 245–7

Pacific Asia Travel Association (PATA) website, 49, 211
Parks Canada website, 44
Periodicals, *see* Journals
Personal computers (PCs), 28
  see also Internet
PHILOXENIA programme, 173
Physical Education Index, 128
Primary research, 11–12
  example of, 12–13
Professional Magnetics Ltd, 239
Psychological Abstracts, 128
Public Information Relays, 180
Public libraries, 53
Publication details, 135–6

Quadrant Video, 239
Qualification and Curriculum Authority (QCA), 240
Qualitative research, 14–15
  example of, 16
Quantitative research, 14–15
  example of, 15–16
Quantum Leap Group Ltd, 240

RAPID database, 171
Reflective practitioners, 4
  profile of, 4–6
Reflexivity, 3–4, 8
Regional organizations, 212–14, 216–20
Relevant websites, 42–50, 203
  company information, 42–3
  European Union information, 169–76, 180–2
  general, 42
  government tourism organizations, 46–9
  leisure studies, 44–5
  sport, 45–6

Relevant websites (*cont.*)
 statistics, 154–5
 tourism trade organizations, 49–50
René Waksberg's Tourism Research
 Index, 37
Report literature, 132–3
Research, 2–17, 24
 communication of, 10
 definition of, 9–10
 natural versus social sciences, 10–11
 primary research, 11–13
 qualitative research, 14–15, 16
 quantitative research, 14–16
 secondary research, 11–12, 13–14
 see also Leisure and tourism research;
 Market research
Resources in Education, 132–3
Royal Parks in London case study, 12–13,
 21
Rural Information Centres (EU), 179
 Ireland, 189
 United Kingdom, 186–7

SCAD database, 170–1, 177
SCAN, 129
Scout Report Signpost, 36
Search engines, *see* Internet search
 engines
Secondary research, 11–12
 example of, 13–14
Small-tourism-firms, 40
Social Science Information Gateway
 (SOSIG), 36
Social sciences, 8, 10–11
Social Sciences Citation Index (SSCI),
 120, 129
Social Sciences Index, 129
Sociological Abstracts, 129–30
*Sources of United Kingdom Unofficial
 Statistics*, 144
Special libraries, 45–55
Sport:
 academic journals, 80
 organizations, 211–12
 relevant websites, 45–6, 182
 statistics, 149–50
Sport and Leisure Research on Disc, 134
SportDiscus, 130, 244

Sports Documentation Monthly Bulletin,
 130
Sports Information and Research Centre
 (SIRC), 212
 website, 45, 150, 212
Sportsearch, 130
Sportspages, 247
Statistical Abstract of the United States,
 143–4
Statistics, 58, 138–40
 European Union statistical information,
 168
 expenditure on leisure, 147–8
 participation in leisure activities, 148–9
 sources of, 142–4
 sport, 149–50
 time available for leisure, 149
 tourism, 144–7
 United Kingdom, 145–7
 using indexes and contents lists, 140–2
 websites for, 154–5
Subject trees, 35–6
Supranational organizations, *see*
 International organizations

Taylor, Maureen, 4–6
Technological development, 2–3
Thai women and Western men case
 study, 16
Theses, 58–9, 133–4
Time diaries, 15–16
Tour CD, 245
Tourism:
 academic journals, 80–1
 definitions of, 17
 economic importance of, 7, 24
 organizations, 210–11
 relevant websites, 46–50, 182
 statistics, 144–7
 United Kingdom, 145–7
 see also Leisure and tourism
Tourism discussion list, 41
Tourism Industries Network (TINET)
 website, 48, 145
Tourism multipliers, 8
Tourism Policy Council website, 48
Tourism Policy Group (New Zealand)
 website, 47–8

Trade periodicals, 78–9
Transport Research Web Links, 37
Travel and transport, academic journals, 81–2
Travel Industry Association of America (TIAA) website, 49
TRINET, 41
TV Choice Ltd, 240

UK National Lottery case study, 9, 13–14
UnCover, 131
Union of International Associations (UIA), 204–9
  publications, 208–9
    Yearbook of International Organizations, 206–8
  website, 205, 209
United Kingdom Official Publications Index (UKOP), 131
United Nations (UN) websites, 209
Universal resource locators (URLs), 30
  inaccurate quotation of, 32
  recording for future use, 30–1
Urbadisc, 131

Vancouver (Numeric) citation method, 60, 61–2, 89, 90
Video Plus Direct, 241
Videos, 232–51
  analysis of videos, 233–4
  copyright, 249–51
  information sources, 242–9
    libraries, 247–9
    organizations, 245–7
    publications, 242–5
  video distributors, 234–42

Visitor attractions, academic journals, 82

Wales Tourist Board website, 48
Websites, see Relevant websites; World Wide Web
Weekly Checklist Catalogue, 131
Whitaker's Books in Print (UK), 136
Working Papers in Sport and Leisure Commerce website, 44
World Directory of Non-official Statistical Sources, 144
World Federation of the Sporting Goods Industry (WFSGI) website, 212
World Hospitality and Tourism Trends (WHATT), 131
World Leisure and Recreation Association website, 45
World Tourism Organization (WTO), 144–5, 210–11
  website, 46, 145, 210–11
World Travel and Tourism Council (WTTC) website, 49–50, 211
World Wide Web (WWW), 27, 28, 29–32
  accessing documents, 30–1
  common problems, 31–2
  library catalogues, 57
  recording URLs for future use, 30–1
  slow response times, 31–2
  web browsers, 29–30
  see also Internet; Relevant websites

Yahoo, 36, 210
Yahoo Sports, 37
Yahoo Transportation, 37
Yearbook of International Organizations, 206–8